American Biodefense

A volume in the series

Cornell Studies in Security Affairs

edited by Robert J. Art, Robert Jervis, and Stephen M. Walt

A list of titles in this series is available at www.cornellpress.cornell.edu.

American Biodefense

How Dangerous Ideas about Biological Weapons Shape National Security

Frank L. Smith III

Cornell University Press

ITHACA AND LONDON

Copyright © 2014 by Cornell University

All rights reserved. Except for brief quotations in a review, this book, or parts thereof, must not be reproduced in any form without permission in writing from the publisher. For information, address Cornell University Press, Sage House, 512 East State Street, Ithaca, New York 14850.

First published 2014 by Cornell University Press

Printed in the United States of America

Library of Congress Cataloging-in-Publication Data
Smith, Frank L., III, 1978– author.
   American biodefense : how dangerous ideas about biological weapons shape national
security / Frank L. Smith III.
      pages cm. — (Cornell studies in security affairs)
   Includes bibliographical references and index.
   ISBN 978-0-8014-5271-0 (cloth : alk. paper)
   1. Biological warfare—United States—Safety measures. 2. Biosecurity—United States.
3. National security—United States. 4. Civil defense—United States. I. Title.
   UG447.8.S583   2014
   358'.384—dc23   2014006183

Cornell University Press strives to use environmentally responsible suppliers and materials to the fullest extent possible in the publishing of its books. Such materials include vegetable-based, low-VOC inks and acid-free papers that are recycled, totally chlorine-free, or partly composed of nonwood fibers. For further information, visit our website at www.cornellpress.cornell.edu.

Cloth printing   10 9 8 7 6 5 4 3 2 1

Contents

Acknowledgments

This book is, first and foremost, the product of my many years at the University of Chicago working with Charles Glaser, along with John Mearsheimer, John Padgett, and James Evans. Through the highs and lows, Charlie provided steady support and sage council, for which I am truly grateful. During my research, I also had the good fortune to spend a year at the Center for International Security and Cooperation at Stanford University. It is therefore no accident that I owe much of the theory in this book to Lynn Eden, as well as the confidence to write it. Lynn is a remarkable mentor and I cannot thank her enough.

Critical content for this book was provided by many knowledgeable people whom I had the pleasure of interviewing or corresponding with over the years. In addition to several anonymous contributors, I want to thank Michael Ascher, Kenneth Bernard, Jack Berndt, Robert Boyle, Richard Danzig, Peter Emanuel, Jeffrey Grotte, Anna Johnson-Winegar, Milton Leitenberg, Carol Linden, Joel McCleary, Christina Murata, Joseph Palma, Frank Rapoport, Richard Spertzel, Ernest Takafuji, Victor Utgoff, Jerry Warner, Keith Yamamoto, and Raymond Zilinskas. I am grateful for help from Jeff Karr at the American Society of Microbiology Archives and Robert Wampler at the National Security Archive, as well as the staff at the National Academy of Sciences Archives and the National Archives and Records Administration.

I have also received tremendous assistance and feedback from friends and colleagues along the way. Among many others, I thank Charles Belle, Bruce Bennett, Jonathan Caverley, Brent Durbin, Marc Hernandez, Anne Holthoefer, Patrick Johnston, Jenna Jordan, Adam Kamradt-Scott, Paul Kapur, Adria Lawrence, Michelle Murray, Takayuki Nishi, Seo-Hyun Park, Chetan Patel, Charles Perrow, Keven Ruby, John Schuessler, Jason

[vii]

Sharman, Rebecca Slayton, Lisa Stampnitzky, Paul Stockton, Mika Uehara, Lora Viola, Jessica Weeks, Alexander Wendt, Dean Wilkening, and Robert Zarate.

This is a much better book thanks to comments from Gregory Koblentz, Alexander Montgomery, Nicola Smith, and Kathleen Vogel, as well as editing by Erin Hurley, Bob Irwin, Katy Meigs, and Susan Specter. I could not ask for more from Roger Haydon or the editors of the Cornell Studies in Security Affairs series; working with Roger, in particular, is a sincere pleasure. This book also draws on my article, "A Casualty of Kinetic Warfare: Military Research, Development, and Acquisition for Biodefense," *Security Studies* 20, no. 4 (2011), by permission of the publisher.

Above all, without the love and support of my family, there would have been little point. This book is dedicated in loving memory to my mom, Virginia H. Smith.

Acronyms

ANBACIS	Automated Nuclear, Biological, and Chemical Information System
BARDA	Biomedical Advanced Research and Development Authority
BIDS	Biological Integrated Detection System
BW	biological weapon(s)
CBDP	Chemical and Biological Defense Program
CBR	chemical, biological, radiological
CBRN	chemical, biological, radiological, nuclear
CBW	chemical and biological weapon(s)
CDC	Centers for Disease Control and Prevention
CENTCOM	US Central Command
CIA	Central Intelligence Agency
CWS	Chemical Warfare Service
DARPA	Defense Advanced Research Projects Agency
DHS	Department of Homeland Security
DoD	Department of Defense
DTRA	Defense Threat Reduction Agency
EIS	Epidemic Intelligence Service
FDA	Food and Drug Administration
HHS	Department of Health and Human Services
IED	improvised explosive device
IOM	Institute of Medicine
JBPDS	Joint Biological Point Detection System
JPO-BD	Joint Program Office for Biological Defense
JVAP	Joint Vaccine Acquisition Program

LIDAR	light detection and ranging
MOPP	mission-oriented protective posture
NBC	nuclear, chemical, biological
NIAID	National Institute of Allergy and Infectious Diseases
NIH	National Institutes of Health
NSC	National Security Council
PHS	Public Health Service
SAC	Strategic Air Command
SMART	Sensitive Membrane Antigen Rapid Test
UNSCOM	United Nations Special Commission
USAMRIID	US Army Medical Research Institute of Infectious Diseases
USAMU	US Army Medical Unit
VEE	Venezuelan equine encephalitis
WMD	weapon(s) of mass destruction

American Biodefense

American Biodefense, from Boston to Baghdad

General George Washington faced a serious problem. It was the winter of 1776, less than a year after he assumed command of the Continental Army outside Boston, and his siege against British forces inside the city was being frustrated by smallpox. Not only was this disease rampant in Boston, but British forces were inoculated against it and reportedly conducting biological warfare by spreading smallpox to impede the Continental Army. Even worse, Washington was receiving news of costly losses in Canada, where "smallpox had reached epidemic proportions in the American expeditionary force and severely compromised its ability to maintain the siege of Quebec and hold Montreal."[1] Facing the grim prospect of losing the Revolutionary War, Washington decided to inoculate the Continental Army against smallpox in 1777. At the time, this was a risky decision: vaccine had not been invented, and inoculation caused a contagious and occasionally lethal infection. Thankfully for the future United States, Washington's gamble on biodefense paid off. The incidence of smallpox among Continental forces dropped precipitously, and the rest is history.

More than two hundred years later, General Norman Schwarzkopf faced far more favorable odds as he prepared for the 1991 Gulf War. The US military had benefited more from modern science and technology than any other military in the world, and it enjoyed the preponderance of power in this conflict. Unlike General Washington, however, Schwarzkopf and the Joint Chiefs of Staff were unable and unwilling to fully vaccinate US forces against the anthrax bacteria and botulinum toxin that Iraq planned to use if Baghdad was destroyed.[2] According to the US Government Accountability Office (GAO), "if Iraq had used the biological warfare agents that were available to it . . . there could have been

[1]

enormous fatalities."[3] Fortunately, these weapons were not used, but Iraqi restraint does not explain why Schwarzkopf had such a hard time with biodefense.

General Colin Powell commented on biological weapons and biodefense shortly after the Gulf War. Relative to other threats, "the one that scares me to death," Powell said, "perhaps even more so than tactical nuclear weapons, and the one that we have least capability against is biological weapons. And this was my greatest concern during Operation Desert Storm."[4] After the show of force known as Operation Desert Thunder in 1998, General Anthony Zinni expressed similar concern. Commenting on anthrax, he said "it would be almost impossible for us to conduct our war plans or to implement them if this were to be used on the battlefield."[5] The US military was better prepared for biodefense when it invaded Iraq and headed for Baghdad in March 2003, but even then the armed services struggled to field the medical countermeasures, detection equipment, and physical protection they would need if Iraq actually had the biological "weapons of mass destruction" or "WMD" that were cited as justification for this preventive war.

Given all the advances in science and technology since the Revolutionary War, how could the US military still struggle to defend itself against biological weapons at the dawn of the twenty-first century? Perhaps comparing biodefense during the Revolutionary War to recent wars with Iraq is like comparing apples to oranges. However, a contemporary and more apt comparison between military and civilian biodefense is even more puzzling. On the one hand, as the difficulties during the 1991 Gulf War and 2003 invasion of Iraq suggest, the US military has neglected biodefense. Military research, development, acquisition, and doctrine were deficient for decades, despite the long-standing threat of biological warfare and the vested interests of the armed services. On the other hand, the United States has spent more than $70 billion on biodefense since September 11 and the anthrax attacks in 2001. This is a huge investment in science and technology for national security, but most of the funding now comes from civilian organizations such as the Department of Health and Human Services (HHS) rather than the Department of Defense (DoD).

Why did the DoD neglect biodefense when it eagerly created and used other kinds of science and technology? Conversely, why did HHS sponsor biodefense when biological weapons were traditionally seen as a military problem? Both military neglect and civilian sponsorship are consequential and counterintuitive. All else being equal, we might expect the history of biodefense to have gone quite differently.[6] Much has been written on the US offensive biological weapons program, which began during World War II and ended in 1969.[7] But the history of American biodefense is puzzling and, with few exceptions, largely untold. These puzzles therefore raise the central question of this book: What factors best explain research, development, acquisition, and doctrine for biodefense in the United States?

MY ARGUMENT: ORGANIZATIONAL FRAMES AND STEREOTYPES

In this book I explain how influential ideas at work inside the DoD and HHS caused both military neglect and the rise of civilian biodefense. These ideas are best described as *organizational frames of reference*, which define the problems that organizations such as the military will choose to solve. I also advance organizational frame theory by employing the concept of *stereotypes*, which are simplistic, repetitious, and often inaccurate ideas about groups. Stereotypes explain what can happen to issues that fall outside an organization's dominant frame of reference.

Social stereotypes usually generalize about groups of people (race, gender, religion, etc.), but similar ideas can also apply to other categories of objects and events. Although these ideas are often fallacious, maybe we should not be surprised to learn that complex and otherwise sophisticated organizations use simple stereotypes. Individuals certainly do (consider the "shiftless negro," among countless other examples), and similar ideas figure prominently in state propaganda, ranging from the German "Hun" during World War I (associating Imperial Germany with primitive barbarism) to rhetoric about "WMD" leading up to the Iraq War (lumping radically different weapons together under the same label).[8]

Such simplicity can come at the cost of accuracy. This tradeoff is particularly dangerous for the armed services and other organizations that operate in hostile environments where subtle distinctions can make the difference between life and death. Nevertheless, like other ideas rooted in culture and cognition, stereotypes and frames of reference are usually taken for granted. When at work inside research-intensive organizations, this unquestioned acceptance can have a powerful effect on science and technology.

In particular, I argue that the US military's dominant frame of reference is defined by kinetic warfare involving projectile weapons and explosives. Simply put, bullets and bombs most readily spring to mind when the Army, Navy, Air Force, and Marine Corps consider the weapons of war. This frame is inapplicable in some circumstances, however, and so the armed services struggle to understand nonkinetic problems and solutions that include, among others, biological weapons and

[3]

biodefense. Rather than learn about issues outside its dominant frame, the military has merely paid them lip service through stereotypes such as "chemical and biological weapons" or "chemical, biological, and radiological defense." These stereotypes conflate and confuse very different kinds of nonkinetic threats and countermeasures, and military biodefense has been neglected as a result.

But this neglect was not inevitable. Different ideas produce different results or outcomes, as evidenced by the rise of civilian biodefense. Unlike the kinetic frame inside the DoD, the dominant approach to problem solving inside HHS is defined by what I call the biomedical frame of reference. Here disease is recognized as a salient cause of damage, and, as a consequence, this civilian organization has proved more willing and able to support biodefense than the military. Instead of adopting the military's inaccurate stereotypes, civilian scientists have chosen to construct a new relationship between bioterrorism and the idea of emerging infectious diseases. This socially constructed relationship facilitated the rise of civilian biodefense during the 1990s, as well as the surge in biodefense after September 11 and the anthrax attacks of 2001.

My argument about the influence of these ideas stands in sharp contrast to the conventional wisdom, which would explain biodefense policy as a product of either the threat environment or bureaucratic interests. Explanations based on external threats are derived from realist theory, while domestic interests in funding and autonomy are cited in the scholarship on bureaucratic politics. Both realism and theories of bureaucratic interests find substantial support in the established literature on weapon systems such as missiles, submarines, and aircraft.[9]

However, this literature suffers from a selection bias that undermines its conclusions about the significance of threats and interests. With few exceptions, these studies focus on science and technology that the military has eagerly pursued. This overdetermined demand for some types of knowledge and hardware can conceal the lessons to be learned in cases of neglect. These studies also focus almost exclusively on the armed services, even though some civilian organizations are intimately involved with national security. Therefore, a wider range of causes and consequences must be examined in order to accurately explain research, development, acquisition, and doctrine. In this book I test theories about realism and bureaucratic interests against organizational frames.

These theories make very different predictions about biodefense policy, just as they have different implications for other aspects of science, technology, and security. Before examining these arguments and evidence in greater detail, however, we must first understand how biological weapons differ from other weapons and what it means to defend against them.

Different Form of Firepower, Different Kind of Defense

Biodefense limits the damage caused by biological weapons (BW), which consist of bacteria, viruses, fungi, and the toxins that these organisms produce (coupled with a delivery system). There is no perfect defense against BW, given their characteristics described below, and "it is easier to make a biological weapon than to create an effective system of biological defense."[10] However, the damage that these weapons cause can be limited through a combination of medical countermeasures, detection and identification, and physical protection.

These are the key components of biodefense. Physical protection limits exposure to infection through face masks and filters that reduce the risk of inhaling aerosolized BW agents, for instance, as well as through bleach and other decontamination solutions that remove or destroy pathogens on surfaces such as skin and clothing. Detection and identification can be difficult, as I will soon explain, but the process involves sensors—assays that use antibodies, chemical stains, polymerase chain reactions, microarrays, or other techniques—and surveillance to help determine when a biological attack has occurred and what pathogens might be present. Perhaps most important, medical countermeasures can prevent or treat infection through prophylactic vaccines and therapeutic drugs such as antibiotics.

Biodefense differs from armor and the other kinds of cover that are used to limit damage caused by projectiles and explosives. This is because biological weapons are a different form of firepower, with distinct timing and mechanisms of damage. Biological weapons harm only living organisms because they incapacitate or kill through disease instead of causing blunt or penetrating trauma. Their physical effects are not immediately apparent, since there is an incubation period after exposure, so days may pass before victims start to suffer from the symptoms caused by most pathogens. They are also odorless, colorless, and tasteless. These characteristics make it difficult to detect biological attacks and treat potential victims before they become sick, let alone protect them from exposure in the first place. Consequently, the physical effects of BW exposure are unlike a gunshot wound or shrapnel injury, even though each may result in death or incapacitation.[11]

Many different pathogens can be used for biological warfare or bioterrorism. Some have special characteristics. The most threatening agents and diseases are thought to include *Bacillus anthracis* (anthrax), *Clostridium botulinum* (source of the toxin that causes botulism), *Yersinia pestis* (plague), *Variola major* (smallpox), *Francisella tularensis* (tularemia), and viral hemorrhagic fevers such as *Zaire ebolavirus* (Ebola). The US Centers for Disease Control and Prevention (CDC) prioritizes these agents as

[5]

"Category A" threats, based on attributes including their ease of dissemination, communicability, and mortality rates (e.g., anthrax is not contagious, but it is relatively easy to disseminate and lethal if untreated). In addition, there are other lists that include different pathogens that could also be used as weapons. For example, the Australia Group lists about eighty bacteria, viruses, and toxins as potential threats that warrant export control.[12] Here, as elsewhere, the focus is on pathogens that cause disease in humans, but BW can target livestock and crops as well. As with the difficulty of detection, the range of potential agents complicates biodefense.

Depending on the pathogen and delivery method, the risks to man, plant, or animal may depend on environmental factors. Although anthrax spores are notoriously hardy, for instance, sunlight can kill other types of bacteria, as well as many viruses, thereby eliminating their ability to cause infection. Biological toxins can degrade under similar conditions. When delivered as an aerosol for victims to inhale, the dispersion of BW is also affected by local weather and terrain. That being said, bacteria and viruses are living weapons that reproduce inside their victims and thus very low levels of exposure can still cause infection. Small amounts could therefore produce significant numbers of casualties when used against a large target such as a city, airfield, seaport, or military base.[13] These characteristics further complicate biodefense and distinguish BW from projectiles and explosives.

BW ≠ Chemical Weapons or Nuclear Weapons

Biological weapons also differ in important ways from other nonkinetic weapons that include—most notably—chemical weapons. The fundamental difference is that, unlike biological agents, chemical agents are not alive: they are small and relatively simple molecules that people synthesize through chemistry (e.g., the chemical agent sarin is isopropyl methylphosphonofluoridate). As a result, the physical properties of chemical agents are very different from biological agents. Chemical agents can exist as a solid, liquid, or gas. Some are volatile, and they can penetrate human skin along with other permeable materials. In contrast, life forms are larger and they behave differently. Even microorganisms are relatively large and complex in comparison. They do not exist in a gaseous phase and, with rare exceptions, biological agents do not penetrate intact skin.

Furthermore, since chemical agents are not living organisms, they do not reproduce, and that means they are far less potent than biological agents. Because bacteria and viruses reproduce inside their victims, a few organisms can grow into many, many more and cause widespread

[6]

infection. But chemical weapons do not grow or replicate. This is why the nerve agent VX is thirty thousand times less lethal by weight than anthrax, for example, and why a few pounds of *B. anthracis* can potentially kill more people than a ton of sarin.[14] Again, chemical agents can be absorbed through skin, but they are less potent than BW when inhaled because they are not alive.

Another critical difference is that chemical weapons are easier to detect than biological weapons. First, because chemical weapons are relatively simple molecules, their chemistry is well specified and they react to other chemicals in ways that provide identifiable signatures. But living organisms are more complex and thus harder to specify, as are the toxic proteins that some of them naturally secrete (e.g., botulinum toxin). Second, chemical weapons are not naturally occurring compounds.[15] This makes them easier to detect because chemical weapons are not present in the environment unless people have manufactured and released them by accident or design. In contrast, biological material is ubiquitous in nature (bacteria, viruses, molds, pollen, etc.). Given this background noise, it can be difficult to discriminate between a BW agent such as anthrax, for example, and a bacteria such as *Bacillus globigii*, which is relatively harmless and commonly found in soil. Third, chemical weapons are fast-acting poisons, some of which people can sense or feel short of a lethal dose. Since the effects of most chemical agents are quickly felt, and some of them even have an odor or taste (e.g., mustard gas reportedly smells like burning garlic and phosgene smells like mown hay), it is easier to know when they are around. But biological agents have no odor or taste, their effects are not felt until well after exposure, their initial symptoms may be nondescript (sore throat, fever, headache, etc.), and, since they are more potent, small concentrations can still be effective. Because of all these differences, biological detection is difficult and slow when compared with chemical detection.

It is possible to quickly detect chemical agents—within seconds to a few minutes—before they incapacitate or kill their potential victims. This makes it feasible to warn people in advance and therefore defend against chemical attacks by wearing the suits and masks that the US military calls mission-oriented protective posture (MOPP) gear, as shown in figure I.1. In contrast, it is difficult to detect biological attacks until after the victims have already been exposed, by which time it is too late for physical protection to provide effective cover. Moreover, because chemical weapons are less potent, chemical defense through MOPP is more likely to work, even if the filters, seals, and decontamination procedures are imperfect. In order to be effective against BW, however, biodefense must rely much less on physical protection and depend much more on medical countermeasures.

[7]

FIGURE I.1. A US Army corporal wearing MOPP gear during warrior task training, 25 August 2010. US Navy photo.

The differences between chemical weapons and BW have profound tactical, operational, and strategic implications—not the least of which is that chemical defense is, on balance, a much easier and thus cheaper problem to solve than biodefense. The material differences between these weapons do not disappear even when the relationship between them proves ripe for social construction, as this book will show. In particular, relying on organizational stereotypes that say "chemical and biological weapons" are the same does not make them so. But denying their differences does make the decisions that follow from these stereotypes all the more dangerous.

Just as BW differ from chemical weapons, they also differ from nuclear and radiological weapons. It is conceivable that biological weapons could cause tens of thousands if not hundreds of thousands of casualties—numbers that approach those for nuclear weapons. And nuclear weapons are notable for having both kinetic effects (blast) and nonkinetic effects (thermal and ionizing radiation). Unlike nuclear weapons, however, biological weapons do not destroy physical infrastructure, and they are much cheaper and easier to acquire.[16] Compared to plutonium or enriched uranium, the materials and equipment needed to build BW are inexpensive and readily accessible because they have other applications in industries such as medicine and agriculture. The knowledge required is relatively common as well. Therefore, while nuclear technology and biotechnology are both dual-use (meaning they can be used for both benefit and harm, or, alternatively, they have both military and civilian applications), the Fink Report argues that "it is futile to imagine that access to dangerous pathogens and destructive biotechnologies can be physically restricted, as is the case for nuclear weapons and fissionable materials."[17] The acquisition and effects of biological weapons also differ from enhanced-radiation weapons (i.e., the neutron bomb), as well as from so-called dirty bombs (i.e., explosive devices that spread radioactive contamination).

Finally, and most important for my analysis, the myriad of differences between these various weapons have significant implications for mounting an effective defense. For instance, MOPP may suffice for chemical defense in the military. However, these suits and masks are ineffective for protection against biological attacks without advance warning, which is unlikely given the difficulty of detecting BW. The use of nuclear weapons is not difficult to detect; moreover, the Geiger counter was invented to detect radiation long before the first atomic bomb. But here the utility of MOPP is limited for different reasons: this standard-issue equipment does not protect against thermal radiation, neutron radiation, or gamma rays, and consequently the suit and mask could ignite or melt while the person wearing them burns or cooks to death inside.

So the problems and solutions involved with defense against these weapons are very different, and the differences are neither subtle nor inconsequential. All else being equal, we would therefore expect the military's language and practices to address these differences in painstaking detail, given that it is responsible for defending itself, if not the country, against all kinds of attack. Granted, the general public might not understand or appreciate the distinctions between chemical, biological, or even nuclear weapons, and politicians or arms control advocates might define categories like WMD strategically to support their policy preferences. But when push comes to shove, the armed forces must prepare to confront these very different forms of firepower in the field. Whether the US military actually addresses these differences is another matter, however, and the reasons why it might not are discussed in the chapters that follow.

PLAN AND METHOD OF THE BOOK

In this book I explain military and civilian biodefense through a comparative analysis of research, development, acquisition, and doctrine from World War II through the 2003 Iraq War. I also look back to General Washington and extrapolate into the future. The book is a tale of two organizations. As one of the most powerful organizations in human history, the DoD is home to exceptionally sophisticated problem solving for kinetic warfare. But inaccurate stereotypes about issues outside the kinetic frame have had a deleterious effect on military biodefense. HHS is also flawed in many ways (including red tape, parochial infighting, and waste), but the ideas at work inside this civilian organization are more amenable to the problems and solutions involved with biodefense. Drawing on original interviews, archival research, and other sources, I show how different ideas have influenced America's vulnerability to biological warfare and bioterrorism, the interpretation or definition of threats and interests within the national security establishment, and, ultimately, the trajectory of science and technology.

In chapter 1, I describe the three explanations for biodefense—realism, bureaucratic interests, and organizational frames—that this book will test. First, realist theory predicts that the United States will fear biological weapons and help protect itself through biodefense because the threat is credible. My threat assessment summarizes enemy capabilities and intentions. Rather than write a gruesome account of how infection can affect an individual's body, I focus on how biological weapons can affect military action (especially at the operational level of warfare). Bureaucratic interests provide a second explanation for biodefense policy. In this view, both the DoD and HHS are predicted to compete for funding and autonomy, so I consider who may win or lose bureaucratic turf wars. Finally, after addressing these conventional theories about threats and interests, I describe my argument about organizational frame theory. Here I define frames and stereotypes, illustrate the kinetic frame of reference, and explain why military biodefense is expected to be neglected as a result. But organizational frame theory also predicts that different ideas will produce different results for civilian biodefense: predictions that stand in sharp contrast to realism and bureaucratic interests. Indeed, these differences set up the empirical analysis that follows.

Which theory provides the best explanation for biodefense policy? I answer this question in the context of military research, development, and acquisition in chapter 2. Neglect in each area is evident throughout the period between World War II and the Iraq War, as predicted by organizational frame theory. The US military initially resisted the idea of biological warfare and assigned it to the Chemical Warfare Service despite all of the differences between chemical weapons and BW. Inaccuracies inherent to the stereotype of "chemical and biological weapons" caused problems for offense as well as defense, and these ideas even influenced

President Richard Nixon's decision to end the offensive BW program in 1969. US investment in biodefense soon hit record lows, in spite of the Soviet threat, which helps explain why General Schwarzkopf was unprepared for BW during the Gulf War. Key lessons from this war were not learned, however, and the military's kinetic frame and nonkinetic stereotypes continued to hinder research, development, and acquisition through the Iraq War.

In chapter 3 I examine military doctrine. Here again, the planning and practice of biodefense has relied on stereotypes that are based on fatally flawed assumptions. The persistence and influence of these dangerous ideas is inexplicable from a realist perspective, but it is consistent with my argument. In particular, I reveal how military doctrine has assumed that biological attacks are like chemical attacks and thus detectable in advance, notwithstanding the difficulty of detecting BW. Similar ideas have undermined war games and training as well, so the practice of military biodefense suffered when the armed services actually tried to employ detection systems and vaccines in preparation for war.

Explaining the military's mistakes is important, but organizational frame theory can offer more than a simple "sociology of error" if it also helps explain the rise of civilian biodefense. Therefore, in chapter 4 I treat civilian biodefense as a "natural experiment" to compare with research, development, acquisition, and doctrine in the military, where the threats and interests involved are related but the ideas differ. I argue that HHS and its subsidiaries—including the CDC and the National Institutes of Health (NIH)—have a biomedical frame that differs from the kinetic frame and thus has produced different results. Foreshadowed during the Korean War, the rise of civilian biodefense began in earnest during the 1990s when prominent scientists constructed a new relationship between bioterrorism and emerging infectious diseases. These ideas helped situate BW inside the biomedical frame at HHS, enabling it to respond to increasing demands from the president and Congress. Unlike the military, HHS lobbied hard to win money on the table for biodefense rather than let this funding go to the Department of Homeland Security after September 11 and the anthrax attacks of 2001. Moreover, HHS does not rely on the military's inaccurate stereotypes. While these differences are difficult to explain with theories about realism or bureaucratic interests, they are consistent with my argument.

The history of military and civilian biodefense indicates that ideational factors such as organizational frames and stereotypes can precondition how threats and interests are interpreted. Although all of these variables are needed to provide a complete account for research, development, acquisition, and doctrine, the independent influence of ideas inside organizations is particularly significant. After reviewing these findings, I conclude the book by looking beyond biodefense and applying the lessons learned to other important aspects of science, technology, and security—ranging from improvised explosive devices to cyberspace. In the end, I show that some ideas are integral to national security policy as well as our ability to understand it.

[1]

Science and Technology for National Security

Threats, Interests, and Ideas

Advanced technology plays a defining role in what has been called the "American way of war."[1] Nuclear weapons, the Internet, satellite navigation, drones, and countless other examples highlight how much US national security depends on technology and, in turn, how much the military influences the state of the art. Not only does the military help create scientific knowledge, supplying innovation by researching and developing new applications, it also provides a market, driving demand when the armed services acquire advanced technology. And the military is not alone. Alongside the Department of Defense, civilian agencies such as the Department of Homeland Security, the Department of Agriculture, and the Department of Health and Human Services create and acquire science and technology for national security as well.

The interplay between science, technology, and security is exemplified by military and civilian biodefense: both of which attempt to limit the damage caused by biological weapons. Biodefense also raises important questions about these relationships. For instance, what factors actually explain research, development, and acquisition? Is the same true for doctrine? Why?

Different theories provide different answers, and in this chapter I describe three of the best available explanations. The first is that the threat of biological weapons drives biodefense policy, as predicted by realist theory. After describing realism, I then establish the preconditions needed to test this theory by explaining why biological warfare and bioterrorism are credible threats. The second explanation is that bureaucratic interests determine biodefense policy. I therefore explain what can and cannot be said about bureaucratic turf wars over funding and autonomy.

[13]

The third explanation involves ideas called organizational frames of reference. These ideas are interesting because they offer novel predictions. To show why, I lay out the causal logic of organizational frame theory and relate it to the concept of stereotypes, which is my primary theoretical contribution. I then posit that the military's frame of reference is defined by kinetic warfare and explain what this means for the non-kinetic problems and solutions involved with biodefense. Right or wrong, these predictions are important because they differ from the conventional wisdom about threats and interests.

Threats: A Realist Theory

The most common explanation for research, development, acquisition, and doctrine is that threats cause the creation and use of science and technology for national security. This explanation is closely associated with realist theory, which argues that the international threat environment determines state behavior.[2] Realism makes several important assumptions about states and the international system that have implications for biodefense policy. In particular, it assumes that the international system is anarchic because there is no overarching authority to enforce international law or, more crucially, prevent violence. Realism also assumes that states want to survive because survival is the prerequisite for every other national interest.

Survival is uncertain due to anarchy, however, since any state may use violent force and no state can credibly commit or promise not to threaten others in the future.[3] Given this uncertainty about actions and intentions, states may be threatened by the material power of other states (and perhaps, by extension, some nonstate actors), including their resources such as population and wealth that can be used for violence. One consequence is that states sometimes fear each other. Another is that, when push comes to shove, a state can only rely on its own resources to provide security and thus survival: an outcome that realism refers to as "self-help." Self-help often involves using science and technology for national security, but "many of the means by which a state tries to increase its security decrease the security of others."[4] This dynamic is known as the security dilemma: it rests at the heart of realist theory and explains why conflict between states is likely if not inevitable.

Along with these arguments about how anarchy, survival, and uncertainty can create security dilemmas, realism also anticipates fear and self-help because it assumes that states are unitary and rational actors. Rationality is particularly important when this theory of international politics is used to explain the national security policies of individual

[14]

states.[5] While it need not be strict or formal, rationality is understood to mean that states make deliberate decisions in pursuit of their national interests, the foremost of which is to maximize their chance of survival.[6] These decisions incorporate most if not all of the available information— in this case, about the threat of biological warfare and bioterrorism—and strategic expectations about how other states might react, as well as trade-offs between the costs and benefits of alternative policy options.

Finally, states are assumed to be unitary actors, an assumption that can be relaxed when realism is applied to national security policy but not dismissed. For example, Barry Posen's classic study of military doctrine in France, Britain, and Germany supports a variant of realist theory (i.e., threats determine doctrine). But he also acknowledges that there are gaps between the policy preferences of civilian statesmen and professional soldiers. Posen therefore argues that civilian intervention is sometimes necessary to integrate national political priorities into military policy.[7] The greater this disjunction, however, and the more that military preferences diverge from the national interest (e.g., requiring civilian intervention or remaining unresponsive to it), the less that realism can explain. As a result, this theory is most useful when it can provide a functional explanation for military policy as a coherent and rational expression of the national interest that is responsive to security threats.

Like Posen's study of military doctrine, other scholars support the realist notion that threats drive research, development, and acquisition, even when they pay considerable attention to other factors. According to Michael Brown, for instance, bureaucratic interests influenced the US strategic bomber program but the Soviet threat was the primary driver.[8] Both Brown and Posen argue that arms races during the Cold War were also evidence of self-help through "internal balancing," since each superpower responded to the threat posed by the other, creating the "action-reaction" or "anticipation-reaction" cycles that typify the security dilemma.[9] Similarly, Eugene Gholz and Harvey Sapolsky claim that "the high level of perceived threat" drove the US defense sector during the Cold War, which privileged military expertise and kept the pork barrel politics of Congress in check.[10] Of course, realism is not without its critics in the context of military science and technology, as elsewhere.[11] But the threats emphasized by this theory stand to be a popular and powerful explanation for biodefense.

In general, realism predicts that threats to national security cause fear and thus self-help through research, development, acquisition, and doctrine. In particular, *if other states or nonstate actors have biological weapons, then the United States will fear biological warfare and bioterrorism; consequently, it will invest in biodefense to help mitigate these threats.* Military policy is expected to be especially responsive.

[15]

Since realism predicts that threats determine military priorities, decisions about how to allocate resources between biodefense and other defense programs should be governed by the expected returns for national security—not parochial interests, let alone incomprehension or wishful thinking. These decisions should also be informed by the available evidence, which rationality requires, and updated based on new information. Given imperfect information about the BW threat, realism suggests that the military should be risk averse and place little faith in international regimes such as the Biological Weapons Convention (i.e., the Convention on the Prohibition of the Development, Production and Stockpiling of Bacteriological [Biological] and Toxin Weapons and on Their Destruction).

A Credible Threat

How threatening are biological warfare and bioterrorism? What is the cause for fear, and what is the need for self-help through biodefense? Recall that biological weapons consist of bacteria, viruses, fungi, and the toxins that these organisms produce, which, when coupled with a delivery system, can incapacitate or kill through disease. They are difficult to detect. Biological material is ubiquitous and complex, the symptoms of disease are not immediately apparent, and the pathogens involved are odorless, colorless, and tasteless. Furthermore, biological weapons are potent. Because pathogenic organisms reproduce inside their victims, low levels of exposure can still cause infection and thus result in large numbers of casualties.

Despite their potency and difficulty of detection, however, the utility of biological weapons has been debated more than any other class of weapon. An influential myth in this debate is that biological weapons are useless against the military, with the corollary being that they pose little or no threat. Unfortunately, this myth fails to recognize that military utility is multidimensional. In order to accurately assess the BW threat, it is therefore necessary to disaggregate warfare into the tactical, operational, and strategic levels of military action.

The Utility of BW

Biological weapons have strengths and weaknesses that differ from other forms of firepower, but none of their drawbacks negate their utility at every level of military action. Consider three supposed weaknesses that are sometimes associated with BW effects, defensive measures, and international norms. The first is that biological weapons have delayed effects, some of which are uncertain because exposure depends on environmental factors when the pathogens are dispersed as an aerosol.[12] Given their delayed effects, these weapons are probably not useful for tactics that involve immediate and localized combat. (In contrast, most chemical weapons take effect immediately, so they may be useful in tactical situations.)

But testing has demonstrated that biological warfare is not unpredictable.[13] Moreover, the same characteristics that limit the tactical utility of BW can enhance their impact at the operational level of warfare. This is where biological weapons may be most effective against the military.[14] The operational level refers to the command, control, and logistic functions that are typically housed at military bases behind the front lines, as well as at the airfields and seaports that are needed to move forces and supplies inside the theater of operations. Not only are these facilities crucial for any military campaign but they are also large, immobile, and occupied for extended periods of time. So if biological weapons are used against this kind of target, then their delayed effects can facilitate covert release. Even uncertainty can be advantageous for the attacker because it creates protracted periods of danger during which detection, treatment, and protection stand to impose a heavy psychological toll and operational burden.[15]

Used in this way, biological warfare would be a form of operational interdiction or deep battle. Although the mechanisms differ, the results could be similar to a blitzkrieg (i.e., operational paralysis), and, while biological weapons do not destroy ships, aircraft, or tanks, "they can render these weapons useless by sickening or killing the crews and support personnel."[16] It is also likely that US allies and host nations would suffer from biological warfare on their soil, which might tempt them to limit their exposure by denying the US military access to the local infrastructure it needs to project power overseas.[17] This means that, far from being useless, these weapons threaten both political access and physical access at the operational level of warfare.

A second "weakness" of biological weapons is that the damage they cause can be limited through medical countermeasures, detection and identification, and physical protection—that is, biodefense. However, this technology must be developed and acquired beforehand, in which case it is better evidence of fear and self-help instead of an absence of threat. More important, the protective measures that are often cited as evidence of the military's invulnerability—suits and masks—are ineffective for cover without advance warning, which, again, is unlikely because biological weapons are difficult to detect. The difficulty of detection enhances the operational utility of these weapons against military forces, as well as their utility for strategic warfare and bioterrorism.

[17]

Strategic warfare destroys an adversary's capability or will to fight by either denying them the military means to win or punishing their civilian population. Since these same factors relate to the concept of deterrence, one way to debate the strategic utility of biological weapons is to ask whether they threaten to inflict unacceptable damage and thus help safeguard a state's vital interests. According to Susan Martin, "biological weapons can serve as a strategic deterrent" despite defensive measures "because effective deterrence requires only a small possibility of great destruction."[18] However, as Gregory Koblentz argues, "the availability of defenses against biological weapons places a premium on the attacker achieving surprise," and surprise requires secrecy, which makes it difficult to issue the credible threats that are required for effective deterrence.[19]

While secret weapons are poor deterrents, they are still used for strategic coercion during war (as illustrated by the Manhattan Project and atomic bomb).[20] Terrorism also resembles coercion more than deterrence, and, perhaps more important, nuclear deterrence does not negate the BW threat. To begin with, deterrence through nuclear punishment requires attribution. But assigning blame is easier said than done for biological attacks because they are difficult to detect, trace, or even distinguish in some cases from naturally occurring outbreaks of infectious disease.[21] Here secrecy is advantageous for the attacker since they might remain anonymous.

Even if the perpetrator is identified, nuclear punishment might not be a credible response to biological attacks by terrorists and nonnuclear states.[22] Nor does the strategic logic of nuclear deterrence invalidate vulnerability at lower levels of warfare. Indeed, the "stability-instability paradox" suggests that nuclear states remain sensitive to operational threats, as did America's emphasis on conventional forces during the Cold War. And nuclear deterrence does not account for prominent technology such as ballistic missile defense, which, in theory, defends against a threat that is easily deterred because the trajectory of a ballistic warhead provides a return address for retaliation. Evidently, the United States is sufficiently risk averse that it is unwilling to rely on deterrence even under favorable conditions, since it has spent hundreds of billions of dollars on missile defense. So realism predicts that it will also invest in biodefense to mitigate a threat where nuclear deterrence is more likely to fail.

Finally, the Soviet Union and other nuclear states developed biological weapons for strategic warfare, which suggests that they might have strategic value. The existence of these BW programs also challenges a third "weakness" of biological weapons, namely, that they are rarely used and are prohibited by international law.[23] These laws include the 1925 Geneva Protocol for the Prohibition of the Use in War of Asphyxiating,

Poisonous or Other Gases, and of Bacteriological Methods of Warfare as well as the 1972 Biological Weapons Convention. Perhaps legal prohibitions are bolstered by long-standing taboos against the use of disease as a weapon because "most nations have embraced the norm that deems these weapons especially repugnant."[24] But as Richard Price argues about chemical weapons, norms are social, and "it is by no means clear that this tradition reflects a robust, uncontested, and universal prohibition" or "a taboo uniquely and primordially rooted in human nature."[25] Moreover, unlike Price, realists hold international law in low regard. For despite laws, norms, and taboos, several states and terrorists have still developed and, on occasion, used biological weapons. From a realist perspective, these material capabilities and hostile intentions therefore threaten military forces and civilian populations.

Enemy Capabilities and Intentions

The ability and intent of state and nonstate actors to wage biological warfare and bioterrorism are debated and documented in numerous government reports and historical studies. Some of these are sensational or apocalyptic while others deliberately discount the threat. That being said, the bulk of evidence can be summarized without exaggerating the threat or dismissing the danger: while no states or terrorists admit to having biological weapons today, several adversaries have demonstrated the capability and intention to acquire and use these weapons against the United States.

As for the threat from states, the prime historical example is the Soviet Union, which built the largest BW program the world has ever known. This program began by secret decree in 1928. Although it was soon undermined by Joseph Stalin's purges of prominent scientists and patronage of Trofim Lysenko (who denounced genetics as bourgeois science), the Soviet BW program benefited from prisoners and documents captured from Japan's infamous Unit 731, which had used biological weapons against the Russians and Chinese in World War II.[26] During the Cold War, both superpowers built biological weapons that ranged from anthrax, botulinum, and tularemia to brucellosis, Q fever, and Venezuelan equine encephalitis. Unlike the United States, however, the Soviet Union also developed incurable pathogens, including smallpox and Marburg virus, as well antibiotic-resistant strains of plague and other bacteria.

More troubling, the Soviet Union signed the Biological Weapons Convention in 1972 with no intention of complying. Instead, Leonid Brezhnev secretly expanded and modernized the offensive BW program. This involved a new and nominally civilian conglomerate called Biopreparat, as well as ministries ranging from Defense to Health and Agriculture, with tens of thousands of people working at dozens of facilities across the country. Annual funding exceeded $200 million—ultimately, with the apparent approval of Mikhail Gorbachev.[27] Tons of smallpox and anthrax were stockpiled for use in the event of war. In addition, by multiple accounts, the Soviet Union developed cruise missiles and intercontinental ballistic missiles with biological warheads for strategic use (although it is debated whether warheads were shaped for the SS-18 ICBM, the SS-11, or other missiles).[28] Medium-range bombers such as the Illyushin-28 were also equipped with spray tanks and cluster bombs to attack targets at the operational level of warfare.

The United States was aware of the Soviet BW program throughout the Cold War. Two German scientists captured after World War II (Heinrich Kliewe and Walter Hirsch) reported that the Soviet Union had an active and aggressive BW program, based on information that the Nazis obtained from Soviet prisoners.[29] As a result, early US intelligence estimates concluded that "the USSR almost certainly had an active BW program," and reconnaissance by U-2 aircraft and Corona satellites seemed to confirm that Vozrozhdeniya Island was an active test site.[30] Doubts were expressed during the 1960s but soon swept aside. In 1975 and 1976, intelligence officials even leaked evidence to the press to suggest that the Soviet Union was violating the Biological Weapons Convention at Sverdlovsk and other facilities. These suspicions were reportedly confirmed with the defection of a senior Soviet diplomat, Arkady Shevchenko.[31] In 1979, an accidental release of anthrax from the production facility at Sverdlovsk killed at least seventy people, providing further proof of the BW program.[32] Consequently, intelligence assessments during the 1980s concluded that the USSR continued to develop, produce, and test biological weapons.

Despite these grim assessments, the United States underestimated the size, scope, and sophistication of the Soviet BW program, at least until the defection of bioweaponeers Vladimir Pasechnik in 1989 and Kanatjan Alibekov in 1992.[33] Biological weapons were still a credible threat, however, given the intensity of security competition during the Cold War. First, the information available at the time was threatening enough to warrant a serious response. As Clifford Geertz argues in a different context, "it is not necessary to know everything in order to understand something."[34] And enough was known to understand that the Soviet Union had biological weapons. Second, "rationality further requires that states invest an appropriate amount of effort in collecting and evaluating information that would inform them about their environment."[35] This means that realism, predicated on rationality, cannot excuse or explain away "the intelligence community's lack of investment in collection and analysis of BW intelligence," which "contributed to these gaps and

[20]

shortfalls."[36] Finally, rather than be rendered moot by uncertainty, realist predictions rely on it—not on perfect information. Uncertainty about the Soviet BW program should therefore have increased American fear and self-help through biodefense.

The United States also believed that other hostile states were armed with biological weapons. During Operation Desert Shield, for instance, the CIA reported that "Iraq has been producing large quantities of the agents anthrax and botulinum toxin since 1989. The Iraqis probably have filled limited quantities of these agents into aerial bombs and artillery rockets already and may eventually use BW agents to fill short-range ballistic missile warheads."[37] As anticipated, Iraq deployed approximately 160 R400 bombs and 25 Al Hussein missiles with biological payloads. Field commanders were preauthorized to use them if Baghdad was attacked with nuclear weapons.[38]

While intelligence estimates of Iraqi capabilities were reasonably accurate during the 1991 Gulf War, the same cannot be said about the information used to build the case for invading Iraq in 2003. But since exaggerated threat perceptions—"Saddam Hussein has biological weapons and the capabilities to rapidly produce more"—were a primary justification for the Iraq War, it was reasonable to expect and thus fear that these weapons would be used to counter a US invasion.[39] Accurately or not, the United States has judged that other states have offensive BW programs as well, including Russia, Syria, North Korea, and Iran.[40]

Lastly, terrorists have acquired and actually used biological weapons with hostile intent but mixed results. This indicates that the technical barriers to bioterrorism are neither inconsiderable nor insurmountable. On the one hand, the Japanese cult Aum Shinrikyo was seen as a bellwether for mass-casualty terrorism after it killed more than a dozen people with sarin gas in 1995. But the cult failed in several attempts to use BW against targets in and around Tokyo, including US Navy bases at Yokohama and Yokosuka (home of the Seventh Fleet). Fortunately, the cult used a nonvirulent strain of anthrax and harmless or contaminated strains of botulinum that did not kill anyone.[41] Al Qaeda also attempted to acquire anthrax, but it was disrupted by the war in Afghanistan in 2001.[42]

On the other hand, the 2001 anthrax letters suggest that an individual or group might acquire and use potent biological weapons.[43] Here the apparent culprit, Bruce Ivins, was a senior microbiologist at the military's premier biodefense research facility. This certainly gave him special access and training. But microbiologists are not uncommon, and, while access to such a facility is rare, it is not necessary in order to obtain anthrax. Kathleen Vogel and Sonia Ben Ouagrham-Gormley argue that building biological weapons requires tacit knowledge that is hard to

[21]

acquire, and yet "this does not mean that terrorists would never be able to develop such know-how."[44] Furthermore, a "red team" exercise called BACUS suggests that the barriers to acquisition are not insurmountable, since this small group was able to produce two pounds of anthrax simulant, milled to 1–5 microns, using commercial technology costing less than $2 million.[45] Milton Leitenberg insists that this exercise was not designed to test whether terrorists could build biological weapons but rather "to see if detectable signatures would result" from their attempt.[46] In doing so, however, BACUS still demonstrated that a dozen people with a modest budget could credibly produce BW.[47]

In sum, enemy capabilities and intentions indicate that biological warfare and bioterrorism are credible threats. Realism therefore predicts that the United States—particularly the US military—will fear biological weapons and help protect itself through research, development, acquisition, and doctrine for biodefense. When good intelligence about BW is difficult to acquire, realism predicts that uncertainty will cause fear and self-help rather than blissful ignorance. Of course, biological weapons are not the only threat and resources are limited, so a rational response will require tradeoffs. But these tradeoffs should be proportional. Even if biological warfare is an order of magnitude less threatening than nuclear war, for example, and thus warrants proportionally less expenditure than the tens of billions of dollars that the armed services spend per year on nuclear threats, realism would still predict sizable and long-standing investment in military biodefense.[48]

INTERESTS: A BUREAUCRATIC THEORY

While common, references to realism require rather heroic assumptions about states behaving as if they were unitary actors that respond rationally to their threat environment. States are not unitary, of course, and so any rational response to threats such as biological warfare and bioterrorism might be modified or constrained by divisions inside the government between different bureaucratic agencies. Thus, if threats fail to explain research, development, acquisition, or doctrine, then bureaucratic interests provide an alternative explanation. This theory represents a popular strand of the literature on bureaucratic politics, which assumes that governments are coalitions of organizations and individuals with competing interests in funding and autonomy. Given these interests, biodefense policy is a competitive game, the outcome of which is determined by who plays, each player's stand, and how those stands aggregate into collective action.[49]

[22]

According to Miles' law, "where you stand depends on where you sit," which means that each player's position in the bureaucracy determines his or her policy preferences. But position is a slippery concept. If defined too broadly, for instance, then it will include the personal history that every official brings to his or her office: idiosyncratic baggage that in turn makes the interests supposedly determined by position difficult to predict or falsify. This is one reason why causal ambiguity is endemic in many references to "bureaucratic politics," which are often "too sloppy, vague, and imprecise."[50] To avoid this problem, it is therefore useful to define position narrowly as a formal office.[51]

The officials who occupy these offices are motivated by self-interest, so they perform and promote their particular responsibilities in order to increase their funding and autonomy. These are generic resources. All else being equal, all bureaucracies are assumed to want more money and more independence because, as James Q. Wilson argues, they value autonomy at least as much as their budget.[52] Interests in these generic resources are the same factors that Posen and Jack Snyder cite when they argue that militaries prefer offensive doctrines.[53]

Thus the US military, like other bureaucracies, competes with other agencies for its share of funding and autonomy. Bureaucratic competition is also evident inside the military. The armed services compete with each other because funding is limited and cooperation constrains their independence. Consequently, compromise over issues like biodefense is usually reached through competitive bargaining and the officials involved are expected to be stanch advocates for their parochial programs, protecting if not expanding their turf or fiefdom.

Bureaucratic Turf Wars: Winners and Losers

If policymaking is a competitive game, then who will win? What determines the outcome of bureaucratic struggles between and inside military and civilian agencies? Since all of the players want the same resources, generic interests in funding and autonomy cannot explain the difference between winners and losers. This means that these questions cannot be answered by simply citing bureaucratic interests—at least not without also relying on other theories or tautological arguments.

The tautological argument is that winners are those who won: an answer as accurate as it is useless. According to Sapolsky, "a program's rank in official priorities is frequently used to explain its success or failure," but "the explanation is inadequate because it begs the question of how a high priority status is obtained or maintained."[54] The same can be said about references to "critical tasks" that fail to explain why these tasks are more critical than others, or, similarly, "core competencies" that are only maintained through a series of choices—decisions that could have been different—and thus warrant explanation. For his part, Sapolsky argues that bureaucratic success depends on political skill, as does Graham Allison, who claims "the pulling and hauling that is politics" produces unintended results that are determined in part by "an elusive blend" of power and skill.[55] But power is shared and skill can be learned, so these arguments cannot explain why some programs consistently win or lose over time.

In order to explain persistent patterns of winners and losers, other theories are required. Sapolsky and other scholars adopt what Gholz calls the "bureaucratic-strategic framework," which, as its name suggests, combines bureaucratic interests with an emphasis on the strategic threats highlighted by realism.[56] This framework assumes that the armed services are self-interested and yet competition between them in "the marketplace of policy making" also produces innovation.[57] Here the programs that succeed appear consistent with a rational response to threats and thus serve the national interest. For example, Sapolsky argues that "we are all beneficiaries of the Air Force–Navy competition." Even though interservice rivalry has had its costs, "it forced both services to examine carefully the missiles and operational doctrines that they were developing," and this in turn improved their response to the nuclear threat.[58]

In principle, there is no problem with combining these different theories. As Wilson laments, there is no single, unified, or comprehensive theory of bureaucracy, and therefore some combination of factors is likely (especially when considering the complexity of research, development, acquisition, and doctrine).[59] In practice, however, the bureaucratic-strategic framework suffers from causal ambiguity due to its genesis and testing in overdetermined cases such as missile and bomber programs during the Cold War. Given this selection of cases, it is difficult to distinguish the relative significance of threats versus interests because, as Michael Brown observes, these different factors often "pushed . . . in the same direction at the same time."[60]

Similar problems impede explanations for winners and losers that combine bureaucratic interests with ideational factors. This combination is apparent in arguments about "organizational essence" and "institutional personalities" that are advanced by Morton Halperin and Carl Builder.[61] Both Halperin and Builder argue that each armed service has distinct ideas about its identity—namely, who it is and thus what it is interested in doing with its funding and autonomy. The Air Force loves flying and holds pilots in high regard, for instance, while the US Navy imagines itself as heir to the tradition of British naval supremacy and war as a conventional battle for control of the sea. For its part, the Army identifies itself with proud memories of American soldiers matching the fight across Europe in World War II.

These arguments about ideas are similar to organizational frame theory, which I describe next. But while ideas and interests are related, the causal mechanisms involved are still distinct. In one strand of argument, behavior is explained by generic interests that are common to all organizations; in the other, behavior is explained by ideational factors that are endogenous to a particular organization.[62] This distinction is lost in references to organizational essence and institutional personalities. As described by Halperin, for example, it is not clear whether the Air Force's initial resistance to ballistic missiles was caused by aversion to the idea of having its officers sit in silos rather than fly or, alternatively, because it had to pay for these missiles out of its existing budget (making them an unfunded mandate). Similarly, it is unclear whether the Navy resisted Polaris because the idea of destroying Russian cities had little to do with control of the sea or because it meant paying for more submarines with the same amount of funding.[63] Since these arguments refer to different factors, they can point in different directions and predict different results. It is therefore useful to distinguish between them.

When distinguished from other theories and tautological arguments, bureaucratic interests in budget and autonomy provide more insight into the players and their stands than who actually wins or loses. Win or lose, this theory predicts that the officials who are responsible for biodefense will be staunch advocates for it. *If a bureaucratic organization is assigned responsibility for biodefense, then officials inside that organization will compete for resources by promoting research, development, acquisition, and doctrine.* The officials who are responsible for biodefense should have some bureaucratic power, since "the sources of bargaining advantages include formal authority and responsibility" as well as "expertise and control over information."[64] The special interests of these officials should also provide collective action advantages over any diffuse opposition that they might face. As a result, these officials are predicted to be prominent players in policymaking relating to biodefense. They may not win every turf war, but nor should they always lose.

These predictions about bureaucratic interests should apply to military and civilian organizations alike. More specifically, the Army has a mandate and thus vested interests in biodefense that date back to World War II. The Army is therefore predicted to promote this mission and protect it from outside interference. Not only should Army officials with special interests and expertise in biodefense try to increase their funding and autonomy but they should also be important players in military policy on this issue.

[25]

The Army surgeon general and officials from Fort Detrick—where the military built its BW program—should be particularly influential. Again, Detrick and the surgeon general may not always get their way, especially since some divisions inside the Army are hierarchical and the military takes orders from above. For example, while the DoD should oppose other organizations encroaching on its turf, the president and Congress have the authority to issue competing mandates for civilian biodefense to HHS, as they did in the 1990s. However, the military should still behave like other bureaucracies that are interested in funding and autonomy. As a consequence, this theory predicts that the DoD and HHS will respond similarly to similar mandates for biodefense and compete for more resources.

IDEAS: ORGANIZATIONAL FRAME THEORY

Both threats and interests provide plausible explanations for biodefense policy, but there is at least one more alternative to consider. I argue that ideas can also have a powerful influence on science and technology. This argument is not without precedent. As just shown, organizational essence and institutional personalities also include ideational factors; unfortunately, those ideas are underdeveloped and overshadowed by bureaucratic interests.[65] So, in order to place the independent influence of ideas on a stronger theoretical foundation, my argument draws on sociological institutionalism and social constructivism, as well as related concepts such as technological frames and scientific paradigms.[66]

Organizational frames are the shared assumptions and heuristics that organizations use to solve problems.[67] They define the problems that an organization will solve, diagnose the causes, and prescribe possible solutions. A similar theory is advanced by Lynn Eden, who argues that "frames can be seen, or 'read,' in knowledge-laden organizational routines."[68] These routines include the handbooks and computer programs that are used to solve problems, for instance, and the frames that organizations apply are manifest in the vocabulary and jargon used to discuss problems and solutions. Because they depend on language and practice, organizational frames are socially constructed. As a result, their content is contingent on particular choices and social relationships (i.e., these ideas are not an automatic response to the threat environment). Contingency also means that different organizations—including the DoD and HHS—can have different frames of reference (i.e., their content is not the inevitable byproduct of generic interests in funding and autonomy).

Dominant Frames versus Organizational Stereotypes

Although they vary between different organizations, some assumptions and heuristics are shared by most of the members inside any specific institution.[69] These ideas provide a common framework for interpreting reality. They only highlight certain aspects of reality, however, and so organizational frames both enable and constrain action. Some actions are enabled because the problems and solutions they involve are salient inside the organization's dominant frame of reference. One consequence is that the science and technology used for these problems will benefit from ample if not excessive resources. Unfortunately, other problems and solutions fall outside of the organization's dominant frame, which is what I argue happened to military biodefense.[70] External or residual issues are systematically deprived of resources, regardless of their potential significance, in part because they fall victim to the organizational stereotypes described below.

These divergent outcomes are two sides of the same coin. Actions inside an organization's dominant frame are enabled by a path-dependent process of learning and selective attention. Initially, a wide range of problems and solutions could capture the organization's attention, but those selected early are preferentially elaborated on through learning. Over time, learning builds expertise and capacity to solve similar problems. This positive feedback reinforces the selective attention already being paid to issues inside the emerging frame or paradigm. According to Eden, "the competence and knowledge gained then contrasts all the more strongly with the lack of ability to solve other problems," and so "the problem-solving path taken becomes far more attractive than other potential options."[71] Vested interests also start to develop around these activities, and, more important for my argument, the language and practices that define the organization's dominant frame become increasingly sophisticated and specialized over time.

On the flipside, problems and solutions that do not capture an organization's attention early are disadvantaged later if they fall outside of its dominant frame. While complex organizations like the US military are rarely oblivious to issues that do not fit their primary pattern, perspective, or model for problem solving, I argue that they often acknowledge but dismiss these anomalies through simplistic or inaccurate stereotypes.[72] Organizational stereotypes are another kind of frame—namely, they are another set of shared assumptions and heuristics that are used to solve problems. But not all frames are created equal. Unlike the organization's dominant frame, stereotypes are overgeneralizations created by a lack of knowledge and learning. This ignorance is an unintended

[27]

consequence of the selective attention that organizations pay to issues inside their dominant frame of reference.

Just as psychology suggests for individuals, organizations can form stereotypes when—through lack of knowledge and learning—they construct conceptual relationships between disparate categories and characteristics based on imperfect information. The result is a group or class of phenomena that are assumed to share essential attributes (or at least a family resemblance) even though the association between them is, in fact, artificial and often inaccurate.

One of the most influential stereotypes discussed in this book is the relationship that the military constructed between chemical and biological weapons (CBW) despite potentially overwhelming evidence against this association. Similar stereotypes that combine dissimilar categories and characteristics include weapons of mass destruction (WMD), as well as related phrases and acronyms such as nuclear, biological, and chemical (NBC), and chemical, biological, radiological (CBR), among others. The internal logic of these groups is not consistent (e.g., some include nuclear weapons, which have both kinetic and nonkinetic effects).[73] This incoherence makes organizational stereotypes fascinating to study but imprudent to use.

The socially constructed relationships that define these stereotypes have at least two troubling characteristics. First, they lack the sophistication or nuance of the shared assumptions and heuristics that define an organization's dominant frame. At best, stereotypes are simplistic or overgeneralized; more often than not, they are crude, contradictory, and inaccurate ideas about groups. When a group is inaccurately assumed to share essential attributes, this error is compounded by the belief that ideas about one member apply to other members as well. For example, consider the stereotype "WMD," which is said to include everything from the homemade explosives used in the Boston marathon bombing to Syrian chemical weapons to Soviet stockpiles of smallpox to thermonuclear warheads. This is not a nuanced category. It glosses over extreme differences in kind, and the stereotype incorrectly implies that knowledge about one of these phenomena equates to useful knowledge about the others.

Second, errors in organizational stereotypes persist due to the lack of learning outside the dominant frame. This ignorance is often reified and reinforced by confirmation bias. Organizations and their members usually collect, interpret, and recall evidence that conforms to their categories or schema, "and they ignore, misperceive, or deny events that do not fit."[74] This leads them to find what they expect to find because, in lingo from the philosophy of science, their observations are theory laden. As a result, stereotypes and the dominant frames from which they fall both appear sensible; they both are taken for granted, and so, in both cases, the contingencies inherent to their social construction are often lost or forgotten.[75] But stereotypes are error prone to begin with, and, since they are rarely recategorized, updated, or improved, relying on them can be dangerous.

Organizations do rely on stereotypes, however, and so these ideas have important although unfortunate consequences.[76] While they misrepresent reality, stereotypes allow an organization to repeatedly acknowledge and simultaneously dismiss issues that it does not understand or, more accurately, that it misunderstands. These ideas do work: they pay lip service to issues outside the organization's dominant frame, truncate future learning, and, in doing so, perpetuate rather than compensate for initial inattention.[77] Stereotypes can therefore cause the military to dismiss problems and solutions such as BW and biodefense due to misunderstanding or incomprehension. Even when unintentional, this dismissive neglect can inflict as much or more damage to research, development, acquisition, and doctrine as deliberate opposition or obstruction.

Culture and Cognition

My argument about stereotypes and frames is related to individual cognition, but I describe how knowledge is created and processed by organizations.[78] My argument also relates to culture, but it avoids many of the pitfalls that plague cultural explanations. Like culture, organizational frames include systems of symbols and practices that are meaningful inside a particular community.[79] Plus, like frames, "cultures act as a heuristic for organizational development," which, as described by Jeffrey Legro, "provide a limiting lens for interpreting and selecting what is important amidst uncertainty."[80] For Legro, organizational culture explains why accidents involving submarine warfare and strategic bombing escalated into intentional use during World War II, despite taboos against them, while similar accidents involving chemical weapons were not considered cause for retaliation in kind. He argues that submarine warfare and strategic bombing were compatible with military cultures in Germany and Britain whereas chemical warfare was not. In a similar vein, Elizabeth Kier argues that culture helps explain why—contrary to predictions by Posen and Snyder—the British and French militaries adopted defensive rather than offensive doctrines after World War I.[81]

While many cultural accounts are compatible with organizational frame theory, culture is a broader concept that includes multiple frames and stereotypes, as well as other aspects of identity, norms, and values.

[29]

That breadth can come at the cost of clarity, which is one reason why references to culture are criticized for being imprecise or, alternatively, depending so much on context that they are inapplicable to other cases.[82] In contrast, as a subset of culture, organizational frame theory can clearly specify how influential ideas like stereotypes affect science and technology inside important organizations. Stereotypes and frames also leave a paper trail for analysis because they are manifest in the language and practices that organizations use in their handbooks and computer programs, along with other routines, rules, procedures, and memoranda. Even stories, discourse, myths, images, and humor inside an organization can provide useful evidence. As a result, these ideas are no less observable than threats or interests. In addition, organizational frame theory identifies general mechanisms that are predictive and portable, including the path dependency of selective attention and learning. It therefore improves on cultural accounts and withstands theoretical challenges at least as well as realism and bureaucratic interests.

Frames and stereotypes can also produce outcomes that differ from those anticipated by realism or bureaucratic interests. Instead of pointing to threats or interests, this theory predicts that military biodefense will depend on the dominant frame and attendant stereotypes used inside the DoD, while, all else being equal, civilian biodefense will depend on the ideas at work inside HHS. In either instance, if biological problems and solutions fall outside of that organization's dominant frame of reference, then biodefense might be subject to stereotypes and neglected as a result. I discuss HHS and its "biomedical frame" in chapter 4. But what is the dominant frame inside the DoD? What assumptions and heuristics, if any, are shared by the Army, Navy, and Air Force? And how might these ideas affect military biodefense?

The Military's Kinetic Frame of Reference

I posit that the military's dominant frame of reference has been constructed around kinetic warfare. In abstract, kinetic warfare involves the rapid transfer of energy through mass in motion. In practice, it is interpreted or understood as the work done by projectile weapons and explosives. The defining characteristics of these weapons are (1) how they cause damage, and (2) how quickly they do so. Projectiles and explosives inflict abrupt physical trauma—blunt and penetrating—to both people and matériel.

Like kinetic firepower, the timing and mechanisms of damage caused by hand-to-hand combat are also fast, bruising, and bloody, as are blades and other simple weapons. One might therefore claim that a conceptual lineage links primitive spears from the Stone Age to today's

[30]

precision-guided munitions. Perhaps some variant of the kinetic frame is ancient; then again, the bow and even firearms were once resisted for their lack of nobility (killing at a distance was seen as cruel, weak, effeminate, or cheap). So this particular approach to military problem solving was not inevitable.[83] But at least since the Civil War, the American way of war has been annihilation, according to Russell Weigley, and "the firepower obsession," as another historian adds, "proved a comfortable fit with a preference for the war of annihilation."[84] In fact, for an artillery officer such as Robert Scales, "the American way of war" is defined by "the willingness of Americans to expend firepower freely" in an attempt to conserve the lives of their fellow citizen soldiers.[85] And consistent with the axiom of "send a bullet, not a man," firepower is conceived almost exclusively in kinetic terms.

However, some assumptions and heuristics about kinetic firepower are inapplicable in instances where the timing or mechanisms of damage differ. The rapid trauma caused by projectiles and explosives stands in sharp contrast to the injury done by biological weapons, which, as noted earlier, cause disease over extended periods of time. The relevant ideas differ as well. For example, kinetic concepts like the "kiloton" can be used to measure the destructive power of explosives, but they are meaningless in the context of BW. Conversely, biological concepts like "communicability," "infective dose," and "the basic reproduction number (R_0)" can help analyze the spread of smallpox or plague, but these ideas are inapplicable to blast damage.

Biological weapons are not the only form of nonkinetic firepower, but the military describes the performance of most weapon systems in physical terms like mass and speed that relate to their kinetic properties. This information is also codified in countless knowledge-laden routines used throughout the DoD. For example, Eden shows how a "blast damage frame" caused the Air Force to fixate on the kinetic effects of nuclear weapons while ignoring fire damage—even though "nuclear fire damage is as predictable as blast damage," and it may be more destructive as well.[86] However, fire involves a different mechanism of damage (thermal radiation burns), and long-standing assumptions about bombing with conventional explosives guided learning about nuclear weapons. Based on these assumptions, fire was neglected while the Air Force researched and developed sophisticated methods for predicting blast damage, including the "VNTK system," which incorporates detailed knowledge about kinetic factors such as overpressure, drag, and yield. Extending Eden's argument, I contend that the assumptions and heuristics associated with blast damage are not limited to nuclear targeting, nor do they only apply in the Air Force. Instead, the blast damage frame is part and parcel of a kinetic frame that is shared across the armed services.

[31]

The dominance of this frame is further evidenced by the US military's troubled history of counterinsurgency, given its failed attempts to use kinetic firepower for solving problems where this kind of force is of limited utility. Counterinsurgency is at least partially nonkinetic because "some of the best weapons for counterinsurgents do not shoot," the process is slow, and political factors such as legitimacy are needed to win. "Throughout its history," however, "the US military has had to relearn the principles of counterinsurgency," and it has often done so on the fly, while fighting and sometimes losing. This is not only because the military repeatedly failed to learn from the past but, by the Army's own admission, because it also "falsely believe[s] that armies trained to win large conventional wars are automatically prepared to win small, unconventional ones."[87]

For instance, the Army sought to destroy enemy forces during the Vietnam War using kinetic firepower rather than countering the insurgency by securing the local population.[88] Then, rather than learn from defeat in Vietnam, the Army continued to disregard counterinsurgency and the special forces that may be used to solve this problem. It chose instead to prepare for a conventional war with the Soviet Union in Europe (an important but unlikely scenario), adopting the combined-arms concept of AirLand Battle and buying more armor, aircraft, and missile defense. Like these weapons systems, AirLand Battle was a sophisticated concept (at least when judged by its internal logic). Yet, once again, it was based on the fundamental assumption that kinetic firepower would prevail.[89]

This same assumption survived the end of the Cold War, leaving the Army unprepared to counter insurgencies in Iraq and Afghanistan. Although the disappointing outcomes and unprecedented length of these wars allowed counterinsurgency to garner some attention, the Army and military as a whole remain remarkably resilient to evidence that might disconfirm key assumptions.[90] And long before counterinsurgency operations in Iraq and Afghanistan were over, the Navy and Air Force were emulating the Army after Vietnam and adopting the "similarly designed" concept of Air-Sea Battle for conflict with China. This concept includes cyber operations but is largely consistent with the kinetic frame inside the DoD.[91]

Of course, my characterization of the military's kinetic frame is not beyond reproach. One critique is that the armed services perform several nonkinetic functions. But even here, other aspects of the military's culture reify and reinforce its dominant frame. Consider the distinction between what General Scales calls "shooting wars," wording that illustrates the kinetic frame, versus "non-shooting constabulary missions such as peacekeeping."[92] Although it is often assigned nonshooting missions, the Army resists them, "with many troops referring to Military Operations Other Than War (MOOTW) as 'Military Operations Other Than What I Signed Up For.'"[93] This official and unofficial acronym has all the markings of a stereotype that ignores important differences between "low-intensity conflict" (LIC being another "unappealing acronym"), peacekeeping, counterterrorism, humanitarian assistance, and domestic support, among other operations.[94]

The Army also distinguishes its combat arms—organized around kinetic weapon systems such as artillery—from support branches such as the Chemical Corps, which, in contrast, are typically seen as technical specialties that do not provide the professional background or promotion pathways valued for general officers.[95] It is no surprise that prestige corresponds to the organization's dominant frame: the difference between working inside versus outside this frame mirrors the distinction between "self" and "other" that often feeds the social construction of identity. But like identity, prestige is an idea. It is not a generic resource like budget or autonomy. Moreover, the interpretation of prestige is neither obvious nor inevitable. Even if the US military interprets the use of nonkinetic weapons as lacking prestige, the same logic need not automatically apply to defense against them. For example, arson is not a prestigious crime (at least not compared to grand theft auto, if movies and video games are to be believed), but civilian firefighters still enjoy a very honorable profession. In the armed services, however, the correlation between professional status and the kinetic frame is institutionalized and taken for granted, which suggests that this is a useful way to characterize or caricature the military's dominant approach to problem solving.

A related critique of my argument is that ideas about projectiles and explosives cannot explain the emphasis on computers and information technology following the so-called revolution in military affairs. But the kinetic frame is clearly evident in how the armed services initially used information technology. ENIAC, the world's first electronic computer, was developed by the Army to automate ballistic calculations and thus solve quintessentially kinetic problems about the trajectories of projectiles.[96] Whereas ENIAC was built using vacuum tubes, "the very first application of a transistor to perform a useful circuit function" was the "Gun-to-p-computer switch" in the Gunnery System Simulator that Bell Labs built for the Navy in 1949.[97] As its name suggests, this system also solved kinetic problems; in particular, "it made an important contribution in answering the question—how lethal are anti-aircraft guns in fending off an enemy attack?"[98] The Air Force was not far behind. It sponsored development of TRADIC, the world's "first large transistor digital computer," which was "used to solve bombing and navigation problems."[99] These kinetic solutions were later incorporated into the Nike, Sentinel, and Safeguard missile defense systems. I will consider modern cyber security in the concluding chapter of this book. Given this historical context, however, the military's use of computers appears evolutionary rather than revolutionary, and many of the problems that the armed services chose to solve using information technology support rather than refute my argument.

It might also be argued that the kinetic frame is not uniquely American and that all militaries share these same assumptions and heuristics. Indeed, Theo Farrell argues that "world culture" or global "norms of conventional warfare provide the template for military organization."[100] While organizational frames may mirror broader norms, they can also vary between organizations. Not all militaries are equally constrained by the same ideas (nor are other security services, let alone nonstate actors).

Path dependency suggests that the contingencies of initial conditions are one source of variation. In its first three years, for example, the Red Army lost over 1.3 million men to infectious diseases; typhus alone killed between 2 and 3 million Russians between 1918 and 1922. According to K. David Patterson, "disease had a substantial impact on military activities and the fate of the Bolshevik revolution," and Alibek argues that typhus "made a deep impression on the commanders of the Red Army."[101] This foundational experience may explain why the Soviet military worked on offensive BW—despite its nonkinetic characteristics—before the United States, and why, in the beginning, the Soviet "program to defend against both biological weapons and natural infectious diseases continued side by side with the offensive program."[102]

A final critique of the kinetic frame is that there are other and perhaps better ways to characterize thinking inside the US military. Why not an offensive frame, drawing on the "cult of the offensive" described by Snyder and Stephen Van Evera?[103] Alternatively, what about service-specific frames, a strategic frame, or, for that matter, a tactical frame? Not only are there different characterizations to consider but organizational frames can also be described at different levels of abstraction, just like the problem solving that they entail.[104] Nevertheless, some ideas explain more than others. Perhaps biodefense would be neglected if the military had an offensive frame, but this would not explain why it might neglect offensive BW as well, or why Eden finds the Air Force fixated on blast damage rather than mass fire. Nor would service-specific frames explain why the Army, Navy, and Air Force might suffer from similar stereotypes. Therefore, because it dominates problem solving across the armed services, the kinetic frame stands to explain more than many other ideas.

[34]

What does the dominance of this frame mean for military biodefense? *If kinetic warfare defines problem solving inside the DoD, then biological problems and solutions will fall outside the military's dominant frame, and biodefense will be neglected as a result.* In addition to predicting neglect (unlike realism and bureaucratic interests), organizational frame theory also anticipates a different kind of neglect than might occur in a counterfactual case in which threats or interests are lacking. Most notably, the military should construct stereotypes that conflate and confuse BW with other nonkinetic weapons. Chemical weapons and radiological weapons are likely candidates because their timing and mechanisms of damage differ from projectiles and explosives. Coupled with the kinetic frame, nonkinetic stereotypes should cause the DoD to learn little about these weapons and dismiss the problems and solutions involved with offense and defense alike. Military research, development, and acquisition for biodefense should suffer as a result, and errors in military doctrine should persist as well. Different ideas produce different outcomes, however, and so HHS should respond differently to civilian biodefense if the problems and solutions involved are more salient inside its frame of reference.

In summary, the three theories presented in this chapter provide plausible, although dissimilar, predictions about biodefense policy. Realism predicts that research, development, acquisition, and doctrine will be responsive to the threat environment, and, since biological warfare and bioterrorism are credible threats, we should expect sizable investments in military biodefense. Alternatively, bureaucratic interests lead us to expect that overall support for biodefense might vary with the ebb and flow of competition over turf, but the officials responsible for these programs should be staunch advocates and prominent players in biodefense policy at the DoD and HHS. In contrast, if my argument about organizational frame theory is correct, then the DoD and HHS will respond differently, and, if the kinetic frame and nonkinetic stereotypes are also at work, then the military will tend to misunderstand and neglect biodefense.

Which theory is best? Science and technology can be complex, as is national security, so it is unlikely that any single theory will explain everything. And all of these theories provide probabilistic rather than deterministic predictions. That being said, some theories still explain more than others. Therefore, having considered the causal logic of threats, interests, and ideas, I now turn to the empirical question of which theory helps us understand more about the history of biodefense.

[35]

[2]

Stereotypical Neglect of Military Research, Development, and Acquisition for Biodefense

Science and technology infuse almost every aspect of biodefense, from the drugs that treat infection and the sensors that detect pathogens to the masks and decontamination equipment that limit exposure after an attack. So how can we best understand the creation and acquisition of this science and technology by the US military? Was the Soviet BW threat the determining factor during the Cold War, for instance, or did the armed services' bureaucratic interests in budget and autonomy dominate biodefense? What influence, if any, did the kinetic frame and nonkinetic stereotypes have on the supply and demand for biological facts and technical artifacts?

In this chapter I examine the history of military research, development, and acquisition for biodefense, beginning before World War II and continuing through the 2003 Iraq War. Time and time again, the military failed to understand the problems and solutions involved because its assumptions and heuristics were inaccurate or inapplicable. After first resisting the very idea of biological warfare, the military assigned this mission to the Chemical Warfare Service (CWS) and thereby institutionalized the inaccurate stereotype of "chemical and biological weapons." This stereotype and others like it hindered biodefense, before and after the US offensive BW program was ended in 1969. They also provide the best explanation for why US forces were woefully unprepared during the 1991 Gulf War. Key lessons from this war were never learned, however, and some of the same problems persisted through the invasion of Iraq in 2003. In all likelihood, similar problems will bedevil the military for years to come unless the ideas at their root are more fully addressed.

ORIGINS OF THE US BIOLOGICAL WARFARE PROGRAM:
WORLD WAR II TO 1969

The US biological warfare program began during World War II as a civilian initiative that never became a mainstream military priority. The BW threat had been contemplated during the interwar period, but only rarely, and it was almost always rejected by US military planners. The chief chemical officer dismissed the potential of "bacteriological warfare" in 1926, for example, and an influential article by Leon Fox (assigned to the CWS) argued that biological warfare was impractical in 1933.[1] This assessment "remained the dominant view" in the US military, even though Shiro Ishii read Fox's article and, reaching the opposite conclusion, proceeded to build Japan's offensive biological warfare Unit 731.[2] Japan was not alone: France and the Soviet Union had researched these weapons since the 1920s, and even Britain and Canada were building BW programs by 1940.[3] But not the United States. Moreover, when James Simmons—then a lieutenant colonel in the Medical Corps and a doctor of public health, who, with a PhD in bacteriology, understood biology better than his chemical counterparts—suggested that the country was vulnerable to biological attack in 1937, he received relatively little attention.[4]

The idea that biological weapons were a credible threat therefore gained little if any traction inside the US military until the eve of World War II. It was August 1941 before the special assistant to the secretary of war arranged a meeting about BW and biodefense. This meeting was prompted by requests by Simmons and the Army surgeon general, who wanted to study "all aspects of biological warfare, in order to provide adequate protection of troops against this type of attack," even though they opposed involvement with offensive development. Simmons also noted intelligence from the Bern Report, which, though "obviously inaccurate in many details," suggested that Germany might be investigating botulinum toxin.[5] Based on this meeting, secretary of war Henry Stimson requested that a civilian committee convene under the auspices of the National Academy of Sciences to study biological warfare in greater depth.

The civilian committee reported back to Secretary Stimson in February 1942. It concluded that biological warfare was "distinctly feasible," and so "there is but one logical course to pursue, namely, to study the possibilities of such warfare from every angle, make every preparation for reducing its effectiveness, and thereby reduce the likelihood of its use."[6] These conclusions would seem to have important implications for the military. After all, the United States was now at war with the Axis

[37]

powers, and "some of the scientists consulted believe that this is a matter for the War Department."[7] Nevertheless, the General Staff wanted the biological warfare program to be run by civilians instead of the armed forces.

The rationale for abdicating military control was inconsistent if not disingenuous. On the one hand, it was argued that "a civilian agency would help in preventing the public from being unduly exercised over any ideas that the War Department might be contemplating the use of this weapon offensively." On the other hand, "offensive possibilities should be known to the War Department. And reprisals by us are perhaps not beyond the bounds of possibility any more than they are in the field of gas attack for which the Chemical Warfare Service of the War Department is prepared."[8] So one reason for giving the BW program to civilians was to assure the public that the military was not considering offensive applications, when, in fact, it was doing just that.

Another important inconsistency seen here is the association between biological weapons and chemical warfare. This is a socially constructed relationship between very different threats, and it illustrates how the military understood—or more accurately, misunderstood—BW at an early stage. There is little if any evidence to suggest that the military tried to solve the novel problem of biological weapons by searching for new solutions; from the beginning, they were simply assumed to be like chemical weapons. Biological weapons were also considered in conjunction with chemical weapons for Operation Sledgehammer in April 1942, which was "the first recorded instance in which the problem of BW was considered in planning of a tactical manoeuvre."[9] Moreover, the socially constructed relationship between these nonkinetic weapons correlated with the military's distaste for them. This helps explain why the War Department wanted the BW program run by civilians and why Secretary Stimson could argue that "biological warfare is, of course, 'dirty business,'" in implicit but dubious moral contrast to the damage done by supposedly clean and conventional kinetic weapons.[10]

The US biological warfare program was therefore born inside the civilian Federal Security Agency and named the War Research Service. Directed by George Merck (president of the pharmaceutical company Merck & Co.), the War Research Service was initially responsible for coordinating all research and development related to biological warfare. Its first task was biodefense. The War Research Service drew up plans for protecting food and water from sabotage, for instance, and it recommended additional protection for civilians and troops in the Hawaiian Islands and Panama Canal Zone.[11]

Encouraged by the British, Merck also asked "that the Chemical Warfare Service develop certain of the offensive aspects of the BW program"

[38]

beginning in December 1942.[12] In order to maintain secrecy, laboratory facilities and pilot plants were built at Camp Detrick in Frederick, Maryland. Consequently, as the scientific program progressed, "the responsibility for getting the job done shifted gradually from civilian to military personnel and organizations."[13]

In December 1943, intelligence indicated that Germany might use BW against Britain. This information was meager, inconclusive, and possibly from the same unreliable source as the Bern Report, but it moved the War Research Service to ask the War Department to assume even greater responsibility for BW.[14] Secretary Stimson assigned this responsibility to the Chemical Warfare Service, "*in view of the similarity of application of biological warfare with chemical warfare.*"[15] That no such similarity had ever been demonstrated was increasingly irrelevant. Instead, critical differences between chemical and biological warfare were unexamined or ignored while the military's stereotype conflating the two was further institutionalized. Final transfer of the BW program was completed during the summer of 1944 when President Franklin D. Roosevelt directed the War Department to assume full control. The War Research Service was liquidated, and its responsibilities were assigned to the Special Projects Division of the CWS.[16]

So, on account of unfounded generalizations about these nonkinetic weapons, chemical officers were saddled with the responsibility for biological warfare (despite their having dismissed its potential during the interwar period). The CWS also suffered a low status that corresponded to its nonkinetic responsibilities. Like the BW program in World War II, the CWS had been established during World War I at the insistence of civilians rather than the mainstream military. According to Fredric Brown, "the military establishment, whose primary function was to prepare the country for war, however remote or unpleasant the contingency might be, failed utterly in the fulfillment of this responsibility by ignoring the question of gas warfare. The Army reacted as if chemical warfare did not exist."[17] The civilian Bureau of Mines started research on chemical defense in February 1917, but the Army did not seriously investigate this problem until months after the United States entered the war—a war in which chemical weapons had already been used for several years. The CWS was not formally established until June 1918, and, even then, Leo Brophy contends that "only reluctantly did the War Department provide for its activation."[18]

US forces were unprepared for chemical warfare on the Western Front and therefore needed the CWS. Despite the manifest threat, however, the secretary of war and chief of staff wanted to abolish the CWS immediately after World War I. Congress decided to keep it as a permanent bureau of the War Department in 1920, "in spite of the near unanimous opposition of the military establishment."[19] The CWS was housed at Edgewood Arsenal in Aberdeen, Maryland, and it was also assigned responsibility for smoke and incendiaries: the first in a series of nonkinetic issues that would be lumped together with chemical warfare.[20] The necessity of the CWS "was seriously questioned by some of the highest ranking officers in the General Staff," so "the War Department was not prone to be oversolicitous for the welfare of the new service."[21] In other words, it was treated like a red-headed stepchild in the military family. "Despite twenty years of intensive effort by the CWS to sell itself and chemical warfare, the Army had not assimilated gas [as a weapon]," and the military was once again unprepared at the outset of World War II.[22]

Notwithstanding its low status (and initially dim view of biological warfare), the CWS expanded on what the War Research Service had started, and it proceeded to build a substantial BW program during World War II. In addition to constructing research and development facilities at Camp Detrick, the CWS Special Projects Division built test sites on Horn Island (off the coast of Mississippi) and Granite Peak (near Dugway Proving Ground in Utah), along with the Vigo production facility (outside Terre Haute, Indiana). The Army and Navy surgeons general cooperated on biodefense, and the BW program also involved research contracts with dozens of universities and private companies, as well as close collaboration with Canada and Britain. By the end of World War II, the Special Projects Division involved four thousand people working on almost two hundred projects with both offensive and defensive applications.

Defensive Work

Sometimes work on offense and defense was closely linked, as with botulinum toxin (an agent assigned the secret code letter "X"). The toxin was first isolated by A. M. Pappenheimer, who later worked at Detrick and produced the first botulinum vaccine. This was a toxoid, or an inactivated form of the toxin, which worked as a vaccine by triggering a prophylactic immune response.[23] At the time, the United States feared that Germany might use botulinum toxin against the Allies. The Defensive Division at Detrick therefore worked with commercial contractors to manufacture thousands of gallons of toxoid—enough to immunize hundreds of thousands of troops or more—in preparation for the invasion of Normandy in 1944.[24] This vaccine was never used for mass immunizations, but large quantities of it were shipped to the European and Pacific theaters of operation for fear of Germany or Japan using the toxin.[25]

While research, development, and acquisition of prophylactic vaccines for botulinum toxins were successful, postexposure therapies were less so. The only treatment for "X" remained the passive immunity provided by an antitoxin that was collected from the blood of exposed animals such as horses, which sometimes caused serum sickness when used to treat humans.[26] Conversely, for anthrax and tularemia, greater progress was made in treating these bacteria with new antibiotics than in developing vaccines against them. Penicillin—first mass produced in preparation for D-Day—proved effective against anthrax. Likewise, streptomycin was first isolated in 1943 and studied extensively at Detrick for treating tularemia, in cooperation with Merck & Co.[27] Vaccines for tularemia were also used at Detrick, drawing on work by Lee Foshay. They performed poorly, however, as did the vaccines that were initially investigated for anthrax and other bacterial infections such as brucellosis.[28]

Research on detection and physical protection provided mixed results as well. Sampling and identification techniques were devised and used to detect contamination at BW facilities and to confirm that Japanese balloon attacks against North America had not released pathogens. They were also used to test whether prisoners of war had been immunized against anthrax or other agents, since this might indicate that the Axis powers were prepared to wage biological warfare.[29] Calcium hypochlorite, which was used for decontaminating chemical agents, was demonstrated to work as a disinfectant. Nevertheless, some of the standard "clothing, canisters, and masks" used for chemical warfare proved inadequate for physical protection against biological agents; because of the potency of BW, "leaks . . . are much more serious in the case of disease-producing organisms than with war gases."[30]

Detection for early warning also fell short of desired outcomes, despite "continuous effort . . . directed towards the development of simple and rapid sampling, screening and identification methods for field use."[31] Pathogens are difficult to detect, unlike chemical agents, but the military seemed to assume that rapid BW detection was feasible. Ira Baldwin, one of the senior biologists involved, laughed when he recalled for his memoir "one navy captain . . . who used to insist that he was not going to be satisfied until you had a signal that would ring a bell when a single pathogenic organism came into the room."[32] This feat would require finding the proverbial microscopic needle in a macroscopic haystack of solids, liquids, and gas, since biological material is ubiquitous in the natural environment. It remains beyond the grasp of modern technology, let alone what was available in the 1940s (before DNA was known to be genetic material). Because chemical agents could be rapidly detected, however, military doctrine soon assumed that biological agents could be rapidly detected as well. But the only way to detect BW at the time was to inject mice with samples from the field or, alternatively, wait for people to get sick or die before trying to treat the survivors.[33]

Offensive Applications

Concurrent with defensive work was research, development, and ultimately acquisition of offensive biological weapons, ostensibly for retaliation against enemy use. The history of this side of the BW program has been well documented elsewhere. In order to understand biodefense, however, it is helpful to highlight the interplay between offense and defense, as well as how much the military's ideas about chemical warfare influenced and even impeded development of BW.

Since building biological weapons is, in many ways, easier than defending against them, offensive work stood to enjoy more success. Moreover, the US program was heavily influenced by the British. "Their attitude is that the best defense is an offense. Therefore, scant British effort has been directed to defense," according to one memo. Similarly, another report notes that the British were "most anxious" that defensive work at Detrick "should not interfere with the greatest possible production" of anthrax.[34] Britain asked the United States to manufacture anthrax and botulinum toxin as early as November 1942, and these agents became the focus of America's offensive program.[35]

Despite the focus provided if not insisted on by the British, deciding which germs were best was still a source of some contention at Detrick. During one technical meeting in 1944, for example, two officers "were reprimanded for becoming emotional in an attempt to show that typhus and psittacosis had greater possibilities than anthrax and botulinum as biological warfare agents."[36] It was later "suggested that perhaps the British had been allowed too much voice in these matters," although, by the end of World War II, the Special Projects Division had expanded its studies to include numerous other human, animal, and plant pathogens as potential weapons.[37]

Even more influential than the British was the idea that nonkinetic weapons should resemble each other, notwithstanding all of their differences. As a result, the CWS repeatedly tried and, in many cases, failed to apply its experience with chemical weapons to the manufacture and delivery of biological weapons. For instance, the CWS knew how to fill munitions that dispersed liquid chemicals, and so it favored using wet forms of biological agents. "In cloud chamber and field trials, however, the apparent similarity was found to be superficial," according to Brophy and Rexmond Cochrane. "Neither the degree of fineness nor the concentration of aerosol organisms that were required to ensure infection by inhalation could be compared to chemical experience."[38] The most effective way to deliver BW agents such as anthrax was probably as a dry powder, dispersed as a fine spray using pressurized gas.[39] But this was not how chemical munitions worked, let alone kinetic weapons, and the military was slow in "accepting or even adequately trying unconventional modes of dissemination."[40]

Instead, the CWS tried to use the M47A2 chemical bomb for BW because this device was known to disperse mustard droplets with an explosive charge. The explosion killed most biological agents, however, and it failed to generate particles that were small enough for victims to inhale deep into their lungs (5 microns or less). The M47A2 was ultimately abandoned in favor of the British Type F bomb, which was renamed SPD Mark 1. This bomb was also designed for chemical agents, but, unlike the one hundred–pound M47A2, it was a four-pound cluster bomblet that produced a somewhat more efficient biological aerosol. Though still imperfect, the CWS ordered one million SPD Mark 1 bombs—half which were for the British—to fill with anthrax in June 1944.[41]

Mass production of the anthrax needed to fill these bombs also illustrates how chemical experience was often assumed to be sufficient for solving biological problems. Although Baldwin, as a biologist, "didn't think we'd done enough research work to enable us to build a production plant," the Vigo production facility started to be converted from manufacturing conventional explosives to biological ordnance in May 1944. Then, unsatisfied with the rate of progress, the CWS tried to replace the engineer in charge of pathogen containment at this facility. When Baldwin asked, "What experience in biological engineering has this other gentleman had?" he learned, "Well, he hadn't had any, but he was a competent chemical engineer." Seeing this as an insufficient qualification for the job, Baldwin insisted that he be relieved of responsibility if anything went wrong.[42] World War II ended before the Vigo facility filled any SPD Mark 1 bombs with anthrax. Because of its kinetic frame and nonkinetic stereotypes, however, the military had assumed that chemical experience was synonymous with biological expertise, and these ideas would continue to shape offense and defense for decades to come.

Bureaucratic Conflict

The atomic bombs created by the Manhattan Project produced huge explosions and enjoyed military support after the war. In contrast, the rush to develop biological weapons and biodefense ended on August 10, 1945. Just days before Japan surrendered, General Brehon Somervell, head of Army Service Forces, ordered the Special Projects Division to stop all work on BW.[43] This decision—like others to follow—involved little if any input from the relevant experts. Simmons asked Merck to convince Secretary Stimson that a more intelligent drawdown was needed, arguing "that someone may not realize the importance of these things . . . on the preventive end, and cut them off too quickly."[44] Stimson later endorsed a postwar program, but many contracts were cancelled, workload and personnel at Detrick were cut (staff was reduced by more than 60% within a few months), and operations were suspended at all other BW installations. Eventually, the Vigo production facility was demobilized and sold; the test sites at Horn Island and Granite Peak were closed as well.[45]

Somervell's stop work order caused "considerable turmoil . . . misunderstandings and conflicting actions."[46] Although most accounts of the BW program highlight how much the armed services cooperated during World War II, there was considerable conflict between the CWS and the surgeons general.[47] Recall that chemical officers had discounted BW before the war, unlike medical officers in the Office of the Army Surgeon General. Then, immediately after the war, the CWS tried to monopolize administrative control over the program. The chief chemical officer proposed that he appoint a technical director with "full responsibility for all research and development in the field of biological warfare," relegating representatives from the other services and agencies to an advisory committee with no authority.[48] This proposal welcomed the Navy and Army surgeons general to station personnel at Detrick, but only so long as their duties were assigned by the technical director chosen by CWS.

Opposing this power grab, the Navy surgeon general recommended "the setting up of biological warfare as a special science, *divorced from the chemical warfare service, where it surely has no place.*"[49] The Army surgeon general also opposed the CWS. He argued that biodefense was a prerequisite for safe work on offense, and, "since protection of the workers is primarily and inescapably a responsibility of the Surgeon General it seems obvious that he must have authority." Like his counterpart in the Navy, the Army surgeon general also argued that "little weight should be given to organizational schemes which have existed during the past war," since "planning for the future should not be colored by such expedients or compromises."[50]

In many respects, this was a classic bureaucratic turf war: one that the surgeons general would soon lose. The CWS managed to consolidate its control over the BW program after World War II, even while the Army once again debated disbanding the CWS (as it had tried to do after World War I).[51] Recall that bureaucratic interests are often insufficient to explain the difference between winners and losers. So why did the CWS win these early fights over BW—both discounting the threat before the war, as well as retaining control of the program afterward—when the surgeons general had more biological expertise? How could the CWS dominate these debates and yet still risk elimination by the mainstream military?

[44]

Given its kinetic frame, the military was prone to dismiss chemical as well as biological warfare, and, failing to understand the difference between them because of its stereotypes, it mistook chemical experience as equivalent to biological expertise.[52] Not only do these ideas help explain bureaucratic outcomes, but without them it is hard to understand the military's reluctance to start a BW program or its decision to give this assignment to the CWS, let alone all the attempts to build biological munitions in the image of chemical weapons in spite of countervailing evidence. Granted, the CWS survived the debate over its elimination after World War II, and it was renamed the Chemical Corps in 1946. Yet it was then assigned the new—and once again, very different—nonkinetic problem of radiological protection, which is fully consistent with my argument about the military's assumptions and heuristics.

The Korean War through Project 112

One consequence of bureaucratic conflict over the Chemical Corps' "empire building" was that, for a time, staff in the Office of the Army Surgeon General distrusted Detrick and disparaged it as a "rathole—a bottomless pit."[53] They were also skeptical that the biological weapons conceived by the Chemical Corps would work. This skepticism was not unfounded. As would soon become apparent, "the Chemical Corps was promising more than it could deliver."[54] In part, this was because the Chemical Corps was aggressively promoting itself to combat its low status. But the Chemical Corps also failed to understand the challenges involved with developing and acquiring BW because living organisms are more complex than chemical compounds.

Under the Chemical Corps, the BW program received relatively little funding until the Korean War (on average, less than $5 million per year). While several military and civilian reports argued that this was inadequate, the most influential was produced by the Stevenson Committee. It highlighted the Soviet threat in a report submitted a few days after the Korean War began in June 1950.[55] This report made several recommendations about increasing investment into BW research and development, many of which were approved by the secretary of defense. But the Stevenson Committee also criticized use of nonkinetic stereotypes:

Chemical, biological, and radiological warfare have been mistakenly assumed to have enough significant characteristics in common to warrant their being grouped together . . . but many of the problems connected with these three weapons require totally different treatment. The Committee questions any approach to the weapons which would produce in either the public or military thinking a feeling that there was an inseparable association

[45]

between chemical, biological and radiological warfare . . . there are fundamental differences in the situation with respect to each of them which calls
for different handling in research, development, and production programs.[56]

This committee disparaged the phrase "weapons of mass destruction" as
well. However, like the Navy surgeon general's recommendation to di-
vorce biological warfare from chemical warfare, these criticisms were
ignored.

Along with the Stevenson Committee, it might be argued that increased investment in BW was fueled by heightened threat perceptions
after Communist states accused the United States of using these weapons in the Korean War. One interpretation of these fraudulent accusa-
tions was "to prepare the ground for Soviet use of BW against US or
allied forces," but, according to Leitenberg, "the simplest explanation
has always seemed the most sensible: that the BW allegations were part
of the Soviet, Chinese, and North Korean war effort, meant to discredit
the United States and to weaken international support for the UN intervention."[57] Either way, by the time the main thrust of this disinformation
campaign was launched in February 1952, the US military was already
trying to expand its BW program.

The Chemical Corps was responsible for building biological weapons
and the Air Force was charged with procuring them for strategic use.
Therefore, "based on Chemical Corps predictions of what it could produce," the Air Force vice chief of staff issued the "Twining directive" in
January 1952.[58] This directed at least one wing of the Strategic Air Command (SAC) to be ready to conduct biological warfare within a year, all
SAC units to be ready in three years, and all installations to prepare for
biodefense against overt or covert attack.

The Twining directive was poorly conceived, and it was rescinded in
October 1953. In particular, the Air Force and Chemical Corps pursued it
with a crash program to standardize the M33 cluster bomb filled with the
incapacitating agent *Brucella suis* (brucellosis). This is a delicate organism, and, since the submunitions inside the M33 were based on the Type
F chemical bomb (modified for anthrax during World War II), the explosive charge killed most of the *B. suis*. The M33 was also designed for
World War II aircraft that were obsolete by the time of the Korean War,
and "logistic support of the munition was a nightmare."[59] Furthermore,
rather than actually arm aircraft with biological weapons, SAC planned
to satisfy the Twining directive "by simply writing a standard operating
procedure and briefing some key people." This was probably because
"General Curtis LeMay remained unenthusiastic."[60]

"It was no secret," argues Dorothy Miller, that by this point, "the Air
Force was disappointed with the results of the Chemical Corps research

[46]

in biological warfare."[61] Neither the Chemical Corps nor the Air Force understood the problems or solutions involved with production, support, and delivery of this ordnance. As was discovered during World War II, "much of the equipment and many of the techniques used . . . for chemical and high explosive munitions were not applicable directly to biological warfare."[62] Yet having failed to learn or recall this lesson, the Chemical Corps overpromised and underdelivered during the Korean War. This disappointed Air Force expectations, which were also untempered by applicable knowledge or experience. Instead of trying to fix this problem with education, the Air Force ended a short-lived "100-man" training program that was to have provided it with officers qualified in biological warfare.[63]

Failure to quickly produce operational munitions was a crippling blow to the BW program. Adding insult to injury, the Army tried to get rid of this program through an unsuccessful attempt to outsource it to the Mathieson Chemical Company in 1953. According to Miller, "turning research and development over to the civilian contractor would have meant the loss of considerable control by the military."[64] This was contrary to the military's bureaucratic interest in autonomy but consistent with its apathy toward nonkinetic capabilities. As a result of this organizational upheaval, large numbers of staff resigned from Detrick and at least one British observer reported that the situation there "had never been worse."[65]

Negotiations over outsourcing eventually collapsed, and so the military retained control of the BW program at Detrick. A new production facility was also completed shortly after the end of the Korean War near Pine Bluff, Arkansas. This facility started to mass produce *B. suis* in 1954 and *Francisella tularensis* (tularemia) in 1955.[66] Furthermore, Camp Detrick's name was changed to Fort Detrick in 1956, which symbolized a more permanent status.[67]

Plus, US policy for using chemical and biological weapons changed in 1956 from retaliation only to a first-strike option, with authorization reserved for the president. The Stevenson Committee recommended revoking the retaliation-only restriction in 1950, but it was rejected by the secretary of defense. The Army also recommended this change, consistent with the Chemical Corps' bureaucratic interest, but the Air Force reversed its initial support and opposed the first-strike option in 1954. Ultimately, this debate was resolved by the National Security Council (NSC) under President Dwight D. Eisenhower. Responding to comments by Marshal Georgy Zhukov that suggested the Soviet Union might use these weapons, the NSC decided that "the United States will be prepared to use chemical and bacteriological weapons in general war to the extent that they will enhance the military effectiveness of the armed forces."[68]

[47]

Once again, the appropriate policy for biological weapons was assumed to be the same as that for chemical weapons, despite the different scenarios in which either may enhance military effectiveness.

New Tests, New Organizations, Old Problems

The first-strike option and production facility at Pine Bluff were significant, but so was improved testing, which was prompted by disappointment in the biological weapons initially produced by the Chemical Corps. These tests started to demonstrate and quantify the potency of BW like never before. In particular, the "St. Jo program" began testing the effects of anthrax on urban areas in 1953. The knowledge requirements were clearly specified; logistics were considered alongside research and development; and data was collected from field trials at Dugway Proving Ground, as well as through simulation studies in St. Louis, Minneapolis, and Winnipeg.[69] "There had been nothing else comparable to the St. Jo program in previous efforts," and, at least according to one officer, these tests were "the best thing that had ever happened" in the BW program.[70]

The St. Jo program had important implications for offensive BW, and testing continued throughout the decade. Many of these tests used what were thought to be harmless simulants like *Bacillus globigii* or *Bacillus subtilis* var. *niger*, but field testing at Dugway involved lethal agents (*B. anthracis* and *F. tularensis*) and nonlethal incapacitating agents (*B. suis* and *Coxiella burnettii*). The potential flexibility provided by nonlethal weapons did not escape notice. For instance, President Eisenhower said that "the use of such agents was a splendid idea," but he also argued that "if we tried to use them in a humane manner, our enemy would probably charge us with germ warfare and then would proceed in retaliation to use lethal chemical and biological weapons."[71] (Perhaps this argument about the enemy reflected Eisenhower's own thinking about massive retaliation in the context of nuclear war.)

The pace and scale of field testing increased after reviews and reorganization by the Kennedy administration included biological weapons as part of a flexible response to the Soviet threat.[72] In 1961, secretary of defense Robert McNamara created Project 112 with the objective to "consider all possible applications, including use as an alternative to nuclear weapons."[73] In response, the armed services established the joint Deseret Test Center at Fort Douglas, Utah. They then conducted a wide range of BW field trials in maritime, desert, tropical, and arctic environments, using everything from aircraft and missiles to submarines and surface ships.

For example, a series of trials conducted through Project Shipboard Hazard and Defense (SHAD) included large area coverage tests like

Shady Grove (using live *F. tularensis*) and Speckled Start (using Staphylococcal enterotoxin B, or SEB).[74] Some of these tests also involved new delivery systems such as the A/B45Y series spray tank. This particular system did not use an explosive charge and, according to William Patrick, it "performed outstandingly and . . . was the best munition developed by the United States."[75] These tests proved that biological agents could be used as strategic weapons (e.g., quickly distributed by high-performance aircraft and causing infection over hundreds of square miles), just as vulnerability tests against seaports and subways in the 1950s and 1960s demonstrated their effectiveness against operational targets.

Testing was also important for biodefense, in part because it rebuilt the relationship between Detrick and the Army surgeon general's office that had frayed after World War II. The surgeon general worried about medical defense during the Korean War, which, like the offensive program, relied on data extrapolated from animal studies to make predictions about human vulnerability.[76] In order to reduce the uncertainties inherent to this extrapolation, the Army Medical Service and Chemical Corps agreed to cooperate on research using human volunteers in 1954. A group of military and civilian doctors advised this work; in order to limit potential controversy, they were named the Commission on Epidemiological Survey because this title sounded "vague and noncommittal."[77] The project officer on this commission, Colonel William Tigertt, negotiated with the Seventh-Day Adventist Church to recruit volunteers from its members who were drafted and, despite being conscientious objectors to lethal force, might still cooperate with the US military. More than two thousand Seventh-Day Adventists eventually volunteered for human testing, as did several members of the professional staff at Detrick.[78]

The first dose-response studies were conducted on volunteers in January 1955. Volunteers were exposed to *C. burnetii*—Q fever being a non-lethal infection that responds rapidly to antibiotics—inside the giant test sphere known as the Eight Ball at Detrick.[79] Initially called Project CD-22, these tests were successful enough to provide the preamble to what became known as Project Whitecoat. It continued until the military draft ended in 1973. Along with Q fever, Project Whitecoat exposed human volunteers to tularemia, Venezuelan equine encephalitis (VEE), and Staphylococcal enterotoxin B, among other agents.

Human testing not only generated a new kind of data, it also catalyzed the creation of a new kind of organization for biodefense. Initially, a medical liaison from the Walter Reed Army Institute of Research was stationed at Detrick to oversee Project CD-22. But when the scope and scale of testing increased with Project Whitecoat, the US Army Medical Unit (USAMU) was established at Detrick in June 1956. Under the command of Colonel

[49]

Tigertt, this new unit conducted its first experiments on human volunteers using tularemia. Building on research from World War II, these tests confirmed that infections acquired through inhalation could be controlled with streptomycin and tetracycline but the Foshay vaccine was ineffective. Later, USAMU examined the dose-response rate of aerosol exposure to tularemia, as well as the effectiveness of inhaled vaccines against it.[80]

USAMU conducted similar research on a variety of other diseases, although some were too dangerous for human testing and thus restricted to animal studies. Challenging the immune system of a human volunteer with inhalation anthrax, for instance, could hardly be considered ethical given the likelihood that this infection might prove lethal. Using laboratory animals instead, researchers at Detrick tested a vaccine for anthrax that they patented in 1965. This is the same vaccine—a cellular filtrate—that is still used today.[81]

Animals were used to test the anthrax vaccine, and yet, in a twist of fate, USAMU also used a vaccine for VEE that it had tested on humans in order to fight a natural outbreak of this virus among horses in Central America. In the early 1960s, USAMU partnered with the National Drug Company (affiliated with Merrell National Laboratories) to produce vaccines at a pilot plant in Swiftwater, Pennsylvania. About three million doses of VEE vaccine were prepared and stored at the Swiftwater facility (an ad hoc decision by USAMU, the Commission on Epidemiological Survey, and the surgeon general's office).[82] As a result, when Guatemala and El Salvador asked for help fighting a natural outbreak of VEE in 1969, USAMU had plenty of vaccine on hand. The same vaccine was later used on horses in the United States when this outbreak spread north.

Despite these advances in biodefense (and the occasional civilian application), the mainstream military remained apathetic. Decades would pass before the DoD started stockpiling anthrax vaccine, even though it held the patent. Instead, what little acquisition there was focused on physical protection—particularly the protective mask—due to the military's nonkinetic stereotypes. These assumed that "the biological warfare defense program was related closely to the chemical and radiological warfare programs because one item [the mask] in most instances might serve all three."[83] But masks were ineffective for cover without advance warning, which research on rapid biological detection was yet to provide.[84] The equipment used to identify BW after an attack was inadequate as well. For example, the M17 Biological Agent Sampling Kit was standardized in 1957 to meet the Chemical Corps' formal requirement, yet the Army only acquired a few of them for training because they were unsuitable for field use.[85]

Even offensive BW enjoyed relatively little attention. Interest declined as military involvement in Vietnam increased, notwithstanding the detailed information provided by tests such as Project SHAD and Shady Grove, or what Ouagrham-Gormley describes as the "integrated system" of "knowledge transmission belts" that helped create biological expertise at Fort Detrick.[86] Therefore, while the BW program had ramped up in response to Secretary McNamara's request for Project 112, several participants noted that it still "suffered from a lack of general and sustained appreciation and support." As was true during the Korean War, this resulted in "vacillating and contradictory directives, excessive fluctuation in program emphasis and in the availability of competent personnel, low morale of the scientific staff . . . and a failure to develop strong defensive capabilities."[87] And these problems were only about to get worse.

The Nixon Decision

Because biological warfare fell outside of the kinetic frame, the military leadership ultimately did little to resist when the Nixon administration decided to end the offensive BW program in November 1969. This decision was catalyzed by Melvin Laird, the secretary of defense. Responding to queries from Congress, Secretary Laird wrote Henry Kissinger in April 1969 and recommended that the NSC review US policy regarding chemical and biological weapons—programs that Laird reportedly opposed because of their cost.[88] The next month, Kissinger issued National Security Study Memorandum (NSSM) 59, which initiated a critical review that would inform Nixon's decision and seal the fate of the offensive BW program.[89]

This review was remarkable, not only for its fateful outcome, but also because it sidelined the Army and involved little or no input from experts at Detrick.[90] Army involvement was tangential because it was only indirectly represented in the NSSM 59 review through representatives of the Joint Chiefs of Staff and, to a lesser extent, the Office of the Secretary of Defense.[91] The Joint Chiefs initially recommended expanding the chemical and biological weapons programs, but Secretary Laird withdrew their draft study, ordered the Army to halt BW production, and directed one of his own offices to rewrite the military's response to NSSM 59. This "resulted in a dramatic shift in the tenor" from support to criticism of these programs.[92] Eventually, the only position paper that the Army might have influenced was removed from the high-level review, according to the historian David Goldman, and "the Army Staff remained uninformed about the deliberations."[93]

The NSSM 59 review resulted in Nixon's decision to renounce the offensive BW program. And, despite the Joint Chiefs' initial recommendation to expand this program, their chairman quickly backed down during the decisive NSC meeting on November 18. Rather than protect their bureaucratic turf, the Joint Chiefs conceded to end the offensive program and accept a "minimal RDT&E [research, development, test, and evaluation] program pointed to defense, guarding against offensive actions by the enemy."[94] Moreover, the military did not hesitate to destroy its BW stockpile. The Army's vice chief of staff supported destroying the munitions at Pine Bluff before he learned that President Nixon was officially renouncing "bacteriological/biological warfare" through National Security Decision Memorandum (NSDM) 35. The Army staff also decided to destroy its biological toxins, which were not mentioned in NSDM 35, before Nixon issued NSDM 44 to this effect.[95]

Ironically, some of the political pressure behind the NSSM 59 review and Nixon's decision was due to the use of chemical herbicides and tear gas in Vietnam, along with several accidents involving chemical rather than biological weapons. These accidents included a botched test of VX nerve agent in Nevada, the unsafe disposal of chemical weapons through Project CHASE, and leaking sarin at a depot in Okinawa. But the biological rather than chemical weapons program was sacrificed, even while Kissinger noted that "the President has decided that . . . the term Chemical and Biological Warfare (CBW) will no longer be used. The reference henceforth should be to the two categories separately."[96] Secretary Laird also argued that this conflated stereotype was dangerous:

> US Government Agencies continue to refer to CBW, i.e. chemical and biological warfare. Such terminology, I believe, is seriously misleading and should be stricken from our lexicon. . . . *It connotes a generic interrelationship between the chemical and biological fields when, in fact, no such relationship exists.* . . . While terminology may seem to be a minor point in some cases, this is one instance in which precise terminology is important. I would also hope that . . . chemical warfare and biological activities of whatever nature would be differentiated and treated separately. To do otherwise will continue to confuse the American public, our allies, our potential adversaries, and even those in our own government responsible for defense programs.[97]

Nevertheless, the military's CBW stereotype remained entrenched, as we will see, and the end of the offensive BW program resulted in deep cuts to biodefense, despite the recognized need to avoid "technological surprise."[98]

To summarize, as evident since World War II, the mainstream military showed little interest in biological warfare, which it conflated with other nonkinetic weapons and neglected as a result. First, civilians essentially forced this program on the US military, which had previously dismissed BW despite enemy research in the field. Second, the program was assigned to the low status Chemical Corps, along with radiological protection, in spite of the different problems and solutions involved. Third, offensive and defensive aspects of biological warfare were repeatedly forced into the mold of chemical warfare, despite ample evidence that this was a poor fit. Offense might have received more support than defense, but an offensive bias is insufficient to explain the neglect of biodefense when the military was apathetic toward all aspects of biological warfare and quick to concede the offensive program in 1969. The preponderance of evidence is therefore consistent with my argument that biological warfare fell outside of the military's kinetic frame and that work suffered as a result of nonkinetic stereotypes.

In contrast, realism has difficulty explaining military policy during this period. Although fear and self-help might explain the decision to stockpile botulinum vaccine before invading Normandy, threats do not explain why the US was the last major power to pursue biological weapons, let alone the military's persistent association between chemical and biological weapons or its temptation to eliminate the Chemical Corps despite known threats. Likewise, heightened threat perceptions during the Korean War help explain increased investment in BW, but the response was poorly conceived. The military even chose to shelve improved intelligence at the time. In 1952, the secretary of defense highlighted "an acute requirement for more reliable information regarding Soviet activities, capabilities and intentions concerning biological warfare," and yet it turned out that "the Defense agencies," which were supposedly under the secretary's control, "do not desire to raise the priority for covert collection of BW intelligence."[99] Tradeoffs between priorities are inevitable, but, like lumping nonkinetic weapons together, this decision to risk ignorance about the BW threat is consistent with an emerging pattern that is hard for realism to account for.

Bureaucratic interests in funding and autonomy are also inadequate. For example, without referring to other theories, bureaucratic interests alone fail to explain the Chemical Corps' longstanding low status. Moreover, generic interests do not help us understand why the military officials with special interests and expertise in biology—whether surgeons general or experts at Detrick—were rarely decisive players in policymaking. Instead, the ideas at work are necessary to understand this initial period and, as path dependency would suggest, what would follow as well.

THE FALL AND PARTIAL RISE OF MILITARY BIODEFENSE: THE END
OF THE VIETNAM WAR TO THE END OF THE COLD WAR

After Nixon's decision, all US research, development, and acquisition
relating to BW was purportedly for biodefense. Some aspects of defensive work are difficult to distinguish from offense, however, given the
dual-use technology involved, and "even clearly defensive programs,
such as vaccine development, can be misused to provide know-how for
those planning to deploy a bioweapon."[100] One consequence is that, long
after Nixon officially ended the offensive BW program, critics claimed
that military biodefense was really a cover for continuing offensive work.
I will address this critique in the concluding chapter, but the largest subterfuge of this sort—known to date—is not American but Russian.[101] As
the US military was dismantling its offensive BW program, the Soviet
Union was building Biopreparat to use civilian research as a cloak for
advancing work on biological weapons.

Subterfuge and secrecy notwithstanding, the expanding Soviet program was increasingly evident during the 1970s, as described in chapter 1
and underscored by the anthrax accident at Sverdlovsk. But despite this
threat and the supposed fear of technological surprise, US investment in
biodefense hit record lows as the United States signed the Biological
Weapons Convention and ratified the Geneva Protocol. Funding fell from
over $30 million in 1969—when the BW program had already started
shrinking—to less than $15 million per year during the 1970s, resulting in
little research and virtually no procurement.[102]

When the US military started to destroy its stockpiles of biological
weapons and demilitarize the production facility at Pine Bluff, it split the
remaining defensive program between Fort Detrick and Edgewood Arsenal. At Detrick, USAMU was renamed the US Army Medical Research
Institute of Infectious Diseases (USAMRIID). Under the direction of the
Army surgeon general, USAMRIID was charged with developing medical countermeasures to biological weapons. In keeping with the CBW
stereotype, however, detection and physical protection were assigned to
the Chemical Corps at Edgewood, which compounded the neglect of
biodefense.

Detection and Physical Protection

Work at Edgewood focused on chemical warfare. Few people addressed biodefense, and those who did suffered "lousy" facilities, little
funding, and lost capabilities.[103] For example, gaseous disinfection—
using ethylene oxide to sterilize equipment—had been pioneered in a lab
at Detrick that was dismantled and sent to Edgewood in 1969, but "the

laboratory was never put together again."[104] More important, the Chemical Corps was almost abolished after the Vietnam War, just like the military debated doing after World War I and again after World War II. As in 1920, Congress prevented it from being totally eliminated, but the Army chief of staff still froze recruitment and promotion.

According to General John Appel, "the Army chose to consider disestablishment of the Corps in the 1970s without consulting me even though I was the principal advisor to the Chief of Staff for NBC at the time."[105] We have seen a similar lack of consultation before (i.e., General Somervell's stop-work order during World War II, as well as President Nixon's decision in 1969). Here, as elsewhere, it defies the predictions derived from bureaucratic theory when officials with special interests and expertise are not prominent players in these critical policy decisions. That being said, the Chemical Corps was later resurrected after an analysis of the equipment used during the 1973 Yom Kippur War indicated that the Soviet Union was prepared for chemical warfare.[106]

Funding for the Chemical Corps grew during the 1980s, due to perceptions of the Soviet threat and increased military spending by the Reagan administration. As the token countermeasure for "chemical and biological warfare," however, chemical defense was the primary beneficiary while biodefense continued to languish. Fewer than fifty out of almost three thousand employees at Edgewood and the Army testing facility at Dugway were funded by the Biological Defense Research Program.[107] The GAO reports that "only $18.9 million (or 6.8 %) of the $276.9 million spent to research and develop chemical and biological detection from fiscal years 1984 through 1989 went for biological detection."[108] Although the Air Force and Navy sponsored competing detection programs in the 1980s, they also focused on chemical warfare and "made even less progress than the Army," according to Albert Mauroni, "due to lack of funds (and a corresponding lack of interest among their combat warriors). This situation is why some people called the NBC defense program a small 'n' small 'b' big 'C' (nbC) program, as the program was practically all chemical detection programs."[109] The end result was that the Navy and Air Force spent almost no money on biodefense.

Furthermore, the Chemical Corps cancelled development of its Biological Detection and Warning System in 1983 and then made virtually no effort to build an alternative. While this system previously received only about $2 million per year, it represented the major if not only thrust to develop BW detection during the 1970s.[110] It consisted of the XM19 Biological Agent Automatic Alarm (which detected airborne material using adhesive tape and chemical luminescence), coupled with the XM2 Biological Sampler (which collected and concentrated aerosol samples for further analysis).[111]

[55]

No doubt the Biological Detection and Warning System was unreliable. This might explain why it was cancelled, except that technical feasibility does not explain the long-standing discrepancy between the difficulty of BW detection and military doctrine (as I describe in the next chapter), let alone the limited investment in solving this problem relative to the ample support that difficult kinetic problems received. For example, consider military aircraft. Brown argues that the Air Force "repeatedly issued performance requirements that demanded major technological advances. The feasibility of these requirements was not adequately assessed," and, as a result, "totally unforeseen technological breakthroughs had to take place."[112] Moreover, despite its demanding requirements, the Air Force still tried to accelerate acquisition by producing aircraft that were still under development.

Likewise, accurate navigation for ballistic missiles was initially thought to be impossible and yet it was eagerly pursued. Even when technically infeasible, bold claims about accuracy were used to promote development of the Navy's Fleet Ballistic Missile program.[113] The same is true for missile defense, which is likened to "hitting a bullet with a bullet," the feasibility of which has been disputed for decades.[114] Unlike these ambitious kinetic systems, however, the Biological Detection and Warning System was cancelled.[115] Work on standoff detection using LIDAR (light detection and ranging) soon ground to a halt as well. Edgewood issued a contract for detecting BW using mass spectrometry in 1987, but advanced development and acquisition of this technology was years away.[116] As a result, the military simply had no detection system in the field.

Medical Countermeasures

Technical feasibility is even less useful for explaining the development and acquisition of medical countermeasures, especially the anthrax vaccine, which the military only started to procure more than twenty years after it was patented by researchers at Detrick. Although USAMRIID was rechristened and, after 1969, responsible for medical countermeasures at Fort Detrick, it fared poorly after Nixon's decision to end the offensive BW program. First, dismantling the offensive program resulted in "the destruction of a large segment of accumulated research results," which set back subsequent work on biodefense.[117] Rather than learn, the military actually lost knowledge that it once had.

Second, ownership of facilities at Detrick was in flux. Nearly seventy buildings were turned over to the National Cancer Institute in 1972.[118] And about 1,200 people were fired with the closure of the Army Biological Defense Research Laboratory at a time when the total compliment of

USAMRIID was fewer than 500 people.[119] Third, USAMRIID studied the pathogenesis and treatment of a variety of diseases (particularly arboviruses such as Rift Valley fever, Chikungunya, and different forms of equine encephalitis), but its annual budget was less than $10 million, and drug development as well as acquisition were at a lull.[120] Only small amounts of vaccine were produced for research staff and these supplies were often depleted. Still, the Army declined to buy the Swiftwater facility, even though it housed the only laboratory that was capable of making many of these vaccines. (The facility was donated to the Salk Institute instead.)[121]

Work at USAMRIID increased during the 1980s, with toxins receiving greater attention after the alleged use of trichothecene mycotoxins in Southeast Asia and Afghanistan during a series of incidents named "Yellow Rain."[122] Vaccines remained a central concern, and researchers investigated viral hemorrhagic fevers as well as other naturally occurring infectious diseases. Some of this work was criticized—particularly by civilian opponents of military involvement in biology—for addressing agents that had not been validated as threats by the US intelligence community.[123] But the Army Medical Research and Development Command insisted that this interpretation of threats was too narrow to serve as a practical guide for defense.

In addition, researchers from USAMRIID sought approval for two new funding and acquisition initiatives. First, in 1985, the commander and a scientist at USAMRIID recommended that the military increase funding for biodefense and acquire a vaccine stockpile, including two million doses for anthrax and botulinum. Despite aggressive support from the Army's vice chief of staff, however, little funding materialized, and the proposed vaccine stockpile went nowhere. For USAMRIID, this outcome was "very disappointing."[124]

A second and smaller initiative was more successful. In 1988, Anna Johnson-Winegar—formerly a researcher at USAMRIID—helped convince the Army surgeon general's office to order three hundred thousand doses of anthrax vaccine: enough to fully immunize about fifty thousand people with a six-dose regimen. In effect, this was the military's first large contract to acquire vaccines for biodefense since World War II, despite the long-standing Soviet threat.[125] Furthermore, this decision was not the result of a comprehensive threat assessment by senior staff but rather the "fortuitous" initiative of an Army major and a civilian employee.[126] The contract was awarded to the Michigan Biologic Products Institute, an antiquated facility run by the Michigan Department of Public Health. It was the only licensed manufacturer of anthrax vaccine in the country. The Michigan facility was given five years to fill this order for anthrax vaccine, and it was awarded another contract for botulinum vaccine in 1989.[127]

This vaccine would soon prove critical, but its acquisition was far too little and late to explain based on the threat alone. On average, the US military spent less than $80 million per year on biodefense during the 1980s, or less than 0.4 percent of its total budget for research and development. At the same time, the Soviet Union was spending more than twice that amount on offensive BW.[128] Even if the Soviet return on investment was deeply discounted, realism would still struggle to account for this difference because "the offense-defense balance in biological warfare strongly favors the attacker."[129] Fear and self-help gained some empirical support from the resurrection of the Chemical Corps after the Yom Kippur War. But realism still fails to explain why the US military seemed to rely on the Biological Weapons Convention despite growing evidence that the Soviet Union was cheating; only started stockpiling vaccine at the end of the Cold War despite having patented the anthrax vaccine in 1965; and neglected BW detection despite doctrine that explicitly—though erroneously—depended on this capability.

Similarly, while bureaucratic interests provide one explanation for why USAMRIID advocated for increased spending and stockpiling in the 1980s, interests alone cannot explain why the Army once again wanted to abolish its own Chemical Corps during the 1970s. References to bureaucratic power beg rather than answer this question. Why was the Chemical Corps habitually so weak, given its wide-ranging responsibilities? The nonkinetic nature of these responsibilities helps explain this weakness, according to my argument, which also explains the litany of evidence that challenges realism.

Again, the Fall and Partial Rise of Military Biodefense: The 1991 Gulf War through the Iraq War

Decades of neglect produced serious deficiencies in military biodefense that were highlighted by the 1991 Gulf War. Many of these deficiencies were apparent at the beginning of Operation Desert Shield in August 1990. "The threat and countermeasures were well known long before Desert Shield/Desert Storm," and the CIA believed that "the Iraqis probably have already deployed militarily significant numbers of biologically filled aerial bombs and artillery rockets."[130] The military rushed to research, develop, and acquire detection systems, computer models, and medical countermeasures in preparation for Operation Desert Storm, which began in January 1991. Because of its failure to understand many of the biological problems and solutions involved, however, it had depressingly little success.

Detection Systems and Computer Models

After sitting dormant for years, development of detection systems was kicked into high gear in August 1990 by General Colin Powell, then chairman of the Joint Chiefs of Staff. In response, the Chemical Corps resurrected the Biological Detection and Warning System that it mothballed in 1983. At the same time, the Defense Nuclear Agency tested three standoff detection systems: a LIDAR system that had been shelved in 1986, a similar device provided by SRI International, and an aircraft-mounted flow cytometer. Unfortunately, the airplane carrying the flow cytometer crashed in October (killing all on board), the SRI system failed, and US Central Command (CENTCOM) did not want to give up hanger space in the Gulf for the LIDAR prototype. The only system left standing was the XM2 component of the old Biological Detection and Warning System, so the Army started to acquire a few of these devices—along with a similar commercial unit called the PM10—in December 1990.[131] However, these detection systems performed poorly and they were nowhere near fast enough to provide advance warning.

Following the fatal plane crash in October, the Defense Nuclear Agency handed its biological detection program over to the Chemical Corps and focused on developing computer models to simulate potential attacks. These models predicted how hazardous materials are transported and dispersed in the atmosphere, providing information that might aid warning and reporting. The Defense Nuclear Agency drew on its experience with nuclear weapons to refine a computer program called the Automated Nuclear, Biological, and Chemical Information System (ANBACIS). This was based on a "non-uniform simple surface evaporation" model that Edgewood previously developed for chemical agents.[132] The refined program, called ANBACIS II, was showcased in January 1991 and run on Cray supercomputers to predict the footprint of contamination in various wartime scenarios.[133]

The value of ANBACIS II was questionable. "It was not used to predict the outcome of any Allied attacks against Iraqi NBC targets," even though this was an important source of possible contamination, and some users preferred the manual method for calculating downwind hazards called ATP-45.[134] Also, consistent with nonkinetic stereotypes, computer programs such as ANBACIS II were based on models for chemical contamination and radioactive fallout: algorithms that might be poorly suited for simulating biological warfare. Dynamics such as contagion were ignored, for instance, and biological weapons were simply treated as a subset of chemical weapons. Moreover, similar algorithms were used after the Gulf War to develop software, including the Hazard

[59]

Prediction and Assessment Capability, which the military used extensively before, during, and after invading Iraq in 2003.

Medical Countermeasures during the Gulf War

While it was developing computer models and detection systems, the military also rushed to acquire medical countermeasures for the anthrax and botulinum toxin that Iraq was believed to have deployed. At the beginning of Operation Desert Shield, the surgeons general and the Armed Forces Epidemiology Board recommended vaccinating US forces immediately and acquiring more vaccine as soon as possible.[135] But the Army only had about 10,000 doses of anthrax vaccine on hand in August 1990. The Michigan facility—the military's sole supplier—was hard pressed to deliver another 140,000 doses over the next few months.[136] Six doses were required for full immunity and so, even with an abbreviated regimen, this was only enough vaccine for tens of thousands of troops and not the hundreds of thousands deployed in the Persian Gulf.

The military's supply of botulinum vaccine was even smaller. More troubling, its sole source of botulinum antitoxin—the entire industrial base for the most advanced military in human history—was a single horse: a single, elderly horse named First Flight.[137] It is almost impossible to imagine the US military tolerating such an absurd lack of surge capacity for critical kinetic systems. According to General Powell, "I'd been kicking around thirty-odd years . . . I was quite aware that we did not have protective equipment or vaccines."[138] But these anomalous facts were routinely ignored, despite the danger, consistent with their nonkinetic character.

Faced with these glaring deficiencies, the military tasked an ad hoc working group called Project Badger to acquire more vaccines and antitoxins. Project Badger bought one hundred horses to supply more botulinum antitoxin, asked every major pharmaceutical company in the country for help making anthrax vaccine, and built a production facility at USAMRIID to manufacture botulinum vaccine. Coupled with acquisition of the antibiotic ciprofloxacin, these efforts were expected to cost between $200 and $400 million.[139]

However, the Gulf War ended before Project Badger enjoyed much success. Few companies had the equipment necessary to make anthrax vaccine, and only one agreed to help, in part because they were not indemnified and thus liable if the vaccine had adverse effects.[140] Procurement of the horses was also delayed, and months of gradual exposure were required for them to produce antitoxin in their blood.[141] Finally, it took more than a year to build a production facility for botulinum vaccine that complied with good manufacturing practices, particularly since

USAMRIID had to recreate a legacy system for making the toxoid version that was developed during World War II. "You want to talk old technology," recalled one participant, "all of that bot-toxoid manufacturing had been done with much older technology. And, in some cases, you couldn't even buy some of the gizmos."[142] Even with technical assistance from the Swiftwater facility, USAMRIID was forced to reinvent the wheel for toxoid production.

Perhaps more important, military leaders did not understand why the production of medical countermeasures could not be accelerated because they failed to appreciate the biology involved. Vaccines and antitoxins are grown, not built like mechanical devices, and some of the requisite knowledge had been lost. According to the chairman of Project Badger's executive committee, "we were faced with a problem that couldn't be solved in the time frame it needed to be solved. The people setting the goals just didn't understand what the issue was."[143] A similar failure to understand the time required to acquire immunity also delayed distribution of what little vaccine was available, and so most troops in the theater of operations were not immunized against anthrax or botulinum toxin during the 1991 Gulf War.

Reorganization

Both the military and Congress tried but failed to solve these problems through reorganization after Operation Desert Storm. In June 1993, the DoD created the Joint Program Office for Biological Defense (JPO-BD), which effectively placed development and acquisition of medical and nonmedical products under the leadership of officers from the Chemical Corps. This was consistent with the CBW stereotype but contrary to advice from the Army Medical Command and a Nobel laureate biologist— Joshua Lederberg—who argued that someone with a background in biology should be in charge of medical products. Once again, those claiming biological expertise lost the bureaucratic fight when the Chemical Corps claimed greater experience in buying military equipment through the traditional acquisition process.[144] In addition to this conflict, neither the Navy nor Air Force was eager to participate in the JPO-BD, and so "it was really rough going in the beginning."[145]

Congress was duly worried that the military would continue to neglect critical countermeasures. Therefore, in November 1993, Congress passed legislation that attempted to raise the priority of these issues by consolidating research, development, and acquisition into the Chemical and Biological Defense Program (CBDP), placed inside the Office of the Secretary of Defense.[146] But the devil is in the details of how this law was implemented. The Army remained the executive agent, and, over the following decade, the CBDP was managed through a shifting series of ineffective committees and ad hoc groups. Repeatedly shifting management indicated "an awareness of the problem but a lack of understanding," which, in turn, prompted yet another round of reorganization just months before the invasion of Iraq in 2003.[147]

On the one hand, acquisition and requirements were streamlined in 2003, creating a slightly less muddled organizational flow chart. On the other hand, another attempt at "slugging it out" failed to separate medical and nonmedical programs. (This time, the unsuccessful effort was spearheaded by the secretary of defense for health affairs.) Instead, management of science and technology was stripped from Detrick, as well as from Edgewood, and given to the Defense Threat Reduction Agency (DTRA). Formerly known as the Defense Nuclear Agency, DTRA had little experience with biodefense beyond forcing BW into the mold of models designed for chemical attacks and radioactive fallout. It also lacked ties to the biological research and development community. Biodefense experts were therefore critical of DTRA, at least initially, and pessimistic about the prospects for improvement under the management structure established immediately before the Iraq War.[148] Plus, several years later, there was "still a great deal of confusion as to who's in charge."[149]

Research, Development, and Acquisition after the Cold War

Despite the deficiencies that prompted reorganization following Operation Desert Storm, the military slashed research and development for biodefense after the Gulf War and the end of the Cold War. Funding and personnel at USAMRIID were cut by more than 30 percent, which was disproportionately greater than the general drawdown in military research and development for the "peace dividend," such as it was, during this period.[150] Put bluntly, USAMRIID "was raped," at least according to one former official.[151]

Other nonkinetic capabilities faced seemingly disproportionate cuts as well. For instance, the Army recommended that the Base Closure and Realignment Commission close the Chemical Defense Training Facility at Fort McClellan and, in 1995, Dugway Proving Ground. The commission demurred.[152] Similarly, by Eden's account, an important initiative to integrate fire damage into nuclear war planning was also terminated after the Cold War.[153] As with attempts to eliminate the Chemical Corps after World War I, World War II, and the Vietnam War, these examples suggest that the prospects for peace or austerity are particularly grim for programs that the military is predisposed to misunderstand and disregard.[154]

[62]

Changing the Trajectory: Civilian Intervention

Cuts to military biodefense would have been even deeper were it not for civilian intervention. Admiral William Owens, the vice chairman of the Joint Chiefs of Staff, planned to cut an additional $1 billion from the chemical and biological defense budget in 1996, due in part to mismanagement of the CBDP and dissatisfaction with the anthrax vaccine.[155] But Owens was opposed by his friend, Richard Danzig, a civilian then serving as under secretary of the Navy.

Although the Navy had little bureaucratic interest in biodefense, Danzig championed it because he had thought about the threat, and, though a civilian, he claimed to have as much standing "in the biological area" as uniformed military officials because "they didn't know any more than I did."[156] Danzig was not alone. Stephen Joseph, another civilian and the assistant secretary of defense for health affairs, was also pushing the anthrax vaccine, and Danzig recruited Joshua Lederberg to help persuade the Joint Chiefs that the BW threat was real and peacetime vaccinations were necessary. He garnered military support from General Charles Krulak, commandant of the Marine Corps, along with the assistant commandant General Richard Hearney. Reportedly, Krulak saw biodefense as a way to gain resources rather than lose them, which suggests that there is nothing inherent to this mission that is antithetical to the military's bureaucratic interests.[157] Krulak and Hearney had the military credentials to make a credible case. With their support, Danzig and Lederberg persuaded the other Joint Chiefs and deputies through an educational campaign— "talking things out" in a series of meetings and presentations—that targeted these leaders' ideas and underlying assumptions about BW.[158]

As an apparent consequence of this persuasion campaign, the Joint Chiefs endorsed peacetime vaccinations against anthrax in 1996. They also reversed their previously planned budget cut, increasing rather than decreasing funding for chemical and biological defense by $1 billion over the next five years. This was an important turning point that marked the beginning of substantially increased investment in military biodefense (see fig. 2.1).

Increased investment and peacetime vaccinations are significant shifts in policy that, at first glance, seem to challenge my argument. After all, I claim that organizational frames and stereotypes are relatively constant, which means that they explain consistency better than change. But the process through which change came about in this case supports the argument that ideas were at least as important as threats or interests. In particular, Danzig and Lederberg did not unveil shocking new intelligence about the BW threat. Nor did they rely on the competitive bargaining or "horse trading" that is often associated with bureaucratic compromise

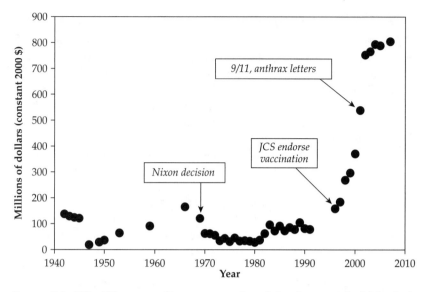

FIGURE 2.1. US military spending on research and development for biological warfare (including offensive work prior to 1969). Budget data for biodefense is incomplete and often indistinguishable from reporting on chemical defense, but the overall pattern is still evident. Data sources include DoD R1 tables and reports to Congress and DoD Committee on Biological Warfare, Research and Development Board, "1950 Program Guidance Report," 24 January 1950; Clendenin, *Science and Technology at Fort Detrick*; SIPRI, *The Problem of Chemical and Biological Warfare: CB Weapons Today*, vol. 2 (Stockholm: Almqvist & Wiksell, 1973), 204; Barton J. Bernstein, "The Birth of the US Biological-Warfare Program," *Scientific American* 256, no. 6 (1987); GAO, *Biological Warfare*; National Research Council, *Giving Full Measure to Countermeasures*; Biological and Chemical Weapons Control Program, *Federal Funding for Biological Weapons Prevention and Defense, Fiscal Years 2001 to 2007* (Washington, D.C: Center for Arms Control and Non-Proliferation, 2007); *Federal Funding for Biological Weapons Prevention and Defense, Fiscal Years 2001 to 2009* (Washington, DC: Center for Arms Control and Non-Proliferation, 2008).

(e.g., using side payments to sweeten the deal and buy off the opposition). Instead, they focused on the ideas at work, persuading the Joint Chiefs to reconsider their assumptions and reinterpret their environment.

Moreover, much of the impetus for change came from civilians and not the mainstream military. On the one hand, this supports Posen's argument that civilian intervention is necessary for military innovation. Reorganization of the CBDP by Congress in 1993 suggests the same, and the shifts in policy that Danzig and Lederberg helped instigate in 1996 were soon reinforced by support from senior civilian leadership, including the secretary of defense William Cohen and President Bill Clinton. The response to September 11 and the anthrax attacks of 2001 further solidified the trend toward increased funding seen in fig. 2.1. In addition, Posen argues that civilians need military "mavericks" to implement innovation inside the armed services, and Generals Krulak and Hearney could be seen as filling this role to change peacetime vaccination policy.[159]

On the other hand, military biodefense also challenges important aspects of Posen's argument. First, Posen claims that successful civilian intervention supports his version of realism. But the very need for such intervention—created by organizational pathologies and the disjunction between military and civilian goals—is inconsistent with realist assumptions about states as unitary and rational actors. The need for civilian intervention is more consistent with organizational frame theory, which, given the shared nature of ideas inside organizations, implies that change is unlikely to originate from inside the military itself.

Second, civilian intervention was not as successful as the spending spike seen in figure 2.1 might otherwise suggest. Just as the military's administration of the CBDP left much to be desired, increased investment into biodefense failed to quickly rectify long-standing neglect by the armed services. The nonkinetic stereotypes at work here were particularly sticky, so the problems caused by these ideas resisted change as well. The limited effect of civilian intervention might therefore provide some support for Stephen Rosen. Contrary to Posen, he argues that successful innovation is not imposed from the outside by civilians or mavericks but rather by "senior military officers with traditional credentials," who, through an "ideological struggle" inside their service, "create a new promotion pathway for junior officers" with skill practicing the new task.[160] Yet the type of internal change that Rosen describes is unlikely to occur for nonkinetic functions: it certainly did not for biodefense. Even with civilian intervention and support from some senior officers, biodefense remained a technical specialty and the military continued to conflate it with chemical defense.

As a result, increased investment eventually halted the decline of research and development. But USAMRIID still suffered in the interim, and projects that had been rushed in preparation for Operation Desert Storm gathered dust during the 1990s. Interest in the production facility for botulinum toxoid waned with the prospect of a recombinant vaccine, for example, and yet the funding that had been available during the Gulf War was lost rather than redirected toward this new countermeasure. Similarly, work on a recombinant anthrax vaccine dated back to the 1980s, but that line of research was delayed in part by reorganization of the CBDP.[161]

The Struggle to Acquire Vaccines

Like research and development, the armed services' emphasis on acquisition waned after the 1991 Gulf War. At the time, Project Badger concluded that the military needed to build its own vaccine production facility because so few companies were willing or able to help.[162] This was not a new idea. Inspired by the military's contract with the pilot plant in Swiftwater, the Armed Forces Epidemiology Board considered building a government-owned, contractor-operated production facility when there was no commercial interest in vaccine for meningitis in 1972.[163] But the Navy and Air Force balked at building such a facility for biodefense in October 1991. Ironically, this was less than one year after the Air Staff was worrying about the Army getting preferential access to the limited supply of vaccine during the Gulf War. Then the Air Force feared that General Schwarzkopf at CENTCOM harbored "an infantryman's concern for his fellow infantrymen."[164] After the war, however, this angst was once again replaced by apathy.

The Army planned to build a production facility in 1995, which, if built at Fort Detrick, was estimated to cost about $260 million.[165] The Army Medical Command and Medical Department supported this plan, but their biological expertise lost out once again. Plans for a production facility were abandoned because Congress and the under secretary of defense for acquisitions and technology—the "acquisition czar" and a former chemist—preferred the traditional process for buying military equipment through prime system contractors, notwithstanding the lack of commercial interest.[166]

Unfortunately, prime system contractors struggled to deliver the anthrax vaccine. The only manufacturer licensed by the Food and Drug Administration was the antiquated Michigan Biologic Products Institute, which the FDA had failed to inspect for several years. When this facility was finally inspected, conditions were so bad that the FDA issued a series of warnings and ultimately threatened to revoke its license in 1997. The military was caught off guard because "it's hard to be proactive when you really don't understand the issue."[167] These problems persisted long after the Michigan facility was sold to BioPort in 1998. It closed for renovation and vaccine production stopped for more than a year, after which BioPort was nearly insolvent and the Army agreed to amend its contract, granting $24.1 million in relief, reducing the number of doses to be delivered from 7.9 million to 4.6 million, and increasing the price per dose from $4.36 to $10.64.[168] The anthrax vaccine remained in critically short supply at least until 2002.

Prime system contractors struggled to deliver other vaccines as well. The military took several years to award a prime contract for vaccines,

[66]

during which time it had no mechanism in place for advanced development and clinical trials.[169] The DoD Joint Vaccine Acquisition Program (JVAP) then awarded its $322 million prime contract to DynPort (a subsidiary of the large defense contractor DynCorp) in 1997. But JVAP was "a disaster" according to General Philip Russell.[170] The military's model for acquisition failed to align with the industry's best practices for vaccine development, and, by 2001, independent experts were calling for the government to build its own production facility—just like Project Badger had previously proposed.[171] Clinical trials for a new botulinum vaccine were "nowhere in sight," for instance, and the DoD had used DynPort to purchase "a ridiculously small amount" of smallpox vaccine for about $75 per dose rather than participate in a parallel contract with the CDC, which bought tens of millions of doses for a few dollars each.[172]

Therefore, when the US military was preparing to invade Iraq in 2003, the DoD was forced to rely on the CDC's stockpile of smallpox vaccine, it failed to acquire an adequate supply of botulinum vaccine through DynPort, and it had a very hard time with the anthrax vaccine from Bio-Port.[173] When the Iraq War ended in 2011, the DoD was once again debating whether to build vaccine production facilities, twenty years after Project Badger made this recommendation during the Gulf War. And protests still persist against vaccine production cannibalizing funding for nonmedical programs.[174] Granted, DoD had pursued platform technologies and broad-spectrum therapies during the Iraq War through its Transformational Medical Technologies Initiative. Despite some progress on treatments for hemorrhagic fevers and influenza, however, this initiative was deemed unsuccessful. DTRA dismantled it in 2011 and redirected the funding toward more traditional projects.[175] Likewise, the Defense Advanced Research Projects Agency has funded biodefense since the late 1990s, but DARPA typically supports research that is neglected by the military at large.

It is difficult to produce new drugs (particularly vaccines) even under the best circumstances. But the technical difficulties involved were compounded by the military's socially constructed ignorance of the problems and solutions at hand. "There has been work over the years trying to align what an FDA milestone for vaccine approval is with a Department of Defense acquisition milestone," but, according to Johnson-Winegar, "they are trying to make a force fit there; it just doesn't seem to work." So, just as "most people . . . were uninformed, didn't appreciate the threat," and "didn't appreciate the difficulty of trying to implement the recommendations of Project Badger" during the Gulf War, "to this day," most military officials "still don't have a full appreciation of what it takes to develop a medical countermeasure, get it approved, get the funding for it, get the policy in place, and implement the logistics of the whole thing. . . . They don't get it."[176]

Biological Detection: Still Difficult

The military had more success acquiring nonmedical products after the 1991 Gulf War, and, in contrast to the Cold War, it finally fielded BW detection systems. Compared to drugs, these devices were easier for the military to fit within its established acquisition system because the hardware more closely resembles the equipment acquired for kinetic warfare. Procurement was still slow, however, and so detection systems remained in short supply during the invasion of Iraq in 2003. Moreover, given its nonkinetic stereotypes, the military still assumed that the performance parameters for biological detection should mirror those for chemical detection—particularly in that rapid or real-time detection is the holy grail. It remains to be seen if this is a fool's errand, but none of the biological detection systems acquired to date are fast enough to provide the advance warning needed for effective use of physical protection. (At times, protective suits and masks were in short supply as well.)[177]

For example, the JPO-BD acquired the M31 Biological Integrated Detection System (BIDS) in 1996. This was an interim non-development item based on existing technology. It consisted of a small lab mounted on a truck that used modified XM2 samplers to concentrate particles from the air for analysis with nonspecific detection instruments (a particle sizer, flow cytometer, and bioluminometer) and specific antibody techniques (including sensitive membrane antigen rapid tests, or SMART cards). In theory, BIDS could detect four types of agent in thirty to forty-five minutes.[178] The military acquired an improved version of BIDS in 1999, which included a mass spectrometer that had been under development for more than a decade. This version could detect eight kinds of agent, but detection times remained around thirty minutes. While half an hour is sufficient to signal that postexposure treatment might be required, it is too long to "detect to protect" using suits and masks.[179]

The JPO-BD also developed and acquired an automated sensor called the Joint Biological Point Detection System (JBPDS). Since the JBPDS could identify ten agents in about twenty minutes, it was slated to further modernize BIDS and serve as a common point detector for all the armed services. This system suffered serious performance problems, however, and so the JBPDS was produced at a low rate and the modernization program was delayed until 2003.[180] More elusive are development and acquisition of technology to detect BW at a distance. Using LIDAR, for example, the Joint Biological Standoff Detection System was once projected to be fully operational by 2012. But this schedule has slipped and it is unlikely that such a system will be fielded for years to come.[181] Finally, fearing even a funded mandate, the military was reluctant to consider civil applications for its detection systems, even with money from other agencies. Thus, in 2002, the DoD went so far as to return—rather than spend—$420 million that the Office of Homeland Security had provided the military to research, develop, and acquire BW detection technologies.[182]

The plight of these detection systems suggests that some of the same problems that plagued military biodefense during the Cold War were still evident before, during, and after the Iraq War. Biological detection is difficult, and trying to replicate rapid chemical or even radiological detection has yet to prove a successful strategy. Conceptual problems are also apparent when we consider medical countermeasures. Failing to understand the biology involved, the military tried and failed to acquire medical countermeasures and detection systems in the months before Operation Desert Storm that require years to develop. The DoD then tried to force vaccines and other drugs to fit into its established but mismatched model for buying equipment through prime system contractors. According to Thomas Monath, "the process of product development was a mild modification of how the army develops a new tank," and, though consistent with the kinetic frame, "the tank mentality doesn't apply to pharmaceuticals very well."[183] The military continued to rely on inaccurate stereotypes as well, as evidenced by the Chemical Corps' lead on medical products and DTRA's mandate to manage research and development based on its nuclear expertise.

Neither these stereotypes nor the kinetic frame explain every outcome. Military research, development, and acquisition are complex, so it is necessary to consider threats and interests in order to understand the complete picture. But the way in which the military interprets these threats and interests suggests that powerful—and often countervailing—ideas are also at work. For instance, the threat perceptions highlighted by realism help explain increased funding for biodefense in the late 1990s, and after September 11 and the anthrax attacks of 2001. The BW threat was long-standing, however, and fear and self-help cannot explain important outcomes that range from cuts to USAMRIID after the 1991 Gulf War to the lack of vaccine throughout the Cold War.

Moreover, almost every major change to military biodefense policy since World War II involved civilian intervention. While this lends some support to Posen's arguments about civilians as the origin of military innovation, realism cannot account for the necessity of civilian intervention without referring to organizational factors. The abject failure of some interventions (e.g., the decision by President Nixon and Secretary Laird to eliminate the CBW stereotype in 1969) and the limited effect of others (e.g., reorganization of the CBDP in 1993 and increased investment in biodefense after 1996) also gives credence to Rosen's claim that "a civilian command to carry out military innovation is by its nature extremely difficult to enforce."[184] Organizational frame theory is not a free-standing theory of change, but both the necessity of civilian intervention into military biodefense and the insufficiency of it are consistent with my argument.

Bureaucratic interests in funding and autonomy are useful explanations as well, at least in so far as they anticipate competition inside and among the armed services. This competition was evident between the Chemical Warfare Service and the surgeons general after World War II, and it continues to this day in conflicts between medical and nonmedical programs. However, bureaucratic interests provide little insight into which players win or lose these fights over time. This is particularly true for the paradox of the CWS and Chemical Corps, which were often victorious over the medical community and yet routinely marginalized by the mainstream military.

So, while the historical record is replete with bureaucratic competition, the outcomes of these turf wars tend to fit with my argument. According to one former official from Detrick, "you were constantly clashing with the chemical people," since "you were always trying to get them out of that pure chemical thinking."[185] As I have started to show, this thinking was enabled by the military's nonkinetic stereotypes, which treated biodefense as a subset of chemical defense. Equally important, these inaccurate stereotypes persisted because the issues involved fell outside the military's dominant frame and thus learning was limited. These ideas help explain the paradox of winners and losers, as well as why some problems endure despite increased investment. Money, though perhaps necessary, is not sufficient to solve problems that are conceptual in nature. Nor can funding conjure up new science or technology out of thin air. Rather, some ideas can cause neglect and confound attempts to rectify it.

[3]

Fatal Assumptions

MILITARY DOCTRINE

Doctrine defines how a military will fight—at least in theory—to support various political goals, including the goal of national security. According to Posen, for example, military doctrine is the component of grand strategy that defines (1) what military means will be used, and (2) how those means will be employed.[1] Doctrine is therefore fundamental to understanding force posture and military operations, which, in turn, affect the probability and outcome of war itself.

In addition to its effects on war and peace, military doctrine is also intimately involved with science and technology. This is particularly true when viewed from a realist perspective. Realism predicts that the threat environment will drive decisions about doctrine and that doctrine will then serve as an intervening variable, informing subsequent decisions about how to create and use science and technology.[2] This prediction now seems suspect, however, since the previous chapter described how military research, development, and acquisition for biodefense were influenced by the kinetic frame and nonkinetic stereotypes at least as much as by the threat environment. Might the same be true for doctrine?

What is US military doctrine for biodefense? How can it be explained? In order to answer these questions, I first address the military's means or method for biodefense by examining its plans and procedures regarding biological warfare. Here doctrine is the standard operating procedure that the armed forces plan to follow in the event of a BW attack: plans and procedures that are documented in numerous handbooks, field manuals, and other military publications. This is how doctrine is commonly referred to, and I argue that the kinetic frame and nonkinetic stereotypes can be seen or read in these documents along with their detrimental effects on biodefense.

[71]

It is worth noting, however, that I treat doctrine somewhat differently than does Eden, for whom doctrine shapes frames and thus "frames are doctrine-in-action."[3] In contrast, I flip this causal relationship to high-light how frames (and stereotypes) shape doctrine. My approach demonstrates that doctrine reflects particular choices, and these choices are influenced by the shared assumptions and heuristics that the military uses to solve problems. Recognition of these choices is consistent with how Posen elaborates on his definition of doctrine to include "judgments" and the "preferred mode of a group."[4] Plus, my approach exploits a wealth of textual data (e.g., military handbooks and field manuals), which allows me to address the otherwise abstract notion of doctrine in very concrete terms.

After examining the military means described in doctrinal texts, I then consider how these means were actually employed for biodefense during training and combat. Unfortunately, as this chapter will show, most aspects or expressions of doctrine rely on dangerously inaccurate and potentially fatal assumptions about biological warfare. Qualitative and quantitative content analysis reveal that military handbooks and field manuals have always been riddled with stereotypes that conflate biological weapons with other kinds of nonkinetic weapons. Over and over again, doctrine describes chemical defense as the token nonkinetic countermeasure, even though biodefense is a different problem and harder to solve. Stereotypes perpetuate this incomprehension and neglect because the issues involved fall outside of the military's kinetic frame.

Aversion to nonkinetic countermeasures is also apparent in doctrinal texts and military training, consistent with my argument. Although General Washington launched a successful campaign against smallpox during the Revolutionary War, the modern American military was unprepared to employ BW vaccines and detection systems during the 1991 Gulf War. Despite the long-standing threat of biological warfare, some of the same problems persisted through the invasion of Iraq in 2003. Military doctrine for biodefense is difficult to reconcile with the rational response to threats that is anticipated by realism, but it does illustrate the profound effect that frames and stereotypes can have on force posture and planning.

READING MILITARY DOCTRINE

Over the years, the armed services have published numerous handbooks and manuals that claim to address biological warfare. These documents define the problems that the military associates with biological weapons, and they specify the solutions that it assumes are appropriate through a series of plans or procedures for biodefense. Some publications are written for relatively narrow audiences such as battalion commanders or medical specialists. But most are intended to be read by service members at large—from enlisted personnel to senior officers—as an integral part of their education and training. As a result, these doctrinal texts reflect and reproduce military thinking about biodefense.

Of course, biodefense is just one of many issues addressed by military doctrine, and so most handbooks and manuals only mention BW in passing if at all. This is not surprising in the Army's Field Manual *Rifle Marksmanship*, for example, or the Air Force's Doctrine Document *Counterair Operations*. Therefore, in order to identify the documents that are most relevant for biodefense, I searched for all official publications that include at least one word with the prefix "bio-" in their title. At least sixty documents like this have been published since the Korean War; most were revisions of previous publications, and about half are still available today.[5] It is noteworthy that few documents refer only to "bio-" in their title, such as *Technical Aspects of Biological Defense*. Rather, most have titles such as the *Armed Forces Doctrine for Chemical Warfare and Biological Defense*, or titles that include abbreviated stereotypes, such as the *NBC Field Handbook*. These titles alone could suggest that military doctrine is predisposed to confuse and conflate BW with other issues.

Titles notwithstanding, what is the military's plan for biodefense? Reading doctrine reveals that, until recently, plans and procedures for biodefense were virtually identical to those for chemical defense. Despite their differences, biological warfare was conflated with chemical warfare and biodefense was subsumed under chemical defense, with chemical defense receiving far more attention. Similarly, as the Joint Strategic Plans Committee observed in 1950, "*only vague and somewhat stereotyped statements*, with respect to these methods of warfare, have been incorporated in our strategic plans. Such statements do not constitute adequate planning guidance"[6]

I argue that military doctrine subsumed biodefense under chemical defense because of the ideas at work in these "stereotyped statements." However, another approach is to refer instead to a "chemical frame," namely shared assumptions and heuristics about chemical warfare that were established during World War I and later applied to BW.[7] While not without merit, one problem with referring to a "chemical frame" is that this approach loses the analytical distinction between issues found inside versus outside an organization's dominant frame of reference. In particular, BW would appear to have been placed inside such a "chemical frame," since the military grouped chemical and biological issues together, but, at the same time, biodefense was still neglected. If an issue can be inside a dominant frame and yet neglected, then how does the frame explain this outcome? Recall that an organization will also learn about issues inside its dominant frame, so the language and practices there become increasingly sophisticated and specialized over time. If a sophisticated "chemical frame" was at work, then why were the differences between chemical and biological weapons not more apparent than their superficial similarities? And why did these differences not become more apparent with learning, driving the military's response to each apart and resulting in increasingly specialized doctrine? Finally, issues inside an organization's dominant frame enjoy ample if not excessive resources. But if the military had a "chemical frame," then why did the Chemical Warfare Service and Chemical Corps struggle to survive?

Referring to a "chemical frame" would therefore raise difficult questions about causal logic. It would also strain to explain behavior that we have already seen to be at odds with the organizational support and learning that Eden associates with the "blast damage frame" in her study of nuclear weapons. This is because not all frames are created equal. In contrast to an organization's dominant frame, stereotypes are different kinds of assumptions and heuristics. Because stereotypes are error prone to begin with, and their errors persist due to limited learning outside the organization's dominant frame, they help explain why the military erroneously conflated chemical and biological weapons in the first place, as well as why it erroneously subsumed biodefense under chemical defense for decades on end.

In addition, the concept of stereotypes helps us notice other aspects of bias against excluded and heterogeneous groups. For instance, the military treats chemical weapons as a token that is assumed to represent a diverse category of nonkinetic weapons, thereby overgeneralizing about issues the organization does not understand. The role of chemical weapons as a token or proxy for the CBW stereotype is evident in military doctrine because the conflation between chemical defense and biodefense is often explicit. According to one Army field manual, for example, "if alerted to a possible chemical or biological attack, personnel will assume that all artillery and air attacks are chemical attacks (until proven otherwise) and will take appropriate defensive actions for a chemical attack."[8] Similarly, "the vocal alarm for any chemical or biological hazard or attack is the word 'GAS,'" even though biological agents do not exist in a gaseous phase (unlike sarin and other volatile chemical agents).[9] Even more important than this sort of explicit conflation are the implicit and potentially fatal assumptions in how the military plans to avoid contamination, provide physical protection, and decontaminate itself in the event of a biological attack.

Contamination Avoidance, Physical Protection,
and Decontamination

Military doctrine for chemical defense and biodefense relies on a three-tiered approach of contamination avoidance, physical protection, and decontamination—each of which assumes that biological agents, like chemical agents, can be rapidly detected. First, doctrine assumes that contamination can be avoided with rapid detection and advance warning, thereby solving the problem by evading exposure in the event of an attack. Building on past practice for chemical warfare, the earliest handbooks and field manuals to mention BW suggest that chemical, biological, and radiological attacks might all be detected in advance through reconnaissance.[10] In this case, contaminated areas could be conveniently marked off with triangular hazard signs—warning against "germs" or "atom," just as they would for "gas"—and avoided altogether.[11]

Second, when contamination cannot be avoided but an attack has been detected, doctrine emphasizes physical protection through impermeable suits and face masks (along with shelters for collective protection). The ensemble of garments, gloves, hood, and mask eventually came to be known as "mission-oriented protective posture," or MOPP. But the mask has always received special attention. For example, according Army and Air Force doctrine in 1971, "the measures taken by troops while under biological attack are similar to those taken while under chemical attack. The most important single item of protective equipment is the mask."[12] This view grew out of the chemical warfare experience during World War I, and, while the name of the mask changed after World War II, the "change in term from 'gas mask' to 'protective mask' involves nomenclature only."[13] Once more, plans previously established for chemical defense were reapplied to biodefense, as well as radiological protection, which was the other new nonkinetic problem at the time. The military's multipurpose mask is too cumbersome to wear for long as a precautionary measure and its integral goggles are probably unnecessary protection for BW. But, here again, the original assumption was that masks and other protective clothing would only need to be worn after an attack was detected.

The last step in the military's three-tiered approach is decontamination, which is done when the mission permits and the chemical or biological attack is over. Doctrine usually assumes that these nonkinetic attacks have distinct phases with a detectable beginning and end, after which cleaning up can limit the risk of further exposure. Moreover, since decontamination requires removing or otherwise neutralizing the hazard, "it is necessary that you know precisely where contamination hazards are," as the Army explained in 1985. "Measurements that determine safe levels are made with detection equipment held 1 inch away from the surface."[14] Though the lack of biological detection equipment capable of making these measurements was briefly noted, this deficiency was rarely if ever reconciled with the apparent necessity of detection for decontamination or, similarly, for issuing the critical "all clear" signal that would let troops know when it was safe to remove their protective gear after decontamination.

So contamination avoidance, physical protection, and decontamination all rest on the fundamental assumption that biological agents are like chemical agents and that they both can be rapidly detected. Unfortunately, this assumption has always been false. Unlike most chemical agents, biological agents cannot be detected fast enough to provide the advance warning needed to avoid contamination. Nor can biological agents be detected fast enough to let troops know when to put on masks and protective clothing during an attack. Biological agents cannot even be detected fast enough for their absence to serve as a practical standard for decontamination in most combat scenarios.

Simply put, there is no reliable "detect to warn" or "detect to protect" capability for BW. Such capability would require that biological samples be collected, analyzed, and identified "in less than 3 to 5 minutes, and preferably in about 1 minute."[15] This time frame is feasible for chemical warfare because automated alarms and hand-held monitors can detect chemical agents in less than 1 minute. But doing so for BW is beyond current technology: biological detection still takes more than 10 minutes. Modern technology notwithstanding, there certainly was no rapid biological detection capability when the military first started applying doctrine for chemical defense to biodefense in the 1940s and 1950s.

Detection that takes any longer than a few seconds or minutes is best described as "detect to treat," which assumes that the target population has already been exposed. However, in sharp contrast to the military's mantra of contamination avoidance, physical protection, and decontamination, treatment and prophylaxis—with vaccines, antibiotics, and other drugs—received scant attention in doctrine during the Cold War. Medical countermeasures are less important for chemical defense: aside from taking pyridostigmine bromide tablets beforehand and injecting atropine afterward, there are few drugs that counteract chemical agents. In contrast, immunization and medical treatment are critical components of biodefense. But military doctrine assumed that biodefense was like chemical defense. Consequently, medical countermeasures received only cursory consideration, on a par with generic advice given about personal hygiene (e.g., doctrine instructing troops to wash their hands and brush their teeth after a BW attack).

[76]

Moreover, what little mention there was of medicine was sometimes inaccurate. For example, according to the armed forces' doctrine in 1976, "immunization available for some enemy-employed biological agents may be administered when biological attack appears imminent."[16] But immunity takes time to acquire, the armed forces had no plans for vaccination before an attack, and they had procured almost no vaccine. For decades on end, the grave implications of these errors were ignored. Instead of giving medical countermeasures serious consideration, the military emphasized plans and procedures for contamination avoidance, physical protection, and decontamination that depend on rapid detection, which, though possible for chemical attacks, has always been unlikely for BW.

These are potentially fatal flaws in the conflation of chemical and biological warfare. They are also inexplicable from a realist perspective, which expects military doctrine to reflect a rational response to threats like BW. Over and over again, doctrine sidelined medical countermeasures and instructed troops to treat biodefense like chemical defense and rely on their masks, even though they were unlikely to learn that a biological attack had actually occurred until long after they were already exposed. According to one Army handbook, "to say that your protective mask is a lifesaver is to state a true and simple fact," but such statements ignore the true and simple fact that these masks are practically useless for cover without rapid detection.[17]

Most handbooks and field manuals acknowledge—in passing—that biological agents are difficult to detect, even as they prescribe plans and procedures for avoidance, protection, and decontamination that rely on detection. Rather than address the difficulty of biological detection and its practical implications, however, these problems were glossed over in older documents. For instance, doctrine during the Cold War suggested that biological attacks would be identified through intelligence, since "there are certain prior indications of an enemy's interest in biological operations that intelligence personnel are trained to look for."[18] But recall that accurate intelligence on BW programs is notoriously hard to come by. Alternatively, "after biological agents have been employed several times, a definite pattern of usage could materialize."[19] While this may be true, the concession to multiple attacks is not coupled with operational plans for mitigating their effects in the interim.

Along with dubious claims about actionable intelligence, Cold War doctrine often claimed that biological attacks could be detected in advance by observing the kinetic systems associated with their delivery. This is consistent with the military's dominant frame of reference. Emphasis is placed on seeing spray released by low-flying aircraft, for example, as well as unusual bombs, artillery shells, missiles, and rockets.

[77]

This faith in observation is not qualified by the difficulty of seeing in the dark, even though nighttime provides some of the most favorable conditions for biological attacks, which may not include visible or audible explosions in any case. Standard operating procedures for reporting these attacks also focus on the kinetic aspects of their delivery. The NBC Warning and Reporting System highlights information such as the "means of delivery . . . number of shells in attack . . . and number of munitions or aircraft," just as older versions of these reports instruct observers to "note the approx. no. of rounds, bombs, or planes" involved.[20]

The difficulty of biological detection is therefore acknowledged but dismissed, thanks in part to the assumption that familiar aspects of kinetic warfare will prevail. Kinetic delivery systems are also emphasized in doctrine about chemical agents. For example, as once described by the Navy, "a chemical attack, in contrast to a conventional shot-and-shell attack, *only begins* when the agent is released. . . . It is as though a chemical machine gun with a huge store of ammunition had been set into automatic operation."[21] This strained analogy illustrates the interpretive power of the kinetic frame. Plus, on rare occasion, the military even acknowledged the contrived nature of its nonkinetic stereotypes. Again, according to the Navy, "while incendiary weapons are now firmly entrenched in the chemical warfare system, their presence there is probably an accident of history, or a convenient lumping together of weapons which were at one time odd or unusual."[22] The same can certainly be said for smoke and radiological protection, as well as for biodefense.

Moreover, doctrine reflects and reinforces the military's aversion to nonkinetic problems and solutions even while it promotes avoidance, protection, and decontamination. These have long been described as "passive" measures, in spite of the fact that "the term *passive defense* had a negative connotation compared with the US military's more action-oriented lingo."[23] Passive defense is also portrayed as onerous and unappealing, especially when compared to more kinetic options. The message is clear when reading between the lines. "While a necessary part of the solution to the NBC threat, passive NBC defense is insufficient in and of itself," according to joint doctrine, and "neutralizing the threat will require the effective application of other military capabilities, in particular active defense measures and counterforce operations."[24]

While downplaying nonkinetic countermeasures in favor of counterforce operations, the military also describes nonkinetic threats in terms that are remarkably graphic or emotive relative to the bland and impersonal language used for other issues.[25] In particular, doctrine is sometimes laced with historical quotes about the horrors of chemical warfare during World War I. "The effects of the successful gas attack were horrible . . . . all the dead lie on their back with clenched fists," according to

[78]

one account quoted in joint doctrine, and, in another, "even in theory the gas mask is a dreadful thing. It stands for one's first flash of insight into man's measureless malignity against man."[26] Whether or not the gas mask is uniquely symbolic of mankind's malevolence, this is an odd account to highlight in doctrine on defense, especially when the same document claims elsewhere that "the mask is the most effective protection against biological and chemical agents." Why not quote a soldier saying, "Sure glad that I had a gas mask in 1918. It saved my life!"? Rather, the military's language implies that kinetic offense and defense are more appealing, for missing are comparable quotes about the flak jacket as a special sign of human cruelty, the agony of being torn apart by flying shrapnel, or the revulsion of seeing a battlefield strewn with bodies ripped asunder by rifle fire.

Kinetic warfare probably appears more appealing in part because it is more comprehensible within the military's dominant frame. This might also explain why the acronym "NBC" is sometimes said—in truthful jest—to mean "No Body Cares." such apathy is consistent with the lack of learning inherent to nonkinetic stereotypes, and it helps perpetuate the erroneous assumption that biodefense is like chemical defense and thus subsumed by it.[27] Biological warfare and bioterrorism are at least as threatening to US forces as chemical attacks (though for different reasons), but military handbooks and field manuals will often discuss chemical weapons first and in greater detail, followed by an abbreviated description of BW. Plans and procedures for biodefense then refer back to chemical defense and the mantra of contamination avoidance, physical protection, and decontamination, even though this three-tiered approach has always been unlikely to work without rapid biological detection.

The dangers inherent in this approach have not gone unnoticed. But recognition is usually confined to a small community of BW experts and, given the nonkinetic issues involved, the controversy is marginalized and thus limited. "That has always been a problem, dating back to ancient times," according to one former official from USAMRIID, "that everything is always chem . . . and bio gets the short end of the stick. The two of them are markedly different, and the concepts and thinking of bio has to be different than it is for chemical."[28] In spite of its resident expertise, however, USAMRIID traditionally had little say on handbooks and manuals about biodefense, most of which were written by the Army Chemical School.

For its part, the Chemical Corps accepted and eventually promoted stereotypes like CBW, NBC, CBR, and CBRN. Had its activities been inside the military's dominant frame, then the Chemical Corps might have specialized instead, only writing doctrine for chemical warfare and acknowledging that biological warfare is very different. But falling outside the kinetic frame, the Chemical Corps had low status, and, desperate to survive on the periphery of the Army, it oversold the general applicability of its expertise. Most important, the resulting flaws in doctrine were tolerated because the mainstream military chose to conflate chemical and biological warfare in the beginning, it did not know any better, and it was disinclined to learn.

Continuity and Change over Time

Doctrine for biodefense remained remarkably static during the Cold War. Although the Chemical Corps revised its doctrine for "NBC defense" during the 1980s, these revisions merely highlighted contamination avoidance, physical protection, and decontamination; they did not fundamentally change the military's long-standing approach.[29] Given the inaccurate assumptions inherent to this approach, doctrine had little practical utility for biodefense. Instead, most military handbooks and field manuals resembled what Lee Clarke calls "fantasy documents," which are rhetorical rather than operational blueprints for action.[30] Like the stereotypes that they may rely on, "the basis of fantasy documents is not knowledge but lack of knowledge."[31] This lack of knowledge helps explain why the US military lacked operational plans for biodefense throughout the Cold War, despite the long-standing Soviet threat.

These conceptual and operational deficiencies were thrown into sharp relief during the 1991 Gulf War, when US forces actually had to mobilize for combat against an adversary armed with biological weapons. Although rapid detection was the linchpin of contamination avoidance, physical protection, and decontamination, Mauroni remarks that, "prior to the Gulf War, no one had seriously addressed the doctrinal or training requirements to implement a biological point detection system." And by failing to understand the difficulty of biological detection, "many soldiers, to include those within the chemical defense community, assume that it should duplicate the current chemical agent point detection system," just as the path dependency of nonkinetic stereotypes might lead us to expect.[32] Moreover, there were no plans for how to use vaccines, antibiotics, or other medical countermeasures.[33] Force employment suffered as a result, as I describe below, and decades worth of doctrine for CBW, NBC, CBR, and similar stereotypes—dating back to the 1950s—proved almost useless for biodefense.

The military's first operational plans for BW detection and vaccination were written on the fly during Operation Desert Shield and after combat commenced during Operation Desert Storm. On the one hand, this interim doctrine for biodefense made some classic but erroneous assertions about rapid detection and, at the insistence of Central Command, the primacy of physical protection.[34] On the other hand, these appear to be the first plans that actually describe in any detail which service members would use vaccines, antibiotics, and other drugs, when they would do so, where biological samples would be transferred for laboratory identification, which tests should be used for medical surveillance, and how casualties might be managed, among other important issues.[35]

In other words, military doctrine only changed as a result of the 1991 Gulf War. This exogenous shock also triggered other forms of external influence, including civilian intervention by Congress to reorganize the Chemical and Biological Defense Program. After 1991, military plans and procedures started to describe the threat differently. Previously, little mention was made of the operational implications of biological warfare: doctrine merely listed the physical attributes of different pathogens, their means of dissemination, and their clinical effects on individual health.[36] Far more relevant for war planning is how these effects could aggregate and affect military operations—listing the effects of infection on an individual is roughly analogous to describing the damage that a bullet causes to soft tissue while ignoring the tactical significance of suppressive and interlocking fields of fire. Doctrine now pays more attention to the operational implications of biological attacks on manpower and mobility. It also concedes that military bases, airports, and seaports are vulnerable, covert attacks are likely, contagious agents might spread, both state and nonstate actors might use BW, and these weapons might affect both US forces and their allies.

Preparation and response are now described differently as well. Recall that, before 1991, doctrine only gave cursory consideration to immunization, merely suggesting that vaccines were available and easy to use when neither, in fact, was true. But, in 1996, civilian intervention into military biodefense helped convince the Joint Chiefs of Staff to endorse peacetime vaccination, after which immunization figured more prominently in planning. For example, the DoD produced detailed plans for using the smallpox vaccine before the 2003 Iraq War, drawing explicitly on guidelines provided by the civilian Centers for Disease Control and Prevention.[37]

Doctrine also acknowledges that specialized medical management is necessary for responding to the large number of casualties that might result from a biological attack. As with immunization, little mention was made of mass-casualty care during the Cold War. Again, doctrine listed the clinical effects of various pathogens on individual health (divorced from their operational implications), while at the same time it suggested that medical treatment of these effects was less relevant to military operations than the procedures for contamination avoidance, physical protection, and decontamination adopted from chemical defense. Dismissing the significance of specialized medical management for biodefense, older handbooks and field manuals simply stated that "personnel who become ill because of a biological attack will be treated in the same way that patients are treated for illness resulting from other causes."[38]

In contrast, doctrine now conceded that "BW exposure . . . may produce disease with clinical features different from the naturally occurring disease," and, similarly, "there are unique aspects of medical management after biological attack."[39] Nevertheless, some of these "unique" aspects of biodefense are still addressed in documents that also purport to address chemical, radiological, and nuclear attacks. This is consistent with nonkinetic stereotypes, and, in keeping with its kinetic frame, the "DOD has not successfully adapted its conventional medical planning to chemical and biological warfare."[40] That being said, the military's plans and procedures for biodefense now consider triage and mass-casualty care, isolation and quarantine, medical logistics, and mortuary affairs, as well as coordination with civilian and foreign agencies, along with other relevant issues.

The extent to which military doctrine has changed, however, is easy to overstate. First, it still relies on the three-tiered approach of contamination avoidance, physical protection, and decontamination—despite the enduring difficulty of detection.[41] Although doctrine for detecting biological attacks is now more detailed and the equipment involved is more capable than in the past, the time required still lags far behind detection of chemical attacks.[42] This lag time undermines the fundamental premise behind the military's three-tiered approach and its applicability to BW. So most doctrine still assumes that biodefense is basically a subset of chemical defense, in spite of exogenous shocks like the 1991 Gulf War and the countervailing influence of countless other factors over the intervening years (including civilian intervention and military reorganization). This overarching continuity tends to support my argument, that is, at least as much as organizational frame theory is challenged by doctrinal change following decades of nearly total stagnation.

Second, just as President Nixon and Secretary Laird failed to eliminate the CBW stereotype in 1969, relatively recent efforts to disaggregate biodefense from chemical defense have also fallen short. After the anthrax letters in 2001, for example, biodefense advocates within the Office of the Secretary of Defense proposed a new operational concept that was less reliant on rapid detection. Instead, it would monitor threat conditions through weather observation, environmental sampling, and medical surveillance. When faced with a high threat, the risks of potential attacks would be mitigated by wearing half-masks. "The principle risk from bio is respiratory," according one advocate for this approach, and so "one can achieve high levels of protection using simple N99 mask/respirators . . . while impacting the performance of military duties minimally," in contrast to cumbersome MOPP gear.[43] After a BW attack, the response would then focus on treating disease, controlling the spread of infection, and restoring military operations.[44]

The proposed concept of "monitor, mitigate, and respond" had notable strengths and weaknesses. Half-masks are cheap and easy to use, for instance, but they also require buying, carrying, and planning for an additional piece of equipment.[45] Be that as it may, this concept challenged some of the tortuous logic and dangerous assumptions needed to apply the same doctrine to both chemical defense and biodefense. However, the armed services and Joint Staff were skeptical of concepts of operation that disaggregated these nonkinetic problems and solutions. They rejected this proposal.[46] As a result, the doctrine used during the 2003 invasion of Iraq continued to conflate important aspects of biodefense with chemical defense.[47]

Shortly after invading Iraq, the US military adopted a new set of principles that were developed by the Army Chemical School and called "sense, shape, shield, and sustain," or 4S.[48] Once again, these principles are applied to chemical, biological, radiological, and nuclear defense alike—another "one size fits all doctrine."[49] And 4S merely repackages the older, three-tiered approach. Here "sense" equates to rapid detection, especially for contamination avoidance; "shield" focuses on physical protection through MOPP gear but adds medical prophylaxis; "sustain" includes decontamination and medical treatment, with an emphasis on the former; and finally, "shape" combines all the preceding elements by referring to situational awareness through command and control. So, while medical treatment and prophylaxis have been folded into this 4S concept, doctrine retains many of the dubious and dangerous assumptions on which it has always rested.

In sum, throughout the Cold War, the military's handbooks and manuals for biodefense were fantasy documents, contrary to realist predictions about doctrine representing a rational response to the threat environment. According to one Army field manual in 1977, "because the magnitude and nature of NBC weapons will have a profound influence on combat operations, the commander should devote as much thought and effort to developing his initial guidance for NBC defense as he does to maneuver planning and fire planning."[50] Few would argue that US Army maneuver and fire planning were far short of excellent. Yet it is apparent that—for decades on end—there was little or no operational planning for biodefense, and procedures that rested on stereotypes like NBC were riddled with errors and contradictions. The difficulty of biological detection and inattention to medical countermeasures are particularly difficult to reconcile with realism.

The discrepancies between the difficulty of detection and doctrine that relies on this capability have diminished since the 1991 Gulf War, and greater consideration is now paid to medical treatment and prophylaxis. Although doctrine is now more consistent with realist predictions than at any time during the Cold War, the military's old mantra of contamination avoidance, physical protection, and decontamination persists to this day. It persists despite all the differences between chemical defense and biodefense. It persists despite the critical changes that first appeared in doctrine written on the fly during Operations Desert Shield and Desert Storm. And it persists despite the enduring difficulty of detecting biological agents. Such striking continuity from the Cold War through today is explained by organizational frame theory. Since the military has difficulty learning outside of its kinetic frame, it relies on inaccurate stereotypes that conflate biodefense with other nonkinetic issues. Doctrine therefore reflects and reinforces the long-standing but dangerous assumption that biodefense is a subset of chemical defense, thereby perpetuating many of the problems revealed here through a close reading of military handbooks and manuals.

COUNTING RELATIONSHIPS AND FREQUENCIES

Of course, there are drawbacks to reading more than a half century's worth of military doctrine. It is a large amount of text, and, as with many instruction manuals, the writing is simplistic or repetitive in some places and in others, dense and technical. More important, a critical reading like mine is vulnerable to the critique that I misinterpret or misrepresent the doctrine at hand. For example, Mauroni (a former chemical officer) has repeatedly defended avoidance, protection, and decontamination as "the right doctrine," claiming that it is not "chem centric," as I and others argue, but instead applies to biodefense and chemical defense in equal measure.[51]

One way to adjudicate between these competing claims is through numbers, namely, quantitative content analysis. I apply two methods: term counts and network text analysis. Both provide useful measures of textual data. Term counts measure the frequency of particular keywords or phrases. These frequencies are important because the content of a document can be defined by the substantive terms that appear most frequently. As a result, this method provides a straightforward way to measure the emphasis that military doctrine places on different words or phrases such as "chemical" versus "biological defense."

Although useful, term counts ignore the context in which these words are used. Network text analysis, in contrast, addresses this context by measuring how words are used in relation to other terms.[52] These relationships are important because they convey the meaning of a document. Relationships can also be measured using established metrics for network analysis.[53] Here documents are treated as semantic networks in which words are the nodes and the relationships between them are represented as lines. I code words that appear in the same sentence as having a relationship.[54] The importance of a given word in a document is

TABLE 3.1 The sample of military doctrine used for quantitative content analysis

Title	Year	Author (doc #)
Defense against CBR Attack	1954	Army (FM 21-40) USAF (AFM 355-9)
Military Biology and Biological Warfare Agents	1956	Army (TM 3-216) USAF (AFM 355-6)
Small Unit Procedures in Atomic, Biological, and Chemical Warfare	1958	Army (FM 21-40)
Soldier's Handbook for Nuclear, Biological, and Chemical Warfare	1958	Army (FM 21-41)
Chemical, Biological, and Nuclear Defense	1966	Army (FM 21-40)
Field CBR Collective Protection	1966	Army (TM 3-221)
Soldier's Handbook for Defense against Chemical and Biological Operations and Nuclear Warfare	1967	Army (FM 21-41)
Chemical, Biological, Radiological, and Nuclear Defense	1968	Army (FM 21-40)
Technical Aspects of Biological Defense	1971	Army (TM 3-216) USAF (AFM 355-6)
Planning and Conducting Chemical, Biological, Radiological (CBR), and Nuclear Defense Training	1973	Army (FM 21-48)

(Continued)

[85]

TABLE 3.1.—Continued

Title	Year	Author (doc #)
Armed Forces Doctrine for Chemical Warfare and Biological Defense	1976	Army (FM 101-40) USN (NWP 36D) USAF (AFR 355-5) USMC (FMFM 11-6)
NBC (Nuclear, Biological, Chemical) Defense	1977	Army (FM 21-40)
US Army Operational Concept for Individual and Collective Measures for Chemical, Biological, and Radiological (CBR) Defense	1982	Army (TRADDOC PAM 525-20)
NBC Decontamination	1985	Army (FM 3-5)
NBC Operations	1985	Army (FM 3-100)
Field Behavior of NBC Agents (including Smoke and Incendiaries)	1986	Army (FM 3-6) USAF (AFM 105-7) USMC (FMFM 7-11H)
NBC Protection	1992	Army (FM3-4) USMC (FMFM 11-9)
Chemical and Biological Contamination Avoidance	1992	Army (FM 3-3) USMC (FMFM 11-17)
NBC Field Handbook	1994	Army (FM 3-7)
Biological Detection Platoon Operations: Tactics, Techniques, and Procedures	1997	Army (FM3-101-4)
Joint Doctrine for Operations in Nuclear, Biological, and Chemical (NBC) Environments	2000	Joint Staff (Joint Pub. 3-11)
Treatment of Biological Warfare Agent Casualties	2002	Army (FM 8-284) USN (NAVMED P-5042) USAF (AFMAN i44-156) USMC (MCRP 4-11.1C)
Multiservice Tactics, Techniques, and Procedures for Nuclear, Biological, and Chemical (NBC) Protection	2003	Army (FM 3-11.4) USN (NTTP 3-11.27) USAF (AFTTP i3-2.46) USMC (MCWP 3-37.2)
Multiservice Tactics, Techniques, and Procedures for Health Service Support in a Chemical, Biological, Radiological, and Nuclear Environment	2009	Army (FM 4-02.7) USN (NTTP 4-02.7) USAF (AFTTP 3-42.3) USMC (MCRP 4-11.1F)
Multi-Service Doctrine for Chemical, Biological, Radiological, and Nuclear Operations	2011	Army (FM 3-11) USN (NWP 3-11) USAF (AFTTP 3-2.42) USMC (3-37.1)

therefore represented by its position in the resulting network, with the most prominent words being centrally located.[55]

The sample I use is listed in table 3.1. This is a large—more than 1.1 million words—and representative collection of military handbooks and field manuals, each of which includes at least one word with the prefix "bio-" in its title. Since "bio-" was the selection criterion, we might expect that words like "biological" will be at least as frequent and central in these documents as words that were not used to select the sample (e.g., "chemical"). This is particularly true if Mauroni is correct and military doctrine is not "chem centric," keeping in mind that biological weapons are at least as threatening to US forces as chemical weapons. However, if my argument is correct and doctrine relies on inaccurate stereotypes that subsume biodefense under chemical defense, then words like "biological" will be less frequent and central.

This sample represents a hard test for my argument. All else being equal, these are the handbooks and field manuals that should discuss biological warfare in greatest detail, using the most sophisticated and nuanced terminology. But term counts reveal that BW is not the most common concept, even in the military handbooks and field manuals that purport to address it. Instead, words and phrases about chemical warfare are far more common. This bias endured for decades (see figure 3.1), and it is statistically significant. Using a paired t-test, "bio-" (mean = .002, standard deviation = .002) is mentioned significantly less often than "chem-" (M = .004, SD = .003), with $t(24) = 2.55$, p < .018 for this sample. Only recently has the corpus of military doctrine that is supposedly about BW started referring to "bio-" more, whereas "chem-" was the token used to typify nonkinetic warfare during and after the Cold War. Even now, as was true then, the majority of documents mention "bio-" on its own less frequently than as part of nonkinetic stereotypes such as CBW, NBC, CBR, and CBRN.

Furthermore, network text analysis demonstrates that "chem-" is more central in these documents than "bio-" and stereotypes are usually the most central of all.[56] This finding correlates with the frequencies above, and it is statistically significant for the three measures of centrality that are commonly used in network analysis (each of which reflects a different definition of what it means to be central in the network of words from a document).[57] The degree centrality of "chem-" (M = .371, SD = .129) is significantly greater than "bio-" (M = .263, SD = .144), with $t(24) = 3.03$, p < .006 for this sample; so is the closeness centrality of "chem-" (M = .615, SD = .05) versus "bio-" (M = .576, SD = .056), with $t(24) = 2.72$, p < .012; and the betweenness centrality "chem-" (M = .023, SD = .021) is also greater than "bio-" (M = .011, SD = .013), with $t(24) = 2.40$, p < .024.[58]

[87]

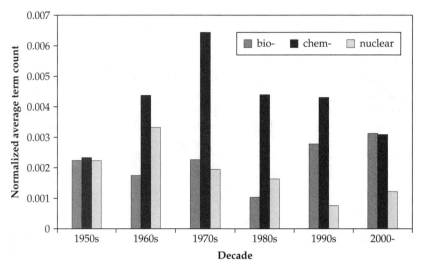

FIGURE 3.1. Frequency of "bio-" words (e.g., biological, biodefense, BW) compared to "chem-" and nuclear words in my sample of military doctrine (excluding the words used together in phrases such as "nuclear, biological, and chemical," CBW, CBRN, etc.).

Similar conclusions are apparent when military doctrine is visualized as a network, as seen in figure 3.2. Not only is "chem-" more central than "bio-" in this particular document, but the most central terms are the stereotypes CBRN and WMD. Network text analysis therefore illustrates and quantifies the extent to which military doctrine is, in fact, "chem centric" and very reliant on stereotypes.

These findings are relatively robust. For example, most documents in my sample are published by the Army, but the same emphasis on stereotypes and "chem-" over "bio-" is evident in doctrine used by the Air Force and Navy. This is puzzling from the perspective of bureaucratic interests. Although the Chemical Corps may have a bureaucratic interest in "chem centric" doctrine, that would not explain why the Army as a whole would accept such a bias, let alone why the other services would acquiesce. Yet they did. Eventually, in the late 1990s, the Air Force started publishing service-specific handbooks for chemical and biological defense to avoid relying on Army or joint doctrine (as it had throughout the Cold War). However, while better than it was before, Air Force doctrine continued to rely on many of the same stereotypes (at least until after the invasion of Iraq in 2003).[59] Moreover, the Navy is well known for

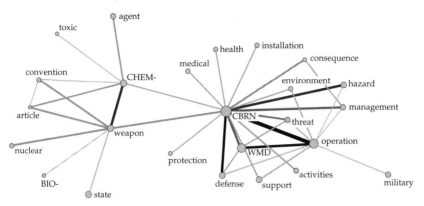

FIGURE 3.2. A representative network of the words and relationships in military doctrine. This network was extracted from the most recent document in my sample: US Army, *Multi-Service Doctrine for Chemical, Biological, Radiological and Nuclear Operations* FM 3-11 / MCWP 3-37.1 / NWP 3-11 / AFTTP 3-2.42 (Washington, DC: Department of the Army, 2011). Node and line size represent the relative frequency of words and their respective relationships. Complete networks were used to calculate centrality, but, to provide a comprehensible image, only the 26 nodes connected by the highest value lines were drawn here using a Kamada-Kawai layout.

insisting on its "stature as an independent institution," but it has rarely published its own doctrine for biodefense.[60] This means that my term counts and network text analysis quantify biases long shared across the armed services.

Quantitative analysis therefore confirms much of what was revealed through my qualitative reading. To recap, military doctrine is demonstrably "chem centric," since it often cites chemical defense as a token of its nonkinetic stereotypes. These stereotypes mask the extent to which doctrine that claims to address biodefense actually says very little about it—a problem that persisted for decades because the military did not learn about issues outside of its kinetic frame. Consequently, doctrine is inconsistent with the rationality of realism, which would anticipate much more learning over time and much less reliance on biased stereotypes. The evidence is also inconsistent with bureaucratic interests. Instead of the variation that intra- and interservice rivalry might otherwise have produced, the same doctrine was often used by all branches of the military. As I discuss next, the ideas behind this pervasive and persistent failure to plan for biodefense adversely affected how doctrine was practiced in training and employed during war.

Individual training and group exercises occupy a halfway house between planning and actually employing force. The saying that "no plan survives contact with the enemy" is attributed to Helmuth von Moltke the Elder, but this expression certainly did not stop him from planning or practicing through war games. And it can also be said that a plan does not really exist until it has been practiced or exercised. This is especially true for the US military. Perhaps more than any other organization in the world, the military trains as a way of life. If not fighting, the armed forces are training for how they plan to fight, often under extremely realistic conditions (e.g., live-fire exercises, among others).

Yet military training for biological warfare has been rare and unrealistic. As doctrine suggests, the armed forces traditionally train service members to treat biodefense as a subset of chemical defense.[61] Individual exercises and drills provide practice in putting on protective masks after detecting a chemical attack (sometimes simulated using tear gas), carrying out routine maneuvers while wearing MOPP gear, and simulating the administration of atropine to counteract nerve agents. In contrast, doctrine provides little guidance for how to train for biodefense, especially given the difficulty of detecting biological attacks. For example, one Army manual from 1973 insists that training "*be realistic* . . . an enemy chemical, biological, or nuclear attack in combat will probably occur without warning. . . . Therefore, training should be conducted so as to prepare troops to react properly to a surprise." However, the same manual goes on to recommend training for biodefense by first warning soldiers that a biological attack is imminent and then releasing colored smoke or talcum powder—both easily visible, unlike BW—in order to practice masking procedures, reporting the attack, and sterilizing kitchen utensils.[62]

While consistent with doctrine that conflates biodefense with chemical defense, this scenario was shockingly unrealistic.[63] The lack of realism was coupled with a lack of practice. Before 1991, "there was hardly ever any training in BW," according to one former NBC officer, and "evaluations never covered BW because we didn't know how to deal with it."[64] Even today, the lack of realistic training remains a persistent problem.[65] This is true for medical training as well, which stands to be particularly relevant for biodefense. In 2002, for example, the Defense Medical Readiness and Training Institute concluded that "an appropriate level of training is not being conducted for first responders, medical planners, and non-medical personnel assigned to medical units."[66] Educational courses were available then, as they are now, but the Army only started to require advanced medical training for nuclear, chemical, and biological events in 2007.[67]

Unit or group exercises are as important as individual training for bio-defense, if not more so, since biological weapons may be most effective at the operational or theater level of warfare. However, as Danzig observed while serving as the under secretary of the Navy, "the Pentagon is remarkably good at working out war games against a whole lot of contingencies, but the answer in the biological arena tended to be historically again and again, we do not understand it enough; it is too difficult to model; and it would disrupt the war game."[68] Given the military's dominant frame, kinetic war games appear more comprehensible and less disruptive than nonkinetic scenarios. "Nobody wants to train on NBC operations, and that's the biggest problem we've always had," recalls one participant. "Even now, when we go out in the field and they have these big field exercises. . . . They'd always tout how much NBC play they were going to have, and then the reality is we never saw any. Commanders don't like the idea of NBC operations messing up the battlefield."[69]

In fact, the US military did not address biological warfare in a major war game until 1995, notwithstanding the Soviet threat throughout the Cold War. This first exercise was called Global 95, and, its "big lesson" was "the realization that we haven't done enough thinking about this."[70] The game simulated an anthrax attack by North Korea, followed by a similar, opportunistic attack by Iraq. Both were devastating. "Global 95 fell apart very fast," according to one senior official. "It was so bad that in order to save the exercise at all, the referees decided to grant the players a 'miracle' for each day . . . one chance to wipe away a bad move or an indefensible mistake."[71] Even with these miracles, US forces still faced defeat in Korea, so when the conflict spread to Iraq, their only remaining response was nuclear retaliation. "While this ended the war game," Mauroni argues, "it did not represent a satisfactory or realistic conclusion."[72]

After Global 95, similar scenarios were played out in war games and seminars such as Coral Breeze in 1997 and Desert Breeze in 1998. The evidence since then is mixed. On the one hand, at least a couple of exercises now mention biological attacks each year, whereas few if any did before Global 95. On the other hand, these exercises often refer to the scenarios as "CBRNE events," and their applicability to biodefense remains doubtful because few involve medical support.[73] There are exceptions to this rule, including Air Force exercises such as Code Silver and Kunsan Focused Effort in 2004 and 2005, as well as planning for pandemic influenza by the combatant commands. But on the whole, "medical play is generally limited."[74]

Because the military has a hard time training itself for biodefense, it also has a hard time trying to train others. In particular, Congress ordered the military to support civil defense training as part of the Defense

Against Weapons of Mass Destruction Act of 1996. This resulted in the DoD Domestic Preparedness Program, which was to train first respond-ers and other civilian officials in hundreds of American cities how to re-spond to terrorist attacks involving WMD, including biological weapons. Unfortunately, Amy Smithson and Leslie-Anne Levy find that much of the training provided through this program received scathing reviews "as 'extremely generic and canned,' or, more bluntly, 'garbage' and 'a big [expletive] waste.' "[75]

Here, as elsewhere, the DoD Domestic Preparedness Program relied on chemical specialists and procedures that were often inapplicable to bioterrorism. For example, one training course dedicated a full day to using MOPP gear, even though civilians neither have access to this pro-tective equipment nor advance warning of biological attacks.[76] Mean-while, the military was "doing absolutely nothing whatsoever on the medical side," according to Donald Henderson, and so it provided little or no instruction on how to diagnose and treat the casualties that such an attack might produce.[77] These problems were symptomatic of the mili-tary's nonkinetic stereotypes, as was its reluctance to participate in the first place. The DoD ultimately extricated itself from this program by turning it over to the Department of Justice in 2000.[78]

In sum, military training and war games suffer because BW falls out-side of the kinetic frame and the armed services depend on nonkinetic stereotypes that conflate biodefense with chemical defense. By focusing on masking procedures, for instance, they ignore the difficulty of biologi-cal detection and the necessity of medical support. Like the military's handbooks and field manuals, individual education and group exercises also lack realism. Training for many nonkinetic contingencies was rare as well, at least until the late 1990s. It was seen to "distract from a tidy mis-sion execution," notwithstanding all of the hypothetical scenarios enter-tained during war games.[79] Training remained variable after the invasion of Iraq in 2003. Though the specter of weapons of mass destruction helped sell this war, by its own admission, "the US military had never trained, organized, or prepared to seize, exploit, and eliminate a nation's WMD program," just as it never trained for biological warfare until years after the 1991 Gulf War.[80] While this lack of training confounds realist predictions about fear and self-help, it is consistent with my argument about organizational frame theory.

BIODEFENSE DURING WAR

Given its training and planning, or lack thereof, how did the US mili-tary actually employ its forces for biodefense during combat operations?

Despite handbooks and field manuals dating back to the 1950s, the military did not start using biological detection systems until the 1991 Gulf War. This was also one of the first times that vaccines were used for biodefense since General Washington inoculated the Continental Army against smallpox during the Revolutionary War. Where Washington was successful, however, given the technology of his day, the modern military struggled to vaccinate US troops and field biological detection systems.

BW Detection

Recall that military doctrine rests on contamination avoidance, physical protection, and decontamination, all of which rely on rapid detection. Therefore, rapid detection—though difficult—has long been the linchpin of military biodefense. But "up to 1991, we had very little in the way of detecting BW attack," according to one former NBC officer, and "the way we dealt with that was we ignored it."[81] This tendency to ignore biological detection was manifest in development and acquisition, as well as in planning and training. The unsurprising result is that US forces had almost no detection equipment to deploy during the 1991 Gulf War, despite doctrine that relied on this capability.

For instance, one of the most advanced detection systems deployed at the time was the Fox NBC Reconnaissance Vehicle. Contrary to its name, however, this system had no biological detection capabilities (only chemical and nuclear equipment), once again illustrating the inaccuracies inherent to stereotypes like NBC and the resulting neglect of biodefense.[82] Recall that the DoD rushed to develop biological detection systems during Operation Desert Shield, but it only deployed the XM2 Biological Sampler (along with a similar, commercial device called the PM10). The XM2 was part of a defunct system that the Chemical Corps had cancelled in 1983, but the military had no other way to detect biological attacks. So it sent this equipment to the Persian Gulf in January 1991—five months after the beginning of Operation Desert Shield. Even then, the advance liaison that put the XM2 into the field had to rent transportation to conduct background and baseline sampling. Mauroni thus describes "the Army's interim biological agent reconnaissance vehicle for the Gulf War" as "a leased Isuzu civilian truck with an XM2 Biological Sampler strapped to its hood."[83]

The XM2s were operated by the 9th Chemical Company, which was in the process of downsizing at the time (the 9th Infantry Division had been deactivated). Beginning on January 15, a detachment of these soldiers—many of whom had never worked together, let alone worked with this equipment—received three days of instruction on how to use the XM2.[84] They then deployed to the Persian Gulf. The first teams arrived more than a week after Operation Desert Storm began with the air campaign against Iraqi forces. Ultimately, a dozen mobile teams were deployed, each consisting of three soldiers operating an XM2. Five stationary teams used the PM10. They were positioned around large concentrations of troops at operational bases in Saudi Arabia, and each team analyzed about two samples per night (when conditions were most favorable for a biological attack).

The people tasked with biological detection performed well, despite the disadvantages of their late arrival and ad hoc organization. The same cannot be said for their equipment. The XM2 and PM10 samplers collected particles from the air and concentrated them in a saline solution that was analyzed using sensitive membrane antigen rapid tests (SMART cards). These test cards were supposed to change color when exposed to anthrax spores or botulinum toxin. They had been rushed into production and suffered quality control problems, however, resulting in an unacceptably high rate of false positives.[85] Even when working properly, SMART cards had a false response rate of nearly 50 percent, and so, as one user observed, "you might as well go out in the field and flip a coin."[86] According to a former UNSCOM inspector, "we jokingly referred to those as not-so-smart cards."[87] It is therefore questionable how accurate this detection system would have been if biological weapons had been used during the 1991 Gulf War. And, with a processing time of about forty-five minutes, it was not nearly fast enough to provide the advance warning needed for physical protection.[88]

These problems prompted the military to deploy better biological detection systems by the late 1990s. While these newer systems were more capable and reliable, some of them continued using XM2 samplers and SMART cards, improvements in detection time were modest, and their deployment was limited. In 1996, for example, the M31 Biological Integrated Detection System (BIDS) was fielded with a detection time of about thirty minutes. This was the military's first credible biological detection system. But the Army only fielded BIDS with the 310th Chemical Company, which was a reserve unit and thus slow to deploy.[89] Part of this unit was deployed to Kuwait during Operation Desert Thunder in 1998, after which BIDS vehicles were fielded with the active duty 7th Chemical Company as well. Apparently, the Chemical Corps resisted pressure to field additional active duty units.[90]

Both the 7th and 310th Chemical Companies deployed during the 2003 Iraq War. Once again, there were not enough BIDS units available, the equipment was out of date, and its use was misunderstood. First, "the main challenge was largely how the combat force viewed the use of BIDS platoons," which, in some cases, "demonstrates a fundamental lack of understanding or appreciation for BIDS capabilities."[91] Second, BIDS had not been modernized as planned. Although the military expected to upgrade these vehicles with the Joint Biological Point Detection System, modernization ran behind schedule. Finally, there were not enough BIDS units to satisfy demand for biological detection in the theater of operations, which included requests by Israel and Jordan, while at the same time provide military support for homeland security in the United States.[92]

There are now more BIDS units, and, in 2003, their equipment started to be upgraded with the newer JBPDS. This joint system is currently installed on hundreds of mobile platforms, including Army trucks and Navy ships, as well as at fixed sites around important military facilities. Yet, like its predecessors, JBPDS has notable limitations. "In the absence of data, they look good," but, according to one former user, "the JBPDS would false alarm all the time. All the time. That is a fantastic diesel detector."[93] A balance must be struck, but like Aesop's fable about the boy who cried wolf, too many false alarms and the warning system risks being disabled or dismissed. In addition, JBPDS takes about twenty minutes to detect BW agents, not including the time required to communicate and respond to this information. The same is true for other detection systems like Joint Portal Shield, which the military has also deployed at hundreds of fixed sites.[94]

These systems likely provide "detect to treat" capabilities, which are useful for a medical response but not fast enough to reconcile with doctrine for contamination avoidance, physical protection, and decontamination. Systems for standoff biological detection, which may provide advance warning, are still under development—as they have been for decades. One day, the military might field a system that is fast enough to "detect to warn" or "detect to protect" against a dense cloud of pathogens approaching from a distance (using LIDAR or other technology). But this hypothetical capability will not retrospectively justify the long-standing discrepancy between doctrine and the biological detection systems available to date, particularly since none were deployed before the 1991 Gulf War and the military did not field a credible detection system until 1996.

Vaccination

Remember that, in the early days of the Revolutionary War, General Washington faced the possibility that the British were using smallpox as a biological weapon. Smallpox was a major factor in the Continental Army's defeat in Quebec—where Thomas Jefferson believed that "this disorder was sent into our army designedly"—and the disease played a pivotal role during the siege of Boston in 1775 and 1776.[95] Therefore, as

[95]

quarantine failed and reports trickled in about British attempts to spread smallpox, Washington concluded that "we should have more to dread from it, than the Sword of the Enemy." He therefore decided to inoculate the Army against "this, the greatest of all calamities that can befall it," on 6 January 1777.[96]

Vaccine would not be invented for another twenty years, and so, at the time, inoculation meant variolation. This carried considerable risks for the military. In particular, variolation created a deliberate infection through an incision in the arm or leg. It produced a milder form of the disease, but the procedure still made soldiers sick, during which time they were too ill to fight; they were also contagious and thus a risk to those around them.[97] Accepting these risks produced considerable rewards for Washington, however, and the incidence of smallpox among American troops dropped considerably after inoculations began in the spring of 1777. According to the historian Elizabeth Fenn, "Washington's unheralded and little-recognized resolution to inoculate the Continental forces must surely rank among his most important decisions of the war."[98]

When juxtaposed against the neglect of military biodefense during the twentieth century, Washington's success against smallpox might seem to confound the path dependency of organizational frame theory. How can the modern military struggle to understand problems and solutions that once gained the attention of the Continental Army? At least part of the answer is organizational discontinuity.[99] After the Revolutionary War, the Continental Army was disbanded and institutional memory of biodefense was lost, just as American military medicine declined precipitously in the decades that followed.[100] Granted, some of the lessons learned during the Revolution did endure. For example, Baron von Steuben's *Regulations for the Order and Discipline of the Troops of the United States*, written at Valley Forge in 1778 and 1779, had a lasting influence on the structure of what later became the US Army, and it included instructions on hygiene and sanitation. But Steuben did not arrive in America until a year after Washington's inoculation order, and the significance of disease as a potential weapon is missing from his *Regulations*. Vaccination eventually replaced variolation, and, before the War of 1812, the secretary of war—a physician—ordered US forces to be vaccinated against smallpox. However, by the time the US military became a permanent and professional institution (around the Civil War), vaccine was seen in the context of preventive medicine for public health more than defense against biological warfare.[101]

While vaccination against naturally occurring diseases became routine, well over a century passed after Washington's inoculation order before American forces were next immunized explicitly for biodefense.

Unfortunately, the modern military's first attempts to employ vaccines for this purpose nearly failed. Recall that James Simmons warned about BW before World War II but received little attention. He was particularly concerned about insect-borne diseases. Therefore, in early 1941, on learning that Japan had tried to acquire samples of yellow fever, Simmons recommended vaccinating all troops in the tropics (e.g., Hawaii) because "this disease might be utilized by the enemy for military purposes."[102] The Rockefeller Institute supplied the yellow fever vaccine, but it was contaminated and caused a massive epidemic of hepatitis B. More than three hundred thousand people received contaminated vaccine, about fifty thousand servicemen were hospitalized, and the Army surgeon general temporarily halted the immunization program in April 1942. Although it resumed a few months later with new vaccine, this program can hardly be considered a complete success.[103]

The Cold War came and went before the military next tried to employ vaccines for biodefense. Though less overtly harmful than the yellow fever fiasco, its attempt to use anthrax and botulinum vaccines during the 1991 Gulf War nearly failed as well. Iraq had bombs and missiles armed with anthrax and botulinum toxin, but the US military could not detect biological attacks fast enough for physical protection—so the 500,000 US troops in the theater of operations had to rely on their vaccines. Yet most were not vaccinated. At the time, immunization against anthrax required six doses of vaccine administered over eighteen months: only 150,000 service members received even a single dose, however, and few of these received more than two shots. Likewise, prophylaxis against botulinum toxin required three doses administered over three months, but only 8,000 troops received even a single dose of this vaccine.[104]

As with biological detection, "no one had really thought about the challenge of vaccinating the total force against the major BW agents" before Operation Desert Shield; but from a realist perspective, as for Mauroni, "it's hard to say why, given concerns about the known scope of the Soviet BW program."[105] This utter lack of preparation is not hard to explain using organizational frame theory, nor are the problems that followed as a result. First, vaccination was hindered by supply shortages. The military did not have an adequate stockpile of vaccine or the surge capacity to make more. Compounding these procurement problems, most military planners wrongly assumed that the MOPP gear for chemical defense was sufficient for biodefense. Thus they were slow to recognize the need for vaccines and other medical countermeasures that might limit the damage of BW. They also failed to understand that the biology involved with making vaccines takes time—there was no quick fix to the vaccine shortage.

[97]

Second, vaccination during the Gulf War was hindered by slow if not poor decisions, which were due in part to the military's difficulty understanding biodefense. In particular, military leaders did not understand how to use vaccines and so they delayed distribution of what little vaccine was available until it was too late. Shortly after Operation Desert Shield began in August 1990, the Army, Navy, and Air Force surgeons general all recommended immediately using the existing vaccine to inoculate US forces.[106] However, the Joint Chiefs were unwilling to make this decision, and, according to one member of the Air Staff, General Schwarzkopf was "looking for an out from having to make the call on who gets inoculated, and who doesn't."[107]

Although military officers are trained to make life-and-death decisions regarding kinetic warfare, they hesitated when faced with this nonkinetic challenge and ultimately waited too long to distribute vaccine.[108] Vaccination teams did not arrive in the Persian Gulf until January 1991, only two weeks before Operation Desert Storm, by which time it was too late for the vaccine to be fully effective during the war.[109] Given its limited supply of vaccine, the military also decided to distribute ciprofloxacin directly to the troops. But this antibiotic still required that an attack be detected in time for treatment, there were problems with its distribution, no instructions on its proper use (by one account, "it is very confusing for the commanders and everyone [is] unfamiliar with it"), and the five-day supply that was issued was no cure for anthrax since the "risk of recurrence remains for at least 60 days because of the possibility of delayed germination of spores."[110]

Similar problems with vaccine supply and vaccination policy persisted long after the 1991 Gulf War. Peacetime vaccinations were proposed shortly after Operation Desert Storm, informed by the failure to effectively employ vaccine before this conflict. Favoring the status quo, however, the Air Force and Navy suggested that troops only be inoculated on the eve of battle—even though this practice would not allow time to provide full immunity.[111] As a result, the military did not establish a vaccination policy for several years, and, when the deputy secretary of defense ordered peacetime vaccinations beginning in 1993, this program was not implemented.[112]

The Joint Chiefs of Staff eventually endorsed peacetime vaccinations for anthrax in 1996, having been persuaded in part by civilians including Danzig and Lederberg. But the secretary of defense did not implement these vaccinations until prompted by General Zinni, who perceived an imminent threat during Operation Desert Thunder in 1998.[113] Then, for better or worse, the military decided to make the Anthrax Vaccine Immunization Program (AVIP) mandatory for the total force of about 2.4 million service members. This particular approach was adopted because

[98]

of the administrative and morale problems that might arise if vaccinations were either voluntary or only required for service members in high-threat areas.[114]

However, mandatory vaccinations prompted a persistent backlash against the AVIP from people concerned about the safety of the anthrax vaccine. Fueling this resistance was fear that the vaccine might have caused Gulf War syndrome—an illness that includes a range of different symptoms—in veterans who served during Operation Desert Storm. Gulf War syndrome was eventually linked to pesticide exposure and pyridostigmine bromide pills (used to counteract potential exposure to chemical agents), with no apparent connection to the anthrax vaccine.[115] But suspicion remains, and the military's rushed reliance on outdated and untested technology in 1991 did not inspire trust. The mandatory vaccination policy was therefore subject to a series of legal challenges. In 2003 and 2004, for example, a court-issued injunction forced the DoD to stop administering anthrax vaccine until it received an emergency use authorization from the Food and Drug Administration, which, in turn, required that vaccinations be voluntary. The legal need for this authorization was later lifted; in 2006, the DoD decided to leave vaccinations voluntary for some but make them mandatory for service members and civilians operating in or around Iraq, Afghanistan, and the Korean Peninsula.[116]

Long-standing supply problems also undermined the AVIP. The military's sole supplier of anthrax vaccine had persistent problems with old equipment, financial accounting, and quality control that ultimately forced it to halt vaccine production in 1998. "There wasn't enough vaccine to go around," according to Johnson-Winegar. As a result, the DoD was forced to repeatedly and drastically curtail anthrax vaccination.[117] The initial plan to vaccinate the entire force was first restricted to service members deployed in the Persian Gulf and Korea, then only to those in the Persian Gulf. By 2001, only special operations units were receiving the anthrax vaccine, although its supply and use increased in preparation for the 2003 Iraq War. Similar supply problems limited the military's use of other vaccines for biodefense, including botulinum vaccine, during the invasion of Iraq.[118]

One exception to the modern military's troubled history using vaccines for biodefense is smallpox. Yet this exception still tends to prove the rule. "Routine vaccination of US military recruits against smallpox was intermittent after 1984," following eradication of the naturally occurring disease, "and it discontinued in 1990."[119] Unfortunately, the Soviet Union manufactured and stockpiled tons of smallpox for use as a biological weapon. The US military was aware of this threat by the early 1990s, but it was not until President Bush announced the National

[99]

Smallpox Vaccination Program in December 2002—in preparation for invading Iraq—that the armed services resumed use of the smallpox vaccine.

More than five hundred thousand service members were soon vaccinated. On the one hand, the smallpox vaccination program succeeded in part because it included an educational campaign that helped troops accept the vaccine.[120] This suggests that the military was finally learning how to employ medical countermeasures. On the other hand, the program's success depended on an adequate supply of smallpox vaccine, and that had to be provided by the CDC Strategic National Stockpile because the DoD had failed to acquire its own supply.[121]

In sum, the military has had difficulty employing BW vaccines as recently as the Iraq War. The same is true for biological detection systems. Force employment for biodefense has certainly improved, which provides belated support for the rationality and thus learning anticipated by realism. Then again, military biodefense could do little but improve. During Operation Desert Shield, for instance, a four-star general needed to ask "What is anthrax?" at a meeting with the Army chief of staff. Now the military leadership is more familiar with this threat and the potential countermeasures.[122] Even so, tensions remain. For example, while the military attempts to quell concerns about the AVIP by arguing that "anthrax vaccinations provide the best protection against a lethal weapon," it still relies on plans and procedures that highlight physical protection through MOPP as the best defense for chemical and biological weapons alike.[123] So stereotypes continue to cause problems, and doctrine suffers as a result.

As we have seen, the kinetic frame and nonkinetic stereotypes have powerful and enduring effects on military doctrine. From the beginning, the military assumed that biological weapons were like chemical weapons. The resulting stereotypes caused the military to likewise assume that biodefense could be achieved using the plans and procedures for contamination avoidance, physical protection, and decontamination previously prepared for chemical defense. Anomalous facts—that is, rapid detection is unlikely for biological attacks and medical countermeasures are more important—were acknowledged but dismissed, and "chem centric" doctrine was not seen as dangerous, since chemical defense and biodefense were assumed to be the same and learning outside of the military's dominant frame was limited. This allowed faulty assumptions to persist for decades on end. Until recently, biodefense was neither planned for on its own terms nor was it not practiced in war games that focused almost exclusively on kinetic warfare. Instead, the military's dominant frame and organizational stereotypes helped create, perpetuate, and mask potentially fatal gaps and errors in planning and training.

Similar gaps and errors are evident in biodefense during wartime. While doctrine depends on rapid detection, the military had never deployed BW detection systems before the 1991 Gulf War. Then it struggled to field antiquated and unreliable equipment. Better detection systems started to reach the field in the late 1990s, but even today they are unlikely to provide the advance warning that doctrine traditionally depends on. The armed services have also struggled with how to use medical countermeasures. Doctrine dating back to the 1950s implied that vaccines were readily available. But the military did not consider how to actually use them until the Gulf War, when it failed to employ vaccines fast enough or in sufficient quantity. More than a decade later, the DoD still faced serious problems with its vaccination policy and drug supply.

Additional problems with deploying decontamination systems could be added to this list, many of which tend to confound realist predictions and support my argument.[124] Granted, if the kinetic frame and nonkinetic stereotypes are relatively constant, then my argument alone cannot explain the changes seen in doctrine after the 1991 Gulf War. But the limits of change are telling as well. Although doctrine improved in response to exogenous shocks and civilian intervention, it did not change quickly or completely (maybe not even adequately). And the evidence suggests that decisions about doctrine were usually driven by an internal and influential set of ideas that resist change. Belated threat perceptions and bureaucratic interests appear to play marginal roles when compared to the momentum of these ideas, whose effects endure to this day.

[4]

An Unlikely Sponsor?

THE RISE OF CIVILIAN BIODEFENSE

Biological weapons and biodefense were widely regarded as military issues throughout the Cold War, even though they were misunderstood and subsequently neglected inside the DoD. The kinetic frame and non-kinetic stereotypes help explain this neglect, but an important part of the puzzle is thus far unexplained because most funding for biodefense now comes from civilian organizations rather than traditional military sponsors. Depending on how you count, the DoD spent about $1.5 billion on biodefense in 2013, while civilian organizations—including the Department of Health and Human Services, the Department of Homeland Security, the Department of Agriculture, and the Environmental Protection Agency, among others—spent almost $5 billion. HHS provides the lion's share of around $4 billion per year.[1] How did this happen? In particular, why did HHS come to be the primary patron of biodefense when this mission had been seen for so long as a matter for the military?

Although security studies tend to focus exclusively on the armed forces, doing so here would provide incomplete if not inaccurate answers to these important questions.[2] When juxtaposed with the military, civilian biodefense also provides a natural experiment for comparing research, development, acquisition, and doctrine in a context in which threats and interests are related but the organizations' ideas differ. Even though biological warfare and bioterrorism are not the same, the BW threat to civilians is related to the operational and strategic threats faced by the military. As a result, military and civilian biodefense involve similar science and technology. In addition, the DoD and HHS are both large bureaucracies that contain several agencies with vested interests in biodefense, since this mission relates to their funding and autonomy. At HHS, these agencies include the Centers for Disease Control and

Prevention, as well as the National Institutes of Health and its subsidiary, the National Institute of Allergy and Infectious Disease (NIAID).

Despite related threats and bureaucratic interests, different ideas are at work inside the DoD and HHS. Whereas the military might be characterized by its kinetic frame, biomedical problems and solutions initially captured the attention of HHS. Consequently, this organization's dominant frame of reference is defined by the idea that disease is the underlying cause of illness.

Before extolling its virtues, it is important to note that the biomedical frame can also be faulted for being asocial and reductionist.[3] According to Allan Brandt and Martha Gardner, "the very nature of the biomedical paradigm was to uncouple disease from its social roots."[4] Similarly, Pricilla Wald argues that an overemphasis on microbes can contribute to an "outbreak narrative," which reifies and reinforces medical approaches to diseases such as HIV/AIDS at the expense of a more comprehensive analysis that considers social context.[5] The deliberate use of diseases for war or terrorism (i.e., malicious intent) is part of the social context and particularly significant for biodefense; to the extent that civilians have a hard time imagining hostile motives, this is one critical reason for not eliminating the military's role in defending against biological attacks. In short, the biomedical frame is no panacea, nor was the dominance of these ideas inevitable inside HHS.

That being said, biomedicine entails a different disposition toward the timing and mechanisms of damage than kinetic warfare. By addressing the damage caused by disease, this frame of reference provides a perspective from which biological weapons and biodefense stand to be comprehensible problems and solutions. I therefore argue that the DoD and HHS used different assumptions and heuristics to solve similar problems, and these ideas caused greater—and seemingly more "normal" or ordinary—support for civilian biodefense. As I describe in this chapter, the differences between military and civilian responses are difficult to explain with realism or bureaucratic interests, but they are consistent with organizational frame theory.

Initial Conditions: World War II and the Cold War

Although HHS agencies like the CDC and NIH/NIAID are now major players in biodefense, they were rarely involved with biological weapons during the Cold War. Granted, the name "Department of Health and Human Services" only dates back to 1980, when HHS was formed from the remnants of the Department of Health, Education, and Welfare, which was the name for what had been, until 1953, the Federal Security

Agency. But many of the agencies involved with science and technology inside HHS have a longer history. For instance, the NIH traces its roots back to the 1880s, when the Hygienic Laboratory was established within the Marine Hospital Service. This laboratory later became the NIH, and the Marine Hospital Service became what is now the Public Health Service (PHS), which, like the military, is a uniformed service with commissioned officers (under the leadership of the US Surgeon General). Likewise, the CDC was established in 1946 from the remnants of a PHS unit that fought malaria during World War II at military installations in the South: an "accident of birth" that resulted in Atlanta becoming its home.[6]

Given their common ancestry, I argue that the CDC, NIH, PHS, and thus HHS as a whole can be characterized—or, like the armed services, caricatured—as sharing a common frame that is dominated by biomedical assumptions and heuristics. This is defensible, despite the differences between these agencies and the alternative ways that their respective missions can be conceived. For example, the CDC was established to help states like Georgia and Alabama respond to communicable diseases, while the NIH focused on chronic diseases and basic research. But these missions frequently overlap in practice.[7] These agencies also share language and practices that conform to the biomedical frame. Even epidemiology, which we might otherwise expect to reflect social models rooted in population health, came instead to focus on biological and often individual risk factors for specific diseases.[8] As a result, the practice of epidemiology at the CDC is not inconsistent with the biomedical frame found inside the NIH and elsewhere at HHS.

While this organizational frame would eventually have important implications for civilian biodefense, initially there was little information available about BW and little opportunity to stimulate even a receptive audience. In December 1940, the NIH concluded that biological weapons had "only a slight nuisance value," and, as a result, the Institute and associated organizations could normally "combat an offensive of this sort."[9] Nevertheless, the NIH still offered lab space to America's fledgling BW program, and it provided the occasional pathogen and piece of equipment to the military during World War II.[10] In the 1950s, at the request of Fort Detrick, the PHS helped survey air samples to determine the background conditions for detecting biological attacks. Representatives from the PHS and NIH also served on advisory committees that considered the safety of field trials at Dugway Proving Ground when the military increased testing after the Korean War.[11]

So the PHS and NIH played minor roles in the military's BW program. For its part, the CDC became involved with biodefense when it established the Epidemic Intelligence Service (EIS) during the Korean War.

[104]

The EIS was the brainchild of Alexander Langmuir, a prominent epidemiologist and proponent of disease surveillance at the CDC. Langmuir was also aware of biological weapons, having served on the DoD Committee on Biological Warfare and the Chemical Corps' Advisory Council; in 1951, he even appeared in a television program titled "What You Should Know about Biological Warfare."[12] Given his understanding of these problems and solutions, Langmuir effectively used the BW threat and Korean War to help build the EIS. He argued that cities like Atlanta and Pittsburgh were ideal targets, for instance, and thus the EIS would detect biological attacks through "epidemiological investigation of all types of epidemics occurring anywhere in the nation."[13]

To a cynical observer, Langmuir's arguments about BW might look like an opportunistic—and thus normal—grab for resources, motivated by bureaucratic interests. They probably were. In the end, the EIS became a training and service program in applied epidemiology. For Langmuir, "even if the epidemic intelligence officers are never needed to counter biological warfare attacks, this program will have fulfilled its ultimate objective of contributing measurably to the understanding and appreciation of epidemiologic approaches to the control of communicable disease."[14] Citing the threat of BW to help achieve this "ultimate objective" is only remarkable when contrasted with the behavior of the military, which often ignored or declined similar opportunities to advance its interests in funding and autonomy. And even if the CDC's initial engagement with biodefense was opportunistic, it was not merely rhetorical. In addition to founding the EIS, researchers at the CDC also worked with their counterparts at Fort Detrick to test sampling devices for BW detection, and they developed fluorescent antibody techniques to identify agents such as anthrax, plague, and tularemia. This pioneering work with florescent antibodies in turn spilled over to help in identifying numerous naturally occurring bacteria.[15]

While the specter of biological attack proved instrumental in promoting research during the Korean War, it vanished soon afterward, and interest in civilian biodefense effectively disappeared for decades. In practice, the capabilities and expertise that Langmuir promoted in the name of biodefense were used to fight natural outbreaks. As Elizabeth Etheridge describes, "CDC's first opportunity to test its response to a hypothetical biological warfare attack came with a naturally occurring polio epidemic," and this crisis, coupled with the Asian flu pandemic in 1957, "ensured that CDC would survive and grow."[16] Meanwhile, the CDC's work on biodefense declined: not only because the organization's bureaucratic interest in survival was now secure, but also because the language and practices that associated epidemiology with biological weapons were left fallow. Socially constructed relationships fade when

[105]

they are not maintained. By 1955, only one EIS officer was working on anthrax. Shortly thereafter, BW was dropped from the EIS curriculum and training focused exclusively on naturally occurring diseases.[17]

This focus on naturally occurring diseases was so effective that the CDC and PHS were eventually victims of their own success, as well as other advances in science and technology. With the antibiotics that became available after World War II, mass inoculations against polio, and other public health victories such as the eradication of smallpox, the burden of infectious disease diminished precipitously in the United States (at least for a time). Consequently, by the 1980s, "the belief that the battle against infectious diseases had been won led to a breakdown in the health infrastructure."[18] As I argue in the next section, beliefs about this breakdown set the stage for renewed fears and bureaucratic opportunities.

Another consequence of focusing on naturally occurring diseases was that CDC officials started to assume all outbreaks had natural causes. This assumption caused the CDC to misidentify a bioterrorist attack by the Rajneeshee cult in 1984. The Rajneeshees had a commune in Oregon, and they tried to sway local elections through a convoluted plot using *Salmonella typhimurium* to sicken county commissioners and residents in a small town called The Dalles. The cult's main attack contaminated the salad bars at several local restaurants, causing at least 751 people to suffer from food poisoning.[19]

CDC initially concluded that this outbreak was caused by unsanitary food handling and not bioterrorism. Moreover, this mistake was only discovered a year later, after the cult's leader accused his followers of betrayal and called for a government investigation that discovered cultures of *S. typhimurium* at the commune and elicited several confessions about the attacks. The initial attribution to natural causes was biased by the fact that the EIS and other investigators had little experience with bioterrorism. According to several of these investigators, "to our knowledge, such an event had never happened," and so, "on the basis of our experience in other investigations, we believed that other hypotheses, although more complicated, appeared more likely."[20] Given this mistake, and fearing copycat attacks, findings from the Rajneeshee investigation were not published until after biodefense reemerged on the national agenda during the 1990s.

Fear of copycats notwithstanding, this incident had little effect on threat perceptions (perhaps because the findings were downplayed). More important, the CDC, PHS, and NIH had no access to classified intelligence about the Soviet BW threat during the Cold War. Since little was known, little was feared. As the PHS surgeon general observed in 1949,

[106]

a fundamental requisite to the effective utilization of civilian agencies in planning defensive measures, is that key professional personnel throughout the country be fully informed as to the present realities and future potentialities of biological warfare. At present, there is almost total lack of information. . . . Heretofore, it has not been possible adequately to inform or to train public health workers in the defensive aspects of biological warfare, because of the high classification placed upon this material.[21]

He urged the military to declassify more information in order to facilitate biodefense planning and professional training, but little information was released over the years and decades that followed. Civilian organizations were effectively left in the dark.

Not knowing better, some civilians even had cause to doubt or discount the anthrax accident at Sverdlovsk in 1979. For more than ten years after this accident, Matthew Meselson—a biologist at Harvard University and outspoken proponent of the Biological Weapons Convention— inadvertently supported the Soviet cover-up by promoting the story that this outbreak was caused by contaminated meat. Inside the military and intelligence community, "there was no question" that Meselson was wrong.[22] But HHS agencies had no access to classified information, and so the Soviet cover-up appeared more credible than it really was.

Given so little information about the BW threat, the lack of civilian biodefense during this period is not surprising from a realist perspective. Nor was there a clear mandate for this mission outside the military.[23] Though Langmuir used the BW threat to promote epidemiology during the Korean War, there was little bureaucratic incentive to invest in biodefense after the EIS was established and the CDC's survival was secure. The knowledge-laden routines of epidemiology persisted, but they did so through language and practices that focused on naturally occurring outbreaks. On the one hand, this focus contributed to the misidentification of bioterrorism by the Rajneeshee cult. On the other hand, the prominence of epidemiology at the CDC and its early association with biological attacks suggests that this organization could accommodate biodefense within its frame of reference.

THE RISE OF CIVILIAN BIODEFENSE: THE 1991 GULF WAR TO SEPTEMBER 2001

Civilian biodefense emerged during the 1990s in response to at least two factors. First, prominent life scientists constructed a relationship between bioterrorism and emerging infectious diseases. Not only did this socially constructed relationship help situate biological weapons inside the organizational frame at HHS, it also provided a strategy for what soon became known as civilian biodefense. Second, threat perceptions increased after Aum Shinrikyo's attacks in Japan, Hussein Kamel's defection from Iraq, and Kanatjan Alibekov's public revelations about the Soviet BW program. The DoD already knew about the Soviet and Iraqi BW programs, but, while the military was willing to cut funding for biodefense, HHS responded differently to similar information about the threat and its emerging mandate. I discuss both factors in turn.

Bioterrorism and Emerging Infectious Diseases

When Langmuir leveraged the relationship between epidemiology and biological warfare during the Korean War, he foreshadowed the rise of civilian biodefense and an important mechanism that would catalyze it, namely, the social construction of particular ideas relating to the biomedical frame of reference. As was the case with Langmuir, prominent scientists were instrumental to this process in the 1980s and 1990s. Particularly important was the biologist and Nobel laureate Joshua Lederberg, who helped coin the phrase "emerging infectious diseases" during a NIH/NIAID conference that was organized by Stephen S. Morse in 1989.[24] At the time, Lederberg and Morse belonged to "a small band of scientists who worry about what they regard as 'complacency' about infectious diseases."[25] Unfortunately, the staggering toll of HIV/AIDS had illustrated that mankind's war with infectious diseases was far from over, and, at least according to Lederberg, "there is no guarantee that we will be the survivors."[26]

Lederberg led this band of worried scientists to write an influential report, *Emerging Infections: Microbial Threats to Health in the United States*, which was coauthored by Robert Shope and published by the nonprofit Institute of Medicine (IOM) in 1992. Even though this report did not explicitly address biological weapons, the authors were cognizant of BW. Shope, for one, had cut his teeth working at Fort Detrick on Project Whitecoat; he also suggested the name "Program for Monitoring Emerging Diseases" for a biodefense project that became ProMED-mail in 1994, and he later held an endowed chair in biodefense at the University of Texas Medical Branch.[27] Likewise, Lederberg was a member of the Defense Science Board who had "access to some of the classified intelligence on the Iraqi biological program," and this information caused him to worry about civilian biodefense.[28] So, as he was organizing the IOM report, Lederberg was also lobbying the White House to protect civilians from biological attacks during the 1991 Gulf War.

Though not inevitable, it is therefore no coincidence that the recommendations made in the IOM report on emerging infectious diseases

[108]

would later be applied to civilian biodefense. They included: (1) increasing research on infectious diseases, (2) strengthening disease surveillance, and (3) acquiring a vaccine stockpile.[29] These recommendations were well received by the CDC and NIAID, which used the IOM report to help lobby Congress and the Clinton administration for more funding. In addition to advancing their bureaucratic interests, these organizations were receptive to this report because it identified problems and solutions that were also salient within their dominant frame of reference. The CDC produced its own plan for addressing emerging infectious diseases through surveillance and research in 1994, but Ruth Berkelman and Phyllis Freeman argue that "it seems highly unlikely that the CDC plan would ever have been conceived" if not for the ideas advanced by Lederberg and his colleagues.[30]

The explicit link between emerging infectious diseases and bioterrorism was still in the making at that time. Lederberg had some success lobbying the George H.W. Bush administration during the Gulf War by arguing that Saddam Hussein might launch a biological attack against the United States using a surrogate or terrorist organization.[31] As a result, civilian biodefense was assigned to Admiral Frank Young and William Clark at the PHS, who, with support from HHS, trained an emergency response team and stockpiled about two-days worth of antibiotics for fifty thousand people near Washington, D.C. These PHS officials continued working on biodefense after the Gulf War as well, notably, through a training exercise called CIVIX 93 that simulated an anthrax attack on a subway in 1993. This was America's first federal bioterrorism exercise—conducted two years before Global 95 (the military's first biological war game). According to Young, it "revealed widespread weaknesses in the response system."[32]

Young and Clark organized a PHS seminar to consider these weaknesses in 1995. This seminar is one of the first times on record that Lederberg and other participants discussed bioterrorism in the context of emerging infectious diseases. Doing so helped construct a persuasive relationship between these threats. For example, in order to illustrate "one aspect of the relationship between naturally occurring infection and biological attack," Lederberg argued that the Black Death in Europe was triggered by biological warfare during the Mongol siege of Caffa in 1346. (The Tartars catapulted cadavers of plague victims into the city, and refugees fleeing Caffa spread the disease to Italy and beyond.)[33] He also noted similarities between the pathogens, research, and emergency responses needed for natural outbreaks and bioterrorism. Young highlighted Metropolitan Medical Strike Teams as one such response, but the specific policies discussed are less noteworthy than the newly constructed relationship that the participants at this seminar helped establish.[34]

[109]

Heightened Threat Perceptions

Though scheduled beforehand, the PHS seminar that helped relate emerging infectious diseases to bioterrorism was held after Aum Shinrikyo attacked the Tokyo subway with sarin gas in March 1995. This chemical attack was followed in April by the Oklahoma City bombing, which killed 168 people using conventional explosives, and, in May, the arrest of Larry Wayne Harris, a white supremacist who had acquired samples of plague through mail fraud. Despite the different motives and capabilities involved, these events galvanized public interest in terrorism using so-called weapons of mass destruction, and references to WMD became an increasingly common but inaccurate stereotype in popular discourse.

Threat perceptions increased yet again after General Hussein Kamel—Saddam Hussein's son-in-law—defected in August 1995. This forced Iraq to admit that it had hidden a sizable biological weapons program and deployed anthrax for potential use during the Gulf War.[35] The growing sense of danger was further amplified in February 1998, when the defector Colonel Kanatjan Alibekov—now named Ken Alibek—first made public his account of the Soviet Union's massive BW program and its work on smallpox along with other dangerous pathogens.[36]

Prior to these public revelations, HHS was largely unaware of the Soviet and Iraqi BW programs because it lacked access to classified intelligence. Outside the military and intelligence community, such access was only occasionally granted to a few biologists like Lederberg and the rare public health official. For example, Michael Osterholm, an epidemiologist with the Minnesota Department of Health, was allowed to meet Alibek in 1993. As with Lederberg's response to intelligence about the Iraqi program during the Gulf War, this meeting caused Osterholm to worry about civilian biodefense.[37] But individual access was the exception rather than the rule. "Alibek was kept under deep cover," according to D. A. Henderson, who was working at that time with the White House Office of Science and Technology Policy. "I didn't know anything about him, and I had every clearance you could imagine." More important was the lack of institutional access. "There was no secure fax machine in the office of the Secretary of Health and Human Services," which did not acquire secure communications facilities until 1999.[38] "For the longest time," according to Margaret Hamburg, then the assistant secretary for policy and evaluation at HHS, "we were not part of those discussions."[39]

In contrast, public revelations about these BW threats could not have surprised the DoD. Unlike HHS, the military had heard everything that Alibek would later reveal to the public when he was debriefed after defecting from Russia in 1992. Furthermore, Kamel's defection merely

confirmed what the military and intelligence community already believed about Iraqi capabilities before the 1991 Gulf War.[40] But, while the
DoD cut funding for military biodefense after the Gulf War and debrief-
ing Alibek, similar information about the BW threat helped increase biodefense funding at HHS.

Threat perceptions outside of these organizations also influenced their
mandates from Congress and the White House. This increased the bureaucratic stakes at play. In June 1995, after the Aum Shinrikyo gas attack and
the Oklahoma City bombing, the Clinton administration issued Presidential Decision Directive (PDD) 39 to provide a framework for counterterrorism policy. It placed the Federal Emergency Management Agency (FEMA)
in charge of consequence management after an attack; FEMA in turn relied
on the Federal Response Plan, which made HHS responsible for health and
medical services.[41] PDD 39 was then cited by another presidential directive
on emerging infectious diseases (PDD NSTC-7), which reinforced the new
relationship between this threat and bioterrorism, along with the response
through research, surveillance, and drug stockpiles recommended in the
1992 IOM report.[42] The roles and responsibilities in PDD 39 were further
clarified by PDD 62, issued in May 1998, which specified the PHS, and thus
HHS, as the lead federal agency for "response to WMD-related medical
emergencies."[43] Nevertheless, the DoD was also mentioned in each of these
directives, even as they started codifying a new mandate for HHS on what
was becoming civilian biodefense.

More important than these formal directives was President Clinton's
personal interest in biodefense. As Alibek was about to go public in 1998,
Clinton was reading *The Cobra Event*, a science fiction novel about bioterrorism that was written with input from Lederberg, Danzig, Osterholm,
and other biodefense advocates. The novel's literary merit is doubtful. Its
political impact, in contrast, may have been significant because it reportedly inspired Clinton to discuss the BW threat with a small group of scientists and public health officials—including Young and Lederberg.[44]
Their recommendations informed PDD 62, which Clinton announced as
an initiative "to aid our preparedness against terrorism, and to help us
cope with infectious diseases that arise in nature."[45]

Not only was the relationship between terrorism and disease now
voiced with presidential authority but Clinton also highlighted how this
threat would be countered through detection and warning, research, and
drug stockpiles. In essence, these were the same recommendations made
in the 1992 IOM report (coupled with the Metropolitan Medical Strike
Teams, which were designed by Young's office at PHS). Moreover, Clinton had Lederberg by his side for a speech he made at the National Academy of Sciences (home of the IOM) in which he asked Congress to more
than double funding for civilian biodefense in January 1999.[46]

[111]

Congress had not been sitting idly by. Before Clinton spoke with Lederberg and Young about biodefense, Congress passed the Defense Against Weapons of Mass Destruction Act of 1996 (also known as the Nunn-Lugar-Domenici Act). However, this legislation gave the military the lead role in enhancing emergency response through the DoD Domestic Preparedness Program. As described in the preceding chapter, this DoD program was hindered by the military's kinetic frame and nonkinetic stereotypes, since "it was all focused on 'bang' or on gas release. There was very little attention being paid to biological."[47] Problems like this might have been rectified by the Public Health Threats Emergencies Act of 2000, which concentrated on HHS and authorized increased funding to counter bioterrorism, but this legislation passed too late in the year to receive appropriations from the Congress that approved it.[48]

A New Normal

The particulars of budget appropriations notwithstanding, Congress and the president were now providing money for civilian biodefense like never before (fig. 4.1). Most evidence suggests that HHS agencies were more responsive to this money and mission than their military counterparts because the problems and solutions involved were more salient within the biomedical frame. For example, the NIH and NIAID had sponsored work on anthrax, plague, botulism, and similar pathogens for years, but they increased funding for research related to bioterrorism from less than $20 million in 1998 to about $50 million by 2001, using money drawn from the Institutes' general appropriations.[49] NIAID also started working with USAMRIID to develop a new anthrax vaccine based on a recombinant protective antigen that might replace the cellular filtrate preparation. Furthermore, responding to revelations about the Soviet BW program, NIAID examined treatment options for smallpox, as well as the feasibility of diluting the smallpox vaccine to stretch the available supply.[50]

At the CDC, work on biodefense began when the president and Congress started to fund this mission. First, the CDC incorporated bioterrorism into its plan for emerging infectious diseases in 1998.[51] This relationship, which was almost unheard of a few years earlier, had become the new normal. Second, the CDC's National Center for Infectious Diseases—author of the aforementioned plan, as well as the original version that had been prompted by the IOM report—became home to the new Bioterrorism Preparedness and Response Program. This program was placed under the direction of Scott Lillibridge, an epidemiologist who helped provide public health assessments after Aum Shinrikyo's attacks and the Oklahoma City bombing.

[112]

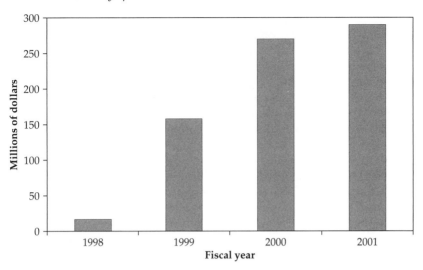

FIGURE 4.1. Total funding for civilian biodefense at HHS (1998–2001). Data sources include Margaret A. Hamburg, MD, "Testimony on Bioterrorism" before the Senate Appropriations Subcommittee on Labor, Health and Human Services, Education and Related Agencies, 25 March 1999; HHS Fact Sheet "HHS Initiative Prepares for Possible Bioterrorism Threat," 18 May 2000; GAO, *Bioterrorism*; Lane, La Montagne, and Fauci, "Bioterrorism"; Ari Schuler, "Billions for Biodefense: Federal Agency Biodefense Funding, FY 2001–FY 2005," *Biosecurity and Bioterrorism: Biodefense Strategy, Practice, and Science* 2, no. 2 (2004): 86–96.

Third, the CDC built the Laboratory Response Network to increase state and local capacity for detecting and diagnosing bioterrorism. Here the effects of classified information on an audience with a receptive frame are evident. As one senior CDC official recalls, "I was receiving classified briefings on what the threat was" and "having nightmares . . . I was so worried that something was going to happen before we got the laboratory response network up and running."[52] Getting this network running involved training more than seven hundred laboratory and public health personnel, as well as improving diagnostic capabilities at the CDC's Rapid Response and Advanced Technology Laboratory.[53] While the CDC only spent about $50 million upgrading its own biodefense capabilities between 1999 and 2001, it awarded almost $180 million to state and local health agencies to help build their capacity.

Finally, during this same period, the CDC spent more than $150 million to build what is now called the Strategic National Stockpile. Since the CDC had no experience or process in place to purchase the thousands of tons of supplies that were required, it partnered with the Department of Veterans' Affairs for procurement, along with the DoD and commercial shipping companies for packaging and delivery. By 2001, this stockpile consisted of eight "push packages"—each weighing fifty tons, carried in wide-body cargo aircraft or tractor trailers, and filled with drugs for agents including anthrax and smallpox, as well as atropine for nerve agents, ventilators, and other equipment.[54] These push packages could be delivered to any state in the country within twelve hours. An additional vendor-managed inventory of supplies could be available within twenty-four to thirty-six hours.

According to Donna Shalala, then secretary of HHS, the rise of civilian biodefense during this period represents "the first time in American history in which the public health system has been integrated directly into the national security system."[55] While true, the magnitude of initial investment and interest should not be overstated. Only a tiny fraction of the government's budget for counterterrorism was spent on biodefense. Even when the ideas involved align, you get what you pay for. Problems therefore persisted, as evidenced by exercises like TOPOFF in May 2000 and Dark Winter in June 2001. These exercises simulated the government's response to scenarios involving plague and smallpox, and they highlighted enduring uncertainty about the relevant roles and responsibilities within the federal system.[56] Furthermore, while HHS agencies entertained a nascent interest in the problems and solutions involved with bioterrorism, not everyone was a true believer. For instance, the director of the CDC, Jeffrey Koplan, drew fire from several biodefense advocates for his managerial approach and lack of enthusiasm.[57]

But complaints about the boss—any boss—are not uncommon, just as poor coordination between local, state, and national leadership has been a defining feature of American federalism since the Revolutionary War. Though poor coordination is a serious problem, it is also normal, as is the way that HHS agencies responded to the emerging mandate and budget for biodefense. Given assumptions and heuristics amenable to the mission, politics as usual prevailed. But this normality is remarkable when contrasted to the anomalous responses to similar threats and interests at the DoD. Furthermore, things could have gone differently, even at HHS. After all, many public health professionals are suspicious of security affairs because of their distaste for armed conflict and resentment over the disproportionate resources that the military often enjoys.[58] Despite this resistance, however, biodefense was comprehensible within the dominant frame at HHS, and so, on balance, the organization was happy to have the money. Rather than shun this mission, as did the DoD, HHS agencies jockeyed for their bureaucratic interests in funding and autonomy. Koplan criticized decisions that gave more money to the NIH than to the CDC, for example, and even the Food and Drug Administration asked for a larger staff and budget by arguing that "the success of the antibioterrorism initiative depends on FDA's involvement."[59]

Because politics as usual prevailed, the biodefense programs established during the Clinton administration continued on a similar path during the first nine months of the George W. Bush administration. For instance, the new HHS secretary, Tommy Thompson, was at least as interested in biodefense as his predecessor had been.[60] In July 2001, Thompson named Lillibridge as his special adviser to lead the ongoing anti-bioterrorism initiative. HHS also released an overview of its "five-year plan for combating bioterrorism" just weeks before the attacks on September 11. This plan proposed increasing the budget for biodefense from about $300 million to $350 million—a modest increase, compared with what was to come—and it continued to emphasize research, surveillance, and stockpiling, harkening back to familiar themes from the 1992 IOM report.[61]

Civilian Plans and Procedures

Not all planning during this period was budgetary. In accordance with PDD 39, for example, HHS produced a plan for responding to chemical and biological terrorism in 1996; later, Hamburg developed strategic plans for what HHS would require to actually accomplish this mission.[62] As previously mentioned, the CDC incorporated bioterrorism into its plan for emerging infectious diseases in 1998. It also developed a strategic plan for terrorism and, along with HHS, provided more specific guidance to state and local health officials in 2001.[63]

These civilian plans rarely if ever refer to their guidelines as "doctrine," so they should be compared to military doctrine with caution because their authors, audiences, and functions differ. Moreover, while the BW threat to civilians is related to the operational and strategic threats faced by the military, there are important differences between these target populations and their respective vulnerabilities that stand to affect plans and procedures. For instance, members of the armed services are a small subset of the general population and more likely to be young, healthy, male, and concentrated on military bases. When attacked, they benefit from specialized training, equipment, and a clear chain of command. In contrast, civilians are more diverse and disorganized. An average cross section of the US population includes men and women, young and old, some sick or immune compromised, with most people concentrated in cities but others widely distributed. Civilians are also weakly regulated by overlapping and often conflicting forms of authority, which

[115]

is one reason why HHS agencies like the CDC do not even pretend to issue orders and expect or enforce compliance like the armed forces.

These differences are noteworthy, but the differences between military doctrine and plans written during the rise of civilian biodefense are even more consistent with the different ideas at work inside the DoD and HHS. First, unlike the military, HHS and the CDC do not assume that biological attacks will be detected in advance. Instead, they focus on responding to covert or unexpected attacks—predicated on the reasonable assumption that contamination will occur and cannot simply be avoided.[64] Second, rather than dismiss the consequences of such attacks, civilian plans and procedures concede that the potential loss of life is significant. Therefore, in addition to anticipating contamination, they also recommend that training and response at the local, state, and federal level prepare for mass casualty care.[65] Finally, quantitative content analysis suggests that the language in civilian plans might differ from military doctrine as well. Granted, when the selection criteria and coding rules described in chapter 3 are applied to civilian documents during this period, the sample is small and the results are not statistically significant.[66] On average, however, "bio-" words are more common and central than either "chem-" words or stereotypes like CBW, CBR, and WMD. This at least hints that HHS agencies use different language from that used by their military counterparts.[67]

So, despite being new to this mission, HHS did not simply adopt the military's long-standing—and thus ready-made—doctrine for biodefense. Nor did civilian plans assume that biodefense is a natural or obvious subsidiary of chemical defense. This means that the military's nonkinetic stereotypes are not an inevitable response to the BW threat: they are socially constructed ideas, and different ideas produce different results. For example, unlike the Army Chemical Corps, NIAID relegated research and development for combating chemical and nuclear terrorism to other agencies in its first strategic plan for biodefense, choosing instead to focus on bioterrorism and not conflate it with other aspects of civil defense.[68] Here, as elsewhere, key differences between military doctrine and civilian plans correspond more closely to the ideas at work than to either the distinction between biological warfare and bioterrorism or the difficulties of protecting civilian populations versus military personnel.

In sum, civilian biodefense emerged during the 1990s, not as a result of 9/11 and the anthrax attacks of 2001. Threat perceptions and bureaucratic interests played an important role, but they did so in part because the socially constructed relationship between bioterrorism and emerging infectious diseases helped situate the problems and solutions involved inside the dominant frame at HHS. Lederberg was particularly influential. "He wasn't the lone individual arguing the case that we really had to be concerned about these issues," according to Henderson, "but he certainly was a towering figure."[69] HHS was more responsive than the DoD to experts like Lederberg, as well as to the growing mandate and budget from the president and Congress, because the biomedical frame did not predispose it to (mis)represent this mission in the same way as the military's kinetic frame and nonkinetic stereotypes did.

The salience of different conceptual relationships depended on the ideas at work inside each organization. Most important, HHS did not rely on the nonkinetic stereotypes that are common and central in military doctrine, and, rather than assume that biodefense is merely a subset of chemical defense, this civilian organization chose instead to relate bioterrorism to emerging infectious diseases. Meanwhile, the DoD made little or no mention of emerging infectious diseases in relation to biological weapons until the mid-2000s. This was long after the military established the DoD Global Emerging Infectious Surveillance and Response System in 1997, which was mandated by PDD NSTC-7, and years after HHS argued that "it is imperative to link bioterrorism preparedness efforts with ongoing disease surveillance and outbreak response activities as defined in CDC's emerging infectious disease strategy."[70]

Neither threats nor interests fully explain these differences. For instance, recall that Aum Shinrikyo's most successful attack was an act of chemical terrorism. Why then did biodefense rather than chemical defense come to dominate research and development for counterterrorism at HHS? Perhaps public revelations about the Soviet and Iraqi BW programs were the reason, but, if so, then why did the military cut biodefense when it had access to similar information years earlier? HHS was a newcomer to the national security establishment in the 1990s, at which time it was dwarfed by the DoD's budget and authority. So why did HHS not simply adopt the military's nonkinetic stereotypes and chem centric approach to biodefense? These questions only challenge observed outcomes—many of which seem normal or ordinary in hindsight—if we ignore the influence of ideas inside these organizations.

THE SURGE IN CIVILIAN BIODEFENSE: AFTERMATH OF THE ANTHRAX LETTERS

Soon after airplanes struck the World Trade Center and the Pentagon on the morning of September 11, US airspace was closed to all traffic. Only four nonmilitary aircraft were permitted to fly that evening: three of which carried supplies from the Strategic National Stockpile to New York City. This was the first time that the CDC used the stockpile, and it suggests that HHS was now alert to the possibility of bioterrorism in a way it might not have been just a few years earlier.[71] "There had been concern that there could have been a biological agent on the planes that hit the World Trade Center," so the CDC monitored hospitals in New York for signs of BW exposure.[72] In addition, Lillibridge was tasked to direct the HHS command center, and Secretary Thompson called Henderson—who had recently helped establish the Johns Hopkins Center for Civilian Biodefense Strategies—into headquarters for advice. Thompson was worried because subsequent attacks might involve biological weapons, the White House did not understand the threat, and the United States was unprepared.[73]

Thompson proved more correct than even he realized. One week after the World Trade Center was destroyed, the first set of anthrax letters was mailed from Trenton, New Jersey. In early October, the first victims of inhalation anthrax were admitted to hospitals in Florida.[74] In one case, a doctor on the scene diagnosed the infection as anthrax and sent samples of the bacteria to the CDC's Laboratory Response Network, where this diagnosis was confirmed. While the CDC organized local, state, and federal teams to investigate the cause, Secretary Thompson and other officials initially suggested that this was an isolated and natural case. However, it was soon recognized as bioterrorism; a second set of anthrax letters was postmarked on 9 October, and other cases of inhalation and cutaneous anthrax were diagnosed in Florida, New York, New Jersey, and Washington, D.C.

In the end, five people died, at least twenty-two were infected, and thousands more were treated using drugs from the vendor-managed inventory of the Strategic National Stockpile.[75] Whereas the military might have relied more on chemical or nuclear expertise during such a crisis, the CDC's response to the Amerithrax case—though imperfect—was coordinated by Julie Gerberding, an infectious disease expert and deputy director of National Center for Infectious Diseases. Secretary Thompson later appointed Gerberding to replace Koplan as head of the CDC. Henderson was consulted about the anthrax letters as well, after which he was appointed to create the new HHS Office of Public Health Preparedness.

Continuity and Change in Biodefense Policy

September 11 and the anthrax letters prompted sweeping changes to national security policy in the United States. Civilian biodefense was no exception. A few months after these attacks, a supplemental appropriations bill increased HHS funding for biodefense by an order of magnitude: from about $300 million in 2001 to almost $3 billion in 2002. HHS lobbied hard to win money on the table for biodefense rather than let it go to what was soon to become the Department of Homeland Security. Although fully consistent with the bureaucratic interests of HHS, this lobbying stands in sharp contrast to the behavior of DoD, which returned rather than spent money that it had been given by the Office of Homeland Security for BW detection.

Unlike the military, NIAID, under the directorship of Anthony Fauci—"sometimes called the J. Edgar Hoover of biology"—enthusiastically accepted additional funding and responsibility for biodefense.[76] Fauci and other NIAID officials argued that the research agenda for bioterrorism "must be given a status similar to that of research in other pressing areas such as malaria, tuberculosis and AIDS." Furthermore, "what began as an area of boutique research . . . is now the center of attention for the biomedical research community," and "we should consider these investigations to be critical components of the broader arena of research on naturally emerging and re-emerging microbes."[77] The annual budget for NIAID was about $2 billion in 2001, but, thanks in large part to lobbying around the surge in civilian biodefense, funding for this institute nearly doubled over the next two years. While only a fraction of the total budget for NIH, which exceeded $26 billion per year in 2003, this increase was still significant.[78]

Similarly, Koplan testified that the CDC needed nearly $3 billion to prepare for a biological attack and, in doing so, he asked Congress for twice the amount that the Bush administration had just requested for his agency.[79] As the saying goes, "a billion here, a billion there, and pretty soon you're talking real money."[80] This is even true for the armed services, but the DoD had no one like Koplan or Fauci aggressively lobbying Congress or the White House for military biodefense. Instead, "it was back to the old, 'it's not that high a priority,'" according to Johnson-Winegar. Despite the military's supposedly generic interests in funding and autonomy, some DoD officials "were not opposed to seeing someone else getting in the game."[81]

Thus, here as elsewhere, the DoD and HHS responded differently to this huge potential influx of money for biodefense. Moreover, the magnitude of money available changed more than the content of research, development, acquisition, and doctrine: consistent with the path dependency of organizational frame theory. The primary beneficiaries of this surge in civilian biodefense were either existing programs or other initiatives that were compatible with ideas from the 1992 IOM report, including research at NIH/NIAID, surveillance at the CDC, and acquisition for the Strategic National Stockpile.

Between 2001 and 2012, for example, the CDC spent nearly $10 billion upgrading state and local public health infrastructure for surveillance, epidemiology, and laboratory testing, along with other aspects of emergency response (drug distribution, interagency coordination, risk communication, etc.). An additional $6 billion was spent on the Strategic National Stockpile.[82] The CDC BioSense Program also sponsored syndromic surveillance, and, through somewhat contentious cooperation with the Department of Homeland Security and the Environmental Protection Agency, the CDC Laboratory Response Network supported Bio-Watch. This BW detection system is now deployed in at least thirty large cities.[83]

BioWatch is a system dedicated to biodefense, but most infrastructure funded by the CDC can be used for responding to both natural and deliberate outbreaks of infectious disease (at least in theory), as well as to other public health emergencies. To an equal or even greater degree, NIAID poured almost $15 billion into basic research between 2001 and 2012, under the rubric of biodefense but with much of the money spent on naturally occurring diseases.[84] In keeping with the socially constructed relationship established during the 1990s, "the NIAID biodefense research effort is integrated into the Institute's larger emerging and re-emerging infectious diseases portfolio."[85] Parroting this relationship, NIAID also established almost a dozen Regional Centers of Excellence for Biodefense and Emerging Infectious Disease Research after 9/11 and the anthrax letters in 2001.

The same ideas that helped director Fauci seek and accept funding and responsibility for biodefense enable, if not encourage, NIAID to blur the distinction between this mission and other issues inside its organizational frame. Therefore, NIAID funded huge amounts of basic research on microbes that ranged from anthrax and smallpox to avian influenza. It also built several high-containment laboratories (i.e., biosafety level 3 and 4 facilities) for working on these and other pathogens.

Vaccines, therapeutics, and diagnostics received some support as well. But here NIAID argued that "basic scientific advances now allow us to go beyond developing countermeasures against individual threats and work toward development of technologies to counter multiple threats," such as non-specific immune responses "that combat a wide array of viruses and bacteria."[86] True or not, this was a deliberate choice. "Central to this research is NIAID's effort to change the paradigm for antimicrobial drug development from a "one-bug, one-drug" approach to a focus on broad-spectrum therapies that could be used against entire classes of pathogens . . . whether naturally emerging or the result of a bioterror attack."[87]

The extent to which this boon for basic research actually translates into development and acquisition of biodefense products is a question that I address later. Basic research is typically seen as a long-term investment, and, in the meantime, the Bush administration pushed forward the

National Smallpox Vaccination Program, which broke with past policy, clashed with HHS recommendations, and ultimately failed to meet its objectives. At the same time, HHS lobbied the White House and Congress to support Project BioShield. Although dwarfed by funding for basic research, BioShield purchased medical countermeasures and was soon coupled with the Biomedical Advanced Research and Development Authority (BARDA). Since these are important initiatives, their respective successes and failures are considered next.

The National Smallpox Vaccination Program

Initially, the CDC took the initiative in preparing for the potential use of smallpox as a weapon, which is poignant because EIS officers had helped eradicate this naturally occurring disease in the 1960s and 1970s. In 2000, the CDC started to augment its supply of Dryvax vaccine (used during the global eradication campaign and grown on calf skin) in the Strategic National Stockpile with a second-generation vaccine produced by Acambis (ACAM1000 and later ACAM2000, both grown in cell culture). Shortly after 9/11 and the anthrax attacks, the CDC vaccinated twenty smallpox response teams, published plans for state and local health agencies to follow in the event of an outbreak, and asked the Advisory Committee on Immunization Practices to review its recommendations on smallpox vaccination. In June 2002, this committee recommended that up to twenty thousand specialized health-care workers should be vaccinated against smallpox as a precautionary measure.[88]

But Vice President Dick Cheney had other plans. At the time, the Bush administration was trying to make a case for war with Iraq based on the threat of "WMD," and, perhaps in the spirit of threat inflation, Cheney favored a nationwide—even compulsory—smallpox vaccination program. Word soon spread that the government was planning to preemptively vaccinate five hundred thousand people as the first step in this larger campaign.[89] "We have no imminent threat," observed Gerberding, then head of CDC, "but we recognize that we are in the process of considering war on our enemies. The context has changed a bit."[90] In addition to rejecting the Advisory Committee on Immunization Practices' recommendation for a more modest program, Cheney's policy preferences clashed with advice from the leadership at HHS. Henderson claims that "our arguments had little effect," even though he, Secretary Thompson, and other health officials reportedly opposed mass vaccinations (particularly using the old vaccine).[91] In spite of this opposition, President Bush announced the National Smallpox Vaccination Program on 13 December 2002. Its goal was to voluntarily vaccinate about 500,000 health-care workers in thirty days, followed by as many as 10 million more first responders.

[121]

The National Smallpox Vaccination Program failed to achieve these objectives. While the military started vaccinating immediately, civilian vaccinations did not begin until 24 January 2003 (the day that liability provisions in the Homeland Security Act went into effect). But even with legal protection against adverse effects from the vaccine, this program was still voluntary, and vaccination against an extinct disease—especially one seen by many to pose no imminent threat—was unprecedented. State and local health officials were therefore reluctant to provide the vaccine, just as potential recipients were reluctant to receive it.

Nationwide, only four people in Connecticut were vaccinated on the first day of the program in January. Fewer than 32,000 people had been vaccinated by April, at which point the CDC abandoned its overdue deadline and suggested that immunizing as few as fifty thousand health-care workers would be sufficient.[92] Standing under the now infamous banner "Mission Accomplished," President Bush declared an end to major combat operations in Iraq in May, and public threat perceptions diminished even further as the justification for this war based on "WMD" quickly unraveled. As a result, civilian vaccinations had slowed to a trickle when the Advisory Committee on Immunization Practices recommended ending the program in June 2003.[93]

Project BioShield and BARDA

While health authorities resisted the vice president on mass vaccinations against smallpox, HHS officials were eager to promote what became the Project BioShield Act of 2004. This legislation originated in part through a request by Secretary Thompson to sketch out a $10 billion civilian biodefense program that Fauci then named "BioShield." Despite debates over vaccine policy, Thompson and his advisers retained a close relationship with the Office of the Vice President, and they pitched this idea to I. Lewis "Scooter" Libby and Cheney. The vice president's office in turn helped push approval for BioShield through the White House and into the 2003 State of the Union address.[94] During this speech, President Bush highlighted the smallpox vaccination campaign and deployment of "the nation's first early warning network of sensors to detect biological attack" (BioWatch). He also asked Congress to fund Project BioShield as part of a $6 billion budget that would "quickly make available effective vaccines and treatments against agents like anthrax, botulinum toxin, Ebola, and plague."

This was the first time in history that botulinum toxin and Ebola were mentioned in a State of the Union address. But Bush's budget proposal was smaller than HHS requested and additional concessions were made during negotiations with Congress. Ultimately, the Project BioShield Act of 2004 authorized advanced appropriation of $5.6 billion over ten years.

[122]

In addition to more money, HHS had also wanted more autonomy. This was consistent with its bureaucratic interests and expressed in a manner befitting the biomedical frame. HHS wanted freedom to use BioShield to buy countermeasures for bioterrorism and naturally occurring diseases (e.g., $100 million for pandemic influenza), as well as to fund development and procurement. However, these aspects of the HHS proposal were opposed by the Office of Management and Budget, the Homeland Security Council, and Congress, so the negotiated result was less money and less autonomy.[95] HHS was forced to share control of BioShield with the Department of Homeland Security, which was responsible for defining the threats and signing the checks, and the program focused on procurement.

In theory, procurement through BioShield provided a market guarantee to drive commercial development of medical countermeasures, thereby supporting if not creating a viable industry.[96] In practice, "investing $5.6 billion for pharmaceutical and biomedical manufacturing is spit in the bucket," according to Robert Kadlec, since most drug candidates fail and even a single success can cost more than $1 billion to bring to market.[97] Not only was this market guarantee too small to attract pharmaceutical companies large enough to have the necessary infrastructure and expertise; the law allowed little or no payment prior to delivery, so it also provided insufficient support for small biotechnology companies to usher their drug candidates across what is called "the valley of death," that is, the difficult transition between the laboratory and market.[98]

When the first BioShield contract was offered for a recombinant anthrax vaccine, the industry giant Sanofi Pasteur dropped out of the bidding. HHS awarded the contract to VaxGen, a small biotech company with technology from USAMRIID but no history of successfully licensing a vaccine. VaxGen committed to an overly ambitious timeline and soon encountered stability problems with its vaccine candidate, rPA102. Meanwhile, the VaxGen contract was assaulted by Emergent Bio-Solutions, which manufactured the old BioThrax vaccine that stood to be replaced by a recombinant version. Emergent spent millions of dollars lobbying Congress and the White House before HHS cancelled its contract with VaxGen in 2006. "National security took a back seat to politics and the power of lawyers and lobbyists," at least according to Philip Russell, a former USAMRIID commander and one architect of BioShield who supported the VaxGen contract.[99] After this contract collapsed, Emergent bought the intellectual property rights to rPA102 for pennies on the dollar from its vanquished competitor.[100] "They bought the technology and buried it," argues Russell, and, as a result, "we are five or six years behind where we should be."[101]

Despite the VaxGen debacle, BioShield successfully contracted with several other companies—including Emergent—to acquire prophylactic and therapeutic drugs. By 2012, BioShield added to the Strategic National Stockpile more than 67,000 doses of antitoxins for treating anthrax, as well as 28 million doses of BioThrax vaccine ("enough anthrax vaccine to respond to a 'three-city attack'"); almost 110,000 doses of botulism antitoxin; nearly 6 million doses of modified vaccinia Ankara for immunocompromised people (augmenting more than 300 million doses of the smallpox vaccine already stockpiled); and about 5 million doses of various treatments for radiation exposure.[102] Additional countermeasures remain under contract.

Furthermore, on the same day that VaxGen's contract was cancelled in 2006, President Bush signed into law the Pandemic and All Hazards Preparedness Act. It attempts to fix some of the problems with BioShield by creating the Biomedical Advanced Research and Development Authority. In particular, BARDA provides milestone grants for drug development to help bridge the valley of death between the lab and market. On the one hand, this means that HHS can now contribute to countermeasures at all phases: from research (NIH/NIAID) and development (BARDA) through to acquisition (BioShield and the Strategic National Stockpile).[103] On the other hand, both development and acquisition are still underfunded. Congress raided BioShield's special reserve fund to support BARDA, and annual appropriations have been lacking as well. According to one prominent and critical review, "the estimated cost of developing the medical countermeasures required to meet the threats identified by the Department of Homeland Security is $3.4 billion a year for the next five years. Appropriation for FY 2010 is less than one tenth of that."[104]

Why All Problems Are Not Equal

Thus while basic research flourished, civilian biodefense only achieved modest gains in development and acquisition during the decade after 2001. These problems call into question the basic distinction that I draw between HHS and the DoD. What difference do the ideas inside these organizations make if military and civilian biodefense are both flawed? The previous chapters showed how the kinetic frame and nonkinetic stereotypes caused military neglect. But if HHS were to suffer the same problems, even with its biomedical frame, then different ideas would not correlate with different outcomes, which would undermine my argument about organizational frame theory.

The problems with military and civilian biodefense are not of the same type, however, and the ideas at work inside the DoD and HHS help us understand why they differ. First, not all of the problems associated with civilian biodefense can be attributed to HHS in the same way that many of the military's problems reside within the DoD. For instance, organizational frames can explain why HHS lobbied for more money and autonomy while the DoD demurred, but these ideas have less influence outside of these organizations—by definition—and the decisions made by Congress and the president have an independent effect on policy.

Therefore, the DoD might be faulted for not lobbying on behalf of military biodefense, but it is harder to blame HHS for not getting all the funding and autonomy it wanted for Project BioShield. Similarly, HHS is responsible for some aspects of civilian biodefense, but it is far from the only agency involved, as illustrated by its joint control of BioShield with the Department of Homeland Security. The biomedical frame may exacerbate coordination problems inside HHS, but it cannot be faulted for poor coordination between all of the different local, state, and federal agencies that share jurisdiction. "Today, there are more than two dozen Senate-confirmed individuals with some responsibility for biodefense," according to the CEO of the bipartisan WMD Center. "Not one person has it for a full-time job, and no one is in charge."[105]

Second, many of the problems with HHS are consistent with its biomedical frame and different from those inside DoD. Consider the disproportionate emphasis on basic research through NIH/NIAID. As Kendall Hoyt argues, here the "investigator-initiated, peer-reviewed grant system generates scientific knowledge and publications, but it falters when the government requests tangible results" such as a vaccine for HIV/AIDS or countermeasures for biodefense.[106] Like the biomedical frame, this approach to problem solving—through highly specialized and individual lines of inquiry—can be faulted for being reductionist and asocial.[107] By missing the forest for the trees or, similarly, believing that basic research automatically drives development (a common but often inaccurate "linear model" of innovation), organizations like NIAID may struggle to integrate the research and development required to create vaccines and other working products.

A good argument can therefore be made that HHS was mistaken to invest as much as it did, in the way that it did, into basic research. HHS officials and other biodefense experts certainly disagree on the best balance to strike between research and development, for example, or on the relative merits of stockpiling "one drug per bug" versus pursuing multipurpose countermeasures and production platforms.[108] But these are relatively sophisticated disputes, informed by shared assumptions and heuristics: they are roughly analogous to debates within the kinetic frame over the sequential versus concurrent procurement of military aircraft, or over the ballistic and logistic tradeoffs between .223 and .308

rifle cartridges.[109] The military's problems with biodefense, however, were of a different type and magnitude. Rather than overemphasizing research, the DoD tended to starve Fort Detrick and then, as seen during the Korean War and the Gulf War, rush to acquire technology at the last minute based on the assumption that chemical experience would suffice. Plus, many other military decisions in the past were more indicative of incomprehension than nuanced disputes over the marginal returns of alternative investment strategies or even the trial and error that might inform learning.

Third, and perhaps most important, HHS appears to be learning faster than the DoD. Organizational frame theory does not predict that organizations are immune to problems inside their dominant frame: only that they usually learn to solve these problems, in contrast to those outside of this frame, which they tend to dismiss. The history of military biodefense demonstrates how the kinetic frame and nonkinetic stereotypes caused the military to dismiss biodefense for more than a half century. There is no doubt that HHS has also made mistakes regarding civilian biodefense. It is more likely to learn from them, however, than to repeat the same errors for decades on end.

An important step in learning—or at least in the search for new solutions—is admitting that you have a problem.[110] Recall that military doctrine was replete with assurances that standard operating procedures for chemical defense were sufficient for biodefense, and that medical countermeasures were available even when they were not. This incomprehension or denial did not help the military learn. In contrast, HHS secretary Kathleen Sebelius acknowledged in 2010 that "the pipeline we rely on to provide those critical countermeasures—diagnostics, vaccines, antivirals, antibiotics—is full of leaks, choke points and dead ends."[111]

HHS appears to be taking corrective action. For better or worse, the BioShield contract with VaxGen was cancelled after two years and replaced with a broader development initiative, whereas the military struggled with the Michigan facility that became BioPort and then Emergent for more than a decade.[112] Responding to gaps in the early stages of technology development, HHS is also seeking to establish an independent strategic investment program to support small companies (modeled on the CIA's venture capital firm, In-Q-Tel).[113] Acknowledging problems at the end stage, the FDA is attempting to reform regulatory science and revise guidance on its Animal Efficacy Rule.[114] When they designed BioShield, HHS officials considered and initially dismissed the idea of building a government-owned facility for vaccine production.[115] Perhaps learning from experience, HHS is now working with industry and academia to build Centers for Innovation in Advanced Development and Manufacturing that fulfill a similar function. HHS is spending

$400 million to establish three centers that will be overseen by BARDA; use a new model for public-private partnerships with GlaxoSmithKline, Emergent, and Novartis (among others); and produce vaccines for pandemic influenza and biodefense.[116]

Of course, the extent to which these and other initiatives actually bear fruit remains to be seen. If, by the year 2040, HHS proves as unprepared for biodefense as the DoD was during the 1991 Gulf War (i.e., fifty years after the military started working on BW at Detrick), then the distinctions that I draw between the kinds of problems that these organizations face will need to be critically reevaluated. Granted, there is no need to wait: the natural experiment that I use to compare the history of military and civilian biodefense is not perfect. But it is difficult to dismiss the large body of evidence that favors my argument about the ideas at work inside HHS and the DoD.

September 11 and the anthrax attacks of 2001 altered American threat perceptions far more than Aum Shinrikyo or revelations about the Soviet and Iraqi BW programs during the 1990s. Funding for biodefense increased as a result. However, the magnitude of funding changed more than the content of biodefense policy because HHS agencies continued to focus on research, surveillance, and stockpiling. This is consistent with the 1992 IOM report and the socially constructed relationship between bioterrorism and emerging infectious diseases. In addition, HHS sought out funding and autonomy for biodefense, unlike the DoD. Fauci used the threat of bioterrorism to promote basic research (like Langmuir used the specter of BW to promote epidemiology during the Korean War), and HHS lobbied the White House and Congress to support Project BioShield. None of these programs are above reproach. But, more often than not, their successes and failures are consistent with the biomedical frame.

Considered in isolation, the rise and subsequent surge in civilian biodefense could support realist predictions about fear and self-help, as well as bureaucratic interests in funding and autonomy. This is politics as usual. Yet these explanations fail to explain why the DOD and HHS responded so differently to similar challenges and opportunities. All else being equal, defending the nation against biological attacks could have become a major military mission like national missile defense. Unlike missile defense, however, biodefense was not salient within the military's dominant frame of reference, so the conventional wisdom about threats and interests failed to apply. Different ideas produced different results, as predicted by organizational frame theory and demonstrated by HHS. This finding makes the otherwise puzzling history of American biodefense far more comprehensible. As I illustrate in the concluding chapter, it also has other important implications for national security policy.

[127]

Biodefense and Beyond

THE INFLUENCE OF IDEAS ON NATIONAL SECURITY

The history of American biodefense is at least as complex as the science and technology involved, especially since artifacts like vaccines and detection systems are shaped by social and political forces at least as much as they shape security policy. Nevertheless, the ideas at work inside the DoD and HHS explain many of the decisions and outcomes that define this history, particularly military neglect and the rise of civilian biodefense. At least three major findings stand out, each of which warrants review before I consider their broader implications. First, biological weapons do not conform to the military's assumptions and heuristics about projectile weapons and explosives. Second, as a consequence of this discrepancy, the armed services have tended to rely on inaccurate stereotypes that conflate BW with other nonkinetic weapons. These stereotypes let the military pay lip service to biodefense while disregarding it as a matter of routine practice. Third, different ideas produce different results. The influence of different ideas on organizational decision making is one major reason why some civilian organizations are more willing and able to support biodefense than are their military counterparts.

Biological weapons are a different form of firepower because their timing and mechanisms of damage differ from projectile weapons and explosives. This means that the problems and solutions involved with BW and biodefense tend to fall outside of the military's kinetic frame of reference. While the ideas that define this organizational frame are powerful social constructs, "the material world is obdurate," as Donald MacKenzie notes in his sociological study of missile guidance.[1] As a result, these ideas still confront what Alexander Wendt calls "rump materialism," because "a technological artifact" like a vial of milled

[128]

anthrax or smallpox vaccine "has intrinsic material capacities."[2] Some ideas are less useful than others for solving problems that relate to such material factors.

Organizations are not mindlessly enslaved to their dominant frames or primary patterns for problem solving, although "it is tempting, if the only tool you have is a hammer, to treat everything as if it were a nail."[3] The US military recognized that biological weapons differ from projectile weapons and explosives. Unfortunately, this recognition truncated the organization's search for more useful ideas. Rather than learn about this different form of firepower, the military constructed simplistic and often inaccurate generalizations that group BW together with other weapons that also fell outside of its dominant frame. I argue that the resulting ideas are best regarded as organizational stereotypes.

Granted, stereotypes are not all bad: they might contain a kernel of truth, and cognitive shortcuts can help simplify a complex world. Simplicity comes at a price, however, and it is dangerous for powerful organizations to rely on flawed categories. The DoD certainly relied on such categories. Time and time again, the military based important decisions about research, development, acquisition, and doctrine on stereotypes that conflated biological weapons with very different kinds of nonkinetic weapons—chiefly chemical weapons. The language of stereotypes about "chemical and biological weapons" was remarkably consequential because, "if the naming is incorrect," as Lee Clarke argues, "then important ways in which things can go awry will be neglected or ignored."[4] And that is what happened to military biodefense.

Using stereotypes that assumed biological weapons are like chemical weapons, the military has treated biodefense as a subset of chemical defense. Chemical defense is another nonkinetic issue that the armed services had previously encountered but never embraced, so problems and solutions associated with chemical warfare were often ignored and the Chemical Corps was almost eliminated on several occasions. However, because the military's stereotypes caused it to mistake chemical experience for biological expertise, chemical defense served as the token countermeasure for both. Biodefense consequently got the shorter end of what was already a very short stick (even though it is a different and harder problem to solve). Being slow to learn about errors outside of its dominant frame, the military also had a hard time comprehending—let alone correcting—this neglect for decades on end.

The military's neglect of biodefense is therefore an example of socially constructed ignorance and inability rather than an inevitable response to the threat environment or bureaucratic interests. This is not to say that threats and interests play no role. There is scattered empirical support for realism over the years, ranging from the decision to stockpile botulinum vaccine before the invasion of Normandy to the critical changes made in military doctrine after the 1991 Gulf War. Likewise, I have described the bureaucratic turf war between the Chemical Warfare Service and surgeons general after World War II, in contrast to the conventional story about how the BW program was especially cooperative, and I show that the Chemical Corps and military medical community have continued to clash over their respective authorities and responsibilities to this day.

As important as these examples are, however, the armed services have often acted contrary to the fear and self-help predicted by realism, and contrary to their bureaucratic interests in funding and autonomy. Realism does not help us understand why military doctrine assumed that biological attacks would be rapidly detected, for instance, particularly when the DoD never had this capability and failed to field BW detection systems of any kind until after the Cold War. The same can be said about the belated acquisition of anthrax vaccine—not to mention sole reliance on First Flight, the horse, for botulinum antitoxin—and the numerous other instances I have documented in which military research, development, and acquisition were unresponsive to the threat environment. Likewise, bureaucratic interests do not explain why the Chemical Corps was always weak (despite its wide-ranging responsibilities), and yet, time and time again, chemical experience prevailed over biological expertise in competition over the management of military biodefense. Nor do generic interests explain why the DoD did not pursue more funding and autonomy on several auspicious occasions, including the aftermath of 9/11 and the anthrax attacks of 2001. So the bulk of evidence is more consistent with my argument about organizational frames and stereotypes.

Finally, different ideas produced different results. In contrast to the military's confused and often dismissive approach to BW, the rise of civilian biodefense appears almost ordinary or "normal," even though weaponry of any sort might seem far afield from the responsibilities HHS has for other programs such as Medicare and Medicaid. We now know why. The timing and mechanisms of damage caused by these weapons are comprehensible and thus salient within the biomedical frame of reference. In addition, the socially constructed relationship between bioterrorism and emerging infectious diseases helped situate biodefense inside the organizational frame at HHS. Rather than rely on the military's inaccurate stereotypes, HHS used different ideas to solve similar problems, and, as a result, agencies such as NIAID and CDC were more sensitive to information about the threat and more interested in maximizing their funding and autonomy for biodefense.

[130]

These findings have several important implications. For instance, critics of American biodefense sometimes suggest that the US military secretly maintained an offensive BW program long after 1969.[5] The good news is that these allegations are probably false. Although certain aspects of offensive work are difficult to distinguish from defense, the military was never very interested in BW, making it unlikely that the DoD intentionally violated the Biological Weapons Convention—not impossible, but unlikely. "Acceptance of a weapon within the military establishment is a prerequisite to employment," at least according to Fredric Brown, but even research and development for biodefense were hard for the armed services to accept because of their kinetic frame.[6]

In addition, the kinetic frame is not unique to the US military. While the content of any organization's dominant frame depends on historical context, other militaries may be constrained by similar ideas about projectile weapons and explosives and therefore might shun biological weapons as well. This suggests that organizational frames can point in the same direction as international laws and norms that prohibit the acquisition and use of these weapons.[7]

But the news is not all good. Frames of reference vary across organizations, and, because they are a local or proximate source of influence, these ideas stand to have a greater impact on organizational behavior than international laws or supposedly global norms.[8] Therefore, other organizations (be they security services or terrorists groups) with different assumptions and heuristics might still develop and use biological weapons, as indicated by Japan's Unit 731, Biopreparat in the Soviet Union, the Iraqi BW program, and Aum Shinrikyo, among other examples. New organizations may adopt different approaches to problem solving as well, and the ideas that might motivate a "lone wolf" or malicious individual such as Bruce Ivans are even more varied.

Perhaps, as an American, I have a harder time imagining threats from institutions close to home, though some critics of biodefense certainly do.[9] A healthy balance should be struck between the freedoms associated with innovation and the controls needed for laboratory safety and security. Given enduring assumptions about the natural causes of disease, I suspect that HHS agencies such as the NIH and NIAID are more likely to support risky research that attempts to anticipate nature—for example, increasing the transmissibility of H5N1 influenza—than they are to violate the spirit of the Biological Weapons Convention. The ideas at work inside the Department of Homeland Security (DHS) warrant further study, as do those of its subsidiaries such as the National Biodefense Analysis and Countermeasure Center. Even if secrecy is justified for some of their research, the shared assumptions and heuristics in these organizations can be studied without revealing classified information, and, if the findings are benign, then this analysis might build confidence that their attempts to anticipate threats will not inadvertently create them.

Although it has been a struggle, the US military is less vulnerable to biological weapons today then during the Cold War. The armed services also benefit from civilian biodefense, which adds some diversity and competition to the marketplace of ideas, along with more science and technology. By reducing the damage that biological weapons might cause, investments in biodefense may also reduce the probability that these weapons will be used in the future. Fortunately, their use has been rare to date. But "luck is not a strategy," as the saying goes, and the danger remains that misunderstanding military biodefense increases the risk to US soldiers, sailors, marines, and airmen, as well as their families and allies. After all, in "the twenty-first century," as Gregory Koblentz contends, "at a time when the United States enjoys overwhelming conventional military superiority, biological weapons may be one of the more attractive means of waging asymmetric warfare."[10]

Beyond Biodefense

My argument about the military's dominant frame and stereotypes helps explain puzzles beyond biodefense. I have already discussed the neglect of nonkinetic capabilities such as chemical defense, predicting nuclear fire damage, and counterinsurgency. But consider explosive mines. James Q. Wilson recalls that "in 1987 the navy began escorting oil tankers in the Persian Gulf to protect them against Iranian attacks," and "it discovered to its embarrassment that it did not have a sufficient fleet of minesweepers to protect the convoys from the ancient mines put in the sea lanes by the pathetically small Iranian Navy."[11] Likewise, Carl Builder asks, "Why was the Navy ready to clear the skies of the Persian Gulf, yet surprised by the mines laid under it?"[12] The answer, according to both Builder and Wilson, is the low status of this mission. Mines are "stepchildren that have still not found the mainstream of the armed services despite their obvious potential," and, because of the Navy's institutional personality, Builder argues that "playing around with mines—sowing them or sweeping them—is simply not the kind of business with which the Navy likes to be associated."[13]

Since mines are explosive devices, their mechanism of damage is consistent with the kinetic frame. This frame is multidimensional, however, and the timing of mine warfare is a poor fit because the damage that these weapons cause is delayed and usually occurs long after their point of release (hours or days, if not longer). As a result, the low status of this mission is consistent with the notion that mines fall—in part—outside of the military's dominant frame. Similar logic might also help explain why US forces were initially unprepared for the improvised explosive devices (IEDs) that caused the majority of US casualties in Iraq and Afghanistan. IEDs use conventional ordinance such as artillery shells to generate an explosive blast, which is consistent with the kinetic frame. But, like mines, IEDs are often put in position long before they are intended to detonate. While many of the problems caused by IEDs were foreseeable, and some of the solutions are familiar (such as ceramic inserts for ballistic vests and armored vehicles with V-shaped hulls), the US military still struggled to acquire and deploy appropriate countermeasures in time.[14]

Similarly, the timing and mechanisms of damage that define the kinetic frame help explain the military's tepid response to "enhanced radiation weapons," that is, the neutron bomb. As Matthew Evangelista asks, "Why was a weapon that was invented in 1958 not produced until the late 1970s?"[15] He finds that "this time lapse was due mainly to the difficulty the ERW's proponents had in gaining support for the weapon within the armed services."[16] Given their kinetic frame, we can understand at least one reason why. The neutron bomb inflicts damage through radiation: a mechanism that leaves physical infrastructure unharmed and yet, depending on the dose, may take minutes to incapacitate people and hours, days, or weeks longer to kill them.[17]

Samuel Cohen famously argued that "the neutron bomb has to be the most moral weapon ever invented." Be that as it may, the Air Force declined this weapon first, followed by the Navy and Army, with the Army only reluctantly reversing its position and adopting the neutron bomb after Congress cancelled all of its other nuclear artillery.[18] But "the Lance neutron warhead was an absolute abomination," according to Cohen:

> If used the way the Army wanted to use it, bursting it close to the ground to make sure there would be a lot of blast (which military folks instinctively trust) besides a lot of radiation (which military folks and civilians who don't like neutron bombs, or know anything about them for that matter, instinctively distrust), it would have caused urban devastation on the scale of the Hiroshima bomb. The artillery warhead was far more reasonable and if properly burst, at an altitude of two or three thousand feet, could have drastically reduced blast damage at the surface. . . . However, like Lance, it was meant to be burst close to the ground.[19]

[133]

In other words, the Army wanted to use these warheads for their explosive blast (a byproduct of the weapon rather than its primary mechanism of damage), which is very difficult to understand without the kinetic frame.

We can therefore place radiation weapons and mines along the two dimensions that define the kinetic frame (see fig. C.1), along with biological weapons and the other examples described earlier. As drawn here, projectiles and explosives define the intersection of timing and mechanisms of damage. The closer that other weapons are to this origin, the more that they conform to the kinetic ideal and, thus, the more likely they are to fall inside this frame (the inside/outside distinction being a matter of degree). In contrast, biological weapons are distant along the diagonal, and so they are doubly disadvantaged by this particular approach to problem solving, as we have seen.

A skeptic could contest the position of different technologies inside each quadrant in figure C.1, but my overarching argument still stands. This schematic also illustrates how organizational frame theory can be reconciled with realism and bureaucratic interests. Threats and interests are viable explanations for research, development, acquisition, and doctrine inside the military's frame of reference (i.e., the lower-left

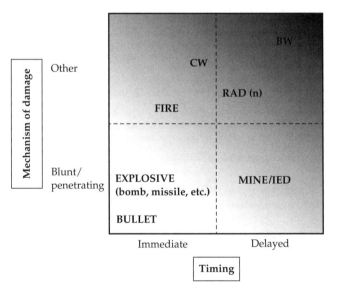

FIGURE C.1. Different kinds of weapons in relation to the interior (core = white) and exterior (periphery = grey) of the kinetic frame.

[134]

quadrant), as demonstrated by the established literature on kinetic weapons and delivery systems such as missiles, submarines, and aircraft. Ideational factors are still at work here, but they are less apparent because these cases are overdetermined. Outside of the kinetic frame, however, the US military might behave contrary to both the threat environment and its own bureaucratic interests, since this frame and the stereotypes associated with it can precondition how the armed services interpret threats and interests in the first place.

A Deviant Case? Implications for Cybersecurity

A skeptic could also claim that military operations in cyberspace are inconsistent with my argument. Maybe cybersecurity will prove to be a deviant case. In many ways, it is a broader and more complicated issue than radiation weapons, mines, or even BW. Yet preliminary evidence suggests that the military's approach to cyberspace is also enabled and constrained by its kinetic frame and nonkinetic stereotypes. If true, then this case is not as deviant as it might initially appear, which in turn points to some troubling signs for the future.

Computer networks are now popular topics at the DoD, as they are in countless other organizations. So it is commonplace to hear that cyber war, cyber espionage, cyber terrorism, and cyber crime threaten everything from military systems and critical infrastructure to financial services and personal privacy.[20] Some of this is hype, but the range of potential targets highlights how ubiquitous information technology has become. Although the military initially focused on using computers for kinetic applications such as ballistics and precision guidance, it is evident that the armed services and society at large have since come to use this technology to solve countless nonkinetic problems as well.

Therein lies the rub, however, since addressing cyberspace in its own right—rather than as merely an enabler of kinetic warfare—requires different assumptions and heuristics. Moreover, consistent with my argument, the military has struggled to find the right words. "In contrast to the case of nuclear and other types of kinetic weapons," several commentators observe that "there are no commonly agreed-upon metrics for reporting the yields of a cyber weapon."[21] Language that relates cyber effects to explosive yields may help link these weapons or tools to the kinetic frame, but then "yield" might be a poor metaphor (just as "kiloton" does not work for BW). According to Martin Libicki, "other misleading metaphors come from ground warfare," and, alongside the military's attempts to relate cyber to concepts such as "firepower" and "maneuver," it also uses terminology with the hallmark inaccuracies of stereotypes from outside its dominant frame.[22] For instance, "cyberspace consists of multiple media," but, for many years, "the concept of information warfare created a false unity binding diverse activities such as cyberspace operations on the one hand and psychological operations on the other. Fruitless hours were spent developing a comprehensive theory covering this agglomeration," just as I argue that decades were wasted on conflated stereotypes like CBW.[23]

Plus, as this language indicates, the military has struggled with the practice of cybersecurity on more than one occasion. Although the DoD established a unified Cyber Command in 2009, threats emanating from the Internet were well-documented by the 1980s—at which time it was doubtful that the military understood the problems and solutions at hand.[24] The Defense Information Systems Agency estimated that 65 percent of attacks were successful in the early 1990s, and, even after the Air Force Information Warfare Center was activated in 1993, an attack on Rome Laboratory (the "Air Force's premier command and control research facility") still seized control of the computer system, stole critical information, compromised other facilities, and remained undetected for several days.[25] When considered in conjunction with subsequent attacks and intrusions such as Solar Sunrise, Moonlight Maze, and Titan Rain, as well as red team exercises such as Eligible Receiver, the history calls into question whether military investment in cybersecurity has really been proportional to the threat.[26]

It remains to be seen how Cyber Command will affect research, development, acquisition, and doctrine in the future. Since Cyber Command is run by the director of the National Security Agency and located at Fort Meade, its dominant frame and stereotypes may resemble those of an intelligence collection agency more than the DoD. Nevertheless, organizational frame theory still suggests some cause for concern. In particular, the military might focus on cyber attacks with immediate or physical effects—consistent with the temporal and damage dimensions of its kinetic frame—but neglect those that involve delay (e.g., backdoors, logic bombs, and malicious hardware) or different mechanisms of damage (e.g., theft or corruption of information). Furthermore, my argument about the kinetic frame is not inextricably linked to an offensive bias, but these ideas are sufficiently compatible to reinforce each other, as seen in the emphasis on counterforce over "passive defense" in the doctrine described in chapter 3. This might not bode well for US cyber defense, especially if the furor over the United States using offensive weapons like Stuxnet—notable for the physical damage it reportedly caused to the centrifuges that Iran uses for uranium enrichment—is a sign of things to come.

Based on her study of nuclear fire damage, Lynn Eden reaches the paradoxical conclusion that "organizations should think about what they are not thinking about—a kind of organizational walking and chewing gum at the same time."[27] The same logic applies to a wide variety of issues, ranging from cybersecurity to biodefense. Perhaps more important, using the concept of stereotypes, we now know what "not thinking" may look like. We can therefore anticipate where organizations are likely to stumble or choke.

This could be valuable information. By signaling error, stereotypes can serve as a useful signpost for where change is needed, ideally providing organizations with the opportunity to take corrective action before disaster, defeat, or disappointment. Even if stereotypes cannot be eliminated, they may be more malleable than an organization's dominant frame. The military's kinetic frame is unlikely to change much, for example, but its nonkinetic stereotypes might, and stereotypes can be improved by increasing their specificity or precision. As a start, this means resisting the siren song of simplicity or habit by differentiating between categories rather than conflating them.[28] Biological weapons differ from chemical weapons; the mass fires caused by nuclear weapons differ from line or forest fires; cybersecurity differs from psychological operations; counterinsurgency differs from peacekeeping; and the list goes on. Sometimes it might be advantageous to further disaggregate these categories; for instance, instead of referring to BW, distinguishing bacteria and viruses from biological toxins. But wherever these lines are redrawn, they should be subject to critical review and revision. An organization that revisits and refines the language and practices it uses to solve problems outside of its dominant frame is more likely to learn and less likely to be defeated by its own stereotypes.[29]

Practical steps include writing military tactics, techniques, and procedures that only refer to a single or more specific category of threat. The current practice, which purports to address different threats under separate sections or chapters in the same document, does not work: the overarching stereotypes drown out the differences and mask discrepancies buried in the body text. Though still the exception to this rule, Army and joint doctrine that addresses biodefense on its own—with little reference to nonkinetic stereotypes—is much more credible.[30] Likewise, if the Air Force actually institutionalizes a Counter-Biological Warfare Concept of Operations without referring to CBW, NBC, CBRN, and the like, then this change will help break these stereotypes and, with them, the lack of learning that has plagued military biodefense for so long.[31]

[137]

Similarly, new organizations such as the DHS should avoid adopting the military's old stereotypes and its habit of deferring to chemical or nuclear expertise for biodefense. The DHS, HHS, and other organizations should also view an "all hazards" approach to planning, preparation, and response with some skepticism.[32] Granted, there are generic principles for emergency management, and, when thoughtful policies for different events overlap, these synergies should be recognized to increase efficiency. But it is dangerous to start with the assumption that disparate phenomena—ranging from disease outbreaks and nuclear accidents to improvised explosives, oil spills, wildfires, and cyber attacks—all share a family resemblance or essential attributes. That is what the military assumed about chemical and biological weapons, among others, and the resulting stereotypes truncated learning and perpetuated error.

Despite their telltale errors, eliminating or improving organizational stereotypes is easier said than done. Organizations are not alone in this regard. Individuals also cling to bad ideas, as do states if not society at large. But unlike states or societies, most organizations are sufficiently small and homogeneous for their stereotypes to remain relatively uncontested inside the institution. Recognizing these bad ideas for what they are means to contest them, however, which is all the more challenging because it requires understanding and admitting—or at least entertaining—the possibility of institutionalized error. This challenge is one reason why organizational change is notoriously difficult (a prominent theme in the study of military innovation, as well as political science, sociology, history, business administration, and public policy).

Yet the necessity for change, albeit difficult, remains. Organizational change is vitally important because, far more than is the case with lone individuals, organizations like the US military are powerful enough for their stereotypes to have significant and deleterious effects on national security. It is hard to overstate how much we depend on our organizations for modern society to function. This makes them a critical locus of influence for good and bad ideas alike. Moreover, the security challenges we face are increasingly complex, as are the science and technology we use. We therefore need military and civilian organizations that can comprehend this complexity and respond accordingly.

Notes

AMERICAN BIODEFENSE, FROM BOSTON TO BAGHDAD

1. Ann M. Becker, "Smallpox in Washington's Army: Strategic Implications of the Disease During the American Revolutionary War," *Journal of Military History* 68 (April 2004): 381–430, 419. "British officers had already demonstrated their willingness to use biological warfare in 1763," when they tried to spread smallpox among Native Americans shortly after the French and Indian War. Elizabeth A. Fenn, *Pox Americana: The Great Smallpox Epidemic of 1775–82* (New York: Hill and Wang, 2001), 88.

2. Judith Miller, Stephen Engelberg, and William Broad, *Germs: Biological Weapons and America's Secret War* (New York: Simon & Schuster, 2001), 105, 112, 116.

3. "US Forces Are Not Adequately Equipped to Detect All Threats" (Washington, DC: GAO, 1993), 1.

4. Statement by Powell to the House of Representatives, Committee on Armed Services, Hearing on National Defense Authorization Act FY 1994, 30 March 1993. Quoted in Graham S. Pearson, "The Essentials of Biological Threat Assessment," in Biological Warfare: Modern Offense and Defense, ed. Raymond A. Zilinskas (Boulder: Lynne Rienner Publishers, 2000), 60.

5. Statement by Zinni to the House of Representatives, Military Personnel Subcommittee, Committee on Armed Services, on the Department of Defense Anthrax Vaccine Immunization Program, 30 September 1999.

6. Frank L. Smith III, "A Casualty of Kinetic Warfare: Military Research, Development, and Acquisition for Biodefense," *Security Studies* 20, no. 4 (2011): 663–96.

7. For example, see Sonia Ben Ouagrham-Gormley, "Barriers to Bioweapons: Intangible Obstacles to Proliferation," *International Security* 36, no. 4 (2012): 80–114; John Ellis Van Courtland Moon, "The US Biological Weapons Program," in *Deadly Cultures: Biological Weapons Since 1945*, ed. Mark Wheelis, Lajos Rozsa, and Malcolm Dando (Cambridge: Harvard University Press, 2006); Jeanne Guillemin, *Biological Weapons: From the Invention of State-Sponsored Programs to Contemporary Bioterrorism* (New York: Columbia University Press, 2005); Simon M. Whitby, *Biological Warfare against Crops* (New York: Palgrave, 2002); and Ed Regis, *The Biology of Doom: The History of America's Secret Germ Warfare Project* (New York: Henry Holt and Company, 1999).

8. See LaDoris Hazzard Cordell, "Black Immigration: Disavowing the Stereotype of the Shiftless Negro," *Judges Journal* 25, no. 19 (Spring 1986); Thomas F. Schneider, ed., *Huns vs. Corned Beef: Representations of the Other in American and German Literature and*

Film on World War I (Gottingen: V&R Unipress, 2007); Gregg Easterbrook, "Term Limits: The Meaninglessness of 'WMD,'" *New Republic*, 7 October 2002; and Christian Enemark, "Farewell to WMD: The Language and Science of Mass Destruction," *Contemporary Security Policy* 32, no. 2 (2011). My use of the concept of stereotypes is related to the metonym, as described in Ido Oren and Ty Solomon, "WMD: The Career of a Concept," *New Political Science* 35, no. 1 (2013): 109–135. However, stereotypes offer additional analytical leverage because they are defined by their inaccuracies; as a result, this concept can inform more concise and often counterintuitive predictions about the consequences of using such language.

9. For example, see Robert J. Art, *The TFX Decision: McNamara and the Military* (Boston: Little, Brown & Co., 1968); Michael H. Armacost, *The Politics of Weapons Innovation: The Thor-Jupiter Controversy* (New York: Columbia University Press, 1969); Harvey M. Sapolsky, *The Polaris System Development: Bureaucratic and Programmatic Success in Government* (Cambridge: Harvard University Press, 1972); Ted Greenwood, *Making the MIRV: A Study of Defense Decision Making* (Lanham, MD: University Press of America, 1975); Michael E. Brown, *Flying Blind: The Politics of the US Strategic Bomber Program* (Ithaca: Cornell University Press, 1992); and Theo Farrell, *Weapons without a Cause: The Politics of Weapons Acquisition in the United States* (New York: St. Martin's Press, 1997).

10. Ken Alibek and Stephen Handelman, *Biohazard* (New York: Dell, 1999), 281. For instance, BW delivery systems do not need to be complex, as illustrated by the envelopes used for the 2001 anthrax letters.

11. Just because kinetic weapons can kill quickly does not mean that they do. Casualties exceed fatalities in war because the wounded outnumber the dead, regardless of the weaponry. In addition, blast and bullet wounds take time to heal, and even the fatal injuries that they inflict do not always mean a fast death. But, lethal or not, the physical trauma is more readily apparent.

12. For the Australia Group's Core List, see http://www.australiagroup.net/en/biological_agents.html. For the Federal Select Agent program list, see http://www.selectagents.gov/Select%20Agents%20and%20Toxins%20List.html.

13. Small samples of bacteria and viruses can also be used to grow more pathogens, potentially providing a perpetual supply for repeat attacks. See the concept of "reload" in Richard Danzig, *Catastrophic Bioterrorism: What Is to Be Done?* (Washington, DC: Center for Technology and National Security Policy, 2003).

14. Brian G. Chow et al., *Air Force Operations in a Chemical and Biological Environment* (Santa Monica, CA: RAND, 1998), viii; Office of Technology Assessment, US Congress, *Proliferation of Weapons of Mass Destruction: Assessing the Risks* (Washington, DC: US Government Printing Office, 1993), 53–54.

15. Even chlorine—an element that has been used as a chemical weapon—is rarely free in nature because it is highly reactive.

16. These differences were apparent at the dawn of the nuclear era. See George W. Merck, *Biological Warfare: Report to the Secretary of War*, 13-II, folder 2, American Society for Microbiology Archives, 3 January 1946, 8; Theodor Rosebury, *Peace or Pestilence: Biological Warfare and How to Avoid It* (New York: Whittlesey House, 1949), 98.

17. Gerald R. Fink et al., *Biotechnology Research in an Age of Terrorism*, ed. Nation Research Council (Washington, DC: National Academies Press, 2004), 23.

1. Science and Technology for National Security

1. Max Boot, "The New American Way of War," *Foreign Affairs* 82, no. 4 (2003): 41–56; Thomas G. Mahnken, *Technology and the American Way of War since 1945* (New York: Columbia University Press, 2008).

2. Among other realists, see Kenneth N. Waltz, *Theory of International Politics* (Reading: MA: Addison-Wesley, 1979); John J. Mearsheimer, *The Tragedy of Great Power Politics* (New York: W. W. Norton, 2001); Charles L. Glaser, *Rational Theory of International Politics: The Logic of Competition and Cooperation* (Princeton: Princeton University Press, 2010).

3. On this commitment problem, see James D. Fearon, "Rationalist Explanations for War," *International Organization* 49, no. 3 (1995): 379–414.

4. Robert Jervis, "Cooperation under the Security Dilemma," *World Politics* 30, no. 2 (1978): 169. Granted, "Jervis did not explicitly frame his analysis in terms of realist theory," but he relies on the same assumptions and most subsequent work about realism refers to this concept. Charles L. Glaser, "The Security Dilemma Revisited," *World Politics* 50, no. 1 (1997): 188. For instance, in addition to being closely associated with defensive realism, "the 'security dilemma,'" according to Mearsheimer, "reflects the basic logic of offensive realism." Mearsheimer, *Tragedy of Great Power Politics*, 35.

5. Although Waltz claims that realism is not foreign policy, realism has clear implications for how individual states should behave. On this debate, see Waltz, *Theory of International Politics*, 121, and "International Politics Is Not Foreign Policy," *Security Studies* 6, no. 1 (1996): 54–57 versus Colin Elman, "Horses for Courses: Why Not Neorealist Theories of Foreign Policy?," *Security Studies* 6, no. 1 (1996): 7–51, and James D. Fearon, "Domestic Politics, Foreign Policy, and Theories of International Relations," *Annual Review of Political Science* 1 (1998): 289–313. Examples of realism applied to foreign policy include Glaser, *Rational Theory of International Politics*, 26; Mearsheimer, *Tragedy of Great Power Politics*, 422; Stephen M. Walt, *The Origins of Alliances* (Ithaca: Cornell University Press, 1987); and Barry R. Posen, *The Sources of Military Doctrine* (Ithaca: Cornell University Press, 1984).

6. Offensive and defensive variants of realism disagree on whether or not rationally increasing security is tantamount to maximizing power and, likewise, over the salience of absolute versus relative gains.

7. Posen, *Sources of Military Doctrine*, 51–54, 74–79. Note that Posen includes organizational dynamics (e.g., the military parochialism that necessitates civilian intervention) in the version of realism (i.e., "balance of power theory") that he claims to test against "organizational theory." This stacks the deck in favor of realism.

8. Michael E. Brown, *Flying Blind: The Politics of the US Strategic Bomber Program* (Ithaca: Cornell University Press, 1992).

9. Ibid., 5, 313; Posen, *Sources of Military Doctrine*, 16–18, 62.

10. Eugene Gholz and Harvey M. Sapolsky, "Restructuring the US Defense Industry," *International Security* 24, no. 3 (1999).

11. For one such critique, see Matthew Evangelista, *Innovation and the Arms Race* (Ithaca: Cornell University Press, 1988).

12. Among others, see Amy L. Stuart and Dean A. Wilkening, "Degradation of Biological Weapons Agents in the Environment: Implications for Terrorism Response," *Environmental Science and Technology* 39, no. 8 (2005): 2736–43.

13. See Interdepartmental Political-Military Group, "US Policy on Chemical and Biological Warfare and Agents," report to the National Security Council in response to NSSM 59, 10 November 1969, National Security Archive, George Washington University, http://www2.gwu.edu/~nsarchiv/NSAEBB/NSAEBB58/RNCBW6a.pdf, 24. Likewise, "these weaponized agents, although never used on the battlefield, were tested in large-scale field tests and achieved area coverages predicted by mathematical models." William C. Patrick III, "Biological Warfare: An Overview," in *Director's Series on Proliferation*, ed. Kathleen C. Bailey (Livermore, CA: Lawrence Livermore National Laboratory, 1994), 1. These models included Kenneth L. Calder, "Mathematical Models for Dosage and Casualty Coverage Resulting from Single Point and Line Source Releases of Aerosol near Ground Level," *BWL Technical Study 3* (Fort Detrick, MD: Office of the Deputy Commander for Scientific Activities, 1957).

14. W. Seth Carus, "'The Poor Man's Atomic Bomb'? Biological Weapons in the Middle East" (Washington, DC: Washington Institute for Near East Policy, 1991); Randall J. Larsen and Robert P. Kadlec, *Biological Warfare: A Post Cold War Threat to America's Strategic Mobility Forces* (Pittsburgh: Matthew B. Ridgway Center for International Security Studies, University of Pittsburgh, 1995); Brad Roberts, "Between Panic and Complacency: Calibrating the Chemical and Biological Warfare Problem," in *The Niche Threat: Deterring the Use of Chemical and Biological Weapons*, ed. Stuart E. Johnson (Washington, DC: National Defense University Press, 1997); Richard A. Falkenrath, Robert D. Newman, and Bradley A. Thayer, *America's Achilles' Heel: Nuclear, Biological, and Chemical Terrorism and Covert Attack* (Cambridge: MIT Press, 1998); Gregory D. Koblentz, *Living Weapons: Biological Warfare and International Security* (Ithaca: Cornell University Press, 2009), 34.

15. With contagious or persistent pathogens, secondary exposure can make even a single attack a continuous problem rather than a discrete event, so they can adversely affect military operations for days, weeks, or longer. The 2001 anthrax letters suggest that these risks might be significant: the death of one Connecticut woman was probably caused by indirect exposure, and experiments conducted in contaminated environments demonstrated the reaerosolization of viable spores. Lydia A. Barakat et al., "Fatal Inhalational Anthrax in a 94-Year-Old Connecticut Woman," *JAMA* 287, no. 7 (2002): 863–68; Christopher P. Weis et al., "Secondary Aerosolization of Viable *Bacillus anthracis* Spores in a Contaminated US Senate Office," *JAMA* 288, no. 22 (2002): 2853–58; Julie A. Layshock et al., "Reaerosolization of *Bacillus spp.* in Outdoor Environments: A Review of the Experimental Literature," *Biosecurity and Bioterrorism: Biodefense Strategy, Practice, and Science* 10, no. 3 (2012): 299–303.

16. Koblentz, *Living Weapons*, 35. Also see Robert A. Pape, *Bombing to Win* (Ithaca: Cornell University Press, 1996), 72. For BW, the blitzkrieg analogy is reinforced by corresponding requirements for defense because, in both cases, "the defender must understand the nature of the threat and how to deal with it, must have the organizational capacity for doing so, and must have the soldiers capable of implementing the solution." John J. Mearsheimer, *Conventional Deterrence* (Ithaca: Cornell University Press, 1983), 46.

17. On antiaccess threats, see Eric V. Larson et al., *Assuring Access in Key Strategic Regions: Toward a Long-Term Strategy* (Santa Monica, CA: RAND, 2004).

18. Susan B. Martin, "The Role of Biological Weapons in International Politics: The Real Military Revolution," *Journal of Strategic Studies* 25, no. 1 (2002): 63–98, 76.

19. Koblentz, *Living Weapons*, 41.

20. Whether such coercion actually works is another question. See Pape, *Bombing to Win*, chap. 4.

21. Among others, see Anne L. Clunan, Peter R. Lavoy, and Susan B. Martin, *Terrorism, War, or Disease? Unraveling the Use of Biological Weapons* (Stanford: Stanford University Press, 2008).

22. Although the 1991 Gulf War is often cited to suggest that nuclear threats prevent the use of BW, the evidence is weak. Scott D. Sagan, "The Commitment Trap: Why the United States Should Not Use Nuclear Threats to Deter Biological and Chemical Weapons Attacks," *International Security* 24, no. 4 (2000): 85–115. Furthermore, if nuclear deterrence has failed, then the marginal utility of a nuclear response is debatable in instances where the US enjoys conventional superiority.

23. For similar logic applied to different weapons, see Nina Tannenwald, "The Nuclear Taboo: The United States and the Normative Basis of Nuclear Non-Use," *International Organization* 53, no. 3 (1999): 433–68; and Richard M. Price, *The Chemical Weapons Taboo* (Ithaca: Cornell University Press, 1997). On the rare use of BW, see Milton Leitenberg, "Assessing the Biological Weapons and Bioterrorism Threat" (Carlisle, PA: Strategic Studies Institute, US Army War College, 2005).

24. Leonard A. Cole, "The Poison Weapons Taboo: Biology, Culture, and Policy," *Politics and the Life Sciences* 17, no. 2 (1998): 119–32, 130.

25. Price, *Chemical Weapons Taboo*, 21.

26. Ken Alibek and Stephen Handelman, *Biohazard* (New York: Dell, 1999), 33–37; Igor V. Domaradskij and Wendy Orent, *Biowarrior: Inside the Soviet/Russian Biological War Machine* (Amherst, NY: Prometheus Books, 2003), 126–32; Milton Leitenberg and Raymond A. Zilinskas, *The Soviet Biological Weapons Program: A History* (Cambridge: Harvard University Press, 2012), 36.

27. Alibek and Handelman, *Biohazard*, 41, 43, 293. On Soviet spending and Gorbachev's knowledge of the BW program, also see David E. Hoffman, *The Dead Hand: The Untold Story of the Cold War Arms Race and its Dangerous Legacy* (New York: Doubleday, 2009), 333, 350.

28. Jonathan B. Tucker, "Biological Weapons in the Former Soviet Union: An Interview with Dr. Kenneth Alibek," *Nonproliferation Review* (Spring-Summer 1999), 2–3; Alibek and Handelman, *Biohazard*, 5; Christopher J. Davis, "Nuclear Blindness: An Overview of the Biological Weapons Programs of the Former Soviet Union and Iraq," *Emerging Infectious Diseases* 5, no. 4 (1999): 509–12, 511; Tom Mangold and Jeff Goldberg, *Plague Wars: The Terrifying Reality of Biological Warfare* (New York: St. Martin's Press, 1999), 83–84. In contrast, for a critical account that rejects most claims regarding these delivery systems, see Leitenberg and Zilinskas, *Soviet Biological Weapons Program*, 309–22.

29. See Jeanne Guillemin, *Biological Weapons: From the Invention of State-Sponsored Programs to Contemporary Bioterrorism* (New York: Columbia University Press, 2005), 134–35; Koblentz, *Living Weapons*, 146–47.

30. CIA, *The Soviet BW Program: Scientific Intelligence Research Aid*, OSI-RA/61-3, Office of Science Intelligence, 24 April 1961, http://www.foia.cia.gov/sites/default/files/document_conversions/89801/DOC_0000250910.pdf, 7. For reconnaissance photographs of Vozrozhdeniya Island from as early as 1957, see http://www.globalsecurity.org/wmd/world/russia/vozrozhdenly.htm.

31. *National Intelligence Estimate: Soviet Capabilities and Intentions with Respect to Biological Warfare*, 11-6-64, 26 August 1964, http://www.foia.cia.gov/sites/default/

files/document_conversions/89801/DOC_0000283835.pdf; Wilton E. Lexow and Julian Hoptman, "The Enigma of Soviet BW," (CIA) *Studies in Intelligence* 9 (Spring 1965); Mangold and Goldberg, *Plague Wars*, 63–65.

32. Experts in the intelligence community did not believe the Soviet cover story that deaths at Sverdlovsk were caused by contaminated meat, even though several arms control advocates inadvertently supported this disinformation campaign. Hoffman, *Dead Hand*, 307; DIA, *Soviet Biological Warfare Threat*, DST-1610F-057-86, 1986, National Security Archives, George Washington University, http://www2.gwu.edu/~nsarchiv/NSAEBB/NSAEBB61/Sverd26.pdf.

33. For details, see Koblentz, *Living Weapons*, 145–69, 196.

34. Clifford Geertz, *The Interpretation of Cultures* (New York: Basic Books, 1973), 20. My thanks to Lynn Eden for this quote.

35. Glaser, *Rational Theory of International Politics*, 30.

36. Koblentz, *Living Weapons*, 169. This lack of investment suggests that influential ideas inside the US intelligence community might mirror the military's kinetic frame. Better intelligence could have been collected: the sheer size of the Soviet BW program suggests that several targets of opportunity were missed. For example, it is reasonable to suspect that collection near Vozrozhdeniye Island might have connected the dots between this known test site and an otherwise inexplicable outbreak of smallpox nearby in 1971. See Jonathan B. Tucker and Raymond A. Zilinskas, eds., *The 1971 Smallpox Epidemic in Aralsk, Kazakhstan, and the Soviet Biological Warfare Program*, Occasional paper 9 (Monterey, CA: Center for Nonproliferation Studies, Monterey Institute of International Studies, 2002).

37. CIA, "Iraq's Biological Warfare Program," August 1990, GulfLINK, http://www.gulflink.osd.mil/declassdocs/cia/19960517/cia_65171_65171_01.html. Also Armed Forces Medical Intelligence Center, "Iraq Biological Warfare Threat," 22 October 1990, GulfLINK, http://www.gulflink.osd.mil/declassdocs/dia/19961031/961031_950901_0408pgf_90.html. Despite accurately anticipating these capabilities and intentions, the US failed to identify Iraq's BW production facilities. Koblentz, *Living Weapons*, 169–76.

38. UN, "UNSCOM Report to Security Council," S/1995/864, 11 October 1995; Raymond A. Zilinskas, "Iraq's Biological Warfare Program: The Past as Future?," in *Biological Weapons: Limiting the Threat*, ed. Joshua Lederberg (Cambridge: MIT Press, 1999).

39. Secretary of State Colin Powell, Speech to the United Nations Security Council, 5 February 2003, Washington Post, http://www.washingtonpost.com/wp-srv/nation/transcripts/powelltext_020503.html.

40. US Department of State, *Adherence to and Compliance with Arms Control, Nonproliferation and Disarmament Agreements and Commitments*, August 2005, http://www.state.gov/documents/organization/52113.pdf.

41. Amy Smithson and Leslie-Anne Levy, *Ataxia: The Chemical and Biological Terrorism Threat and the US Response*, Stimson Report 35 (Washington, DC: Henry L. Stimson Center, 2000), 78; W. Seth Carus, *Bioterrorism and Biocrimes: The Illicit Use of Biological Agents since 1900*, working paper (Washington, DC: Center for Counterproliferation Research, National Defense University, 2001), 50; Richard Danzig et al., *Aum Shinrikyo: Insights into How Terrorists Develop Biological and Chemical Weapons* (Washington, DC: Center for a New American Security, 2011).

42. Thomas H. Kean et al., *The 9/11 Commission Report*, 2004, http://www.9-11commission.gov/report/911Report.pdf, 151.

43. The fact that "only" five people died was in part because these letters explicitly warned about "this anthrax" or said "take penacilin [sic] now." Covert use of the same agent could have caused mass casualties.

44. Kathleen M. Vogel, *Phantom Menace or Looming Danger? A New Framework for Assessing Bioweapons Threats* (Baltimore: Johns Hopkins University Press, 2013), 9; similarly, see Sonia Ben Ouagrham-Gormley, "Barriers to Bioweapons: Intangible Obstacles to Proliferation," *International Security* 36, no. 4 (2012).

45. On BACUS (Biotechnology Activity Characterization by Unconventional Signatures), see Judith Miller, Stephen Engelberg, and William Broad, *Germs: Biological Weapons and America's Secret War* (New York: Simon & Schuster, 2001), 297–98.

46. Leitenberg, "Assessing the Biological Weapons and Bioterrorism Threat," 54.

47. The politics and interpretation of BACUS aside, here the critical question is: Can an individual or small group build BW? The answer is probably yes.

48. Stephen I. Schwartz, *Atomic Audit: The Cost and Consequences of US Nuclear Weapons Since 1940* (Washington, DC: Brookings Institution Press, 1998). Another standard for judging military investment is effectiveness—at least as much as efficiency—given the high costs of failure when national security is involved. This is one reason why the US military can appear insensitive to price and willing to pay a premium for performance. Among others, see Jacques S. Gansler, *The Defense Industry* (Cambridge: MIT Press, 1980); John A. Alic et al., *Beyond Spinoff: Military and Commercial Technologies in a Changing World* (Boston: Harvard Business School Press, 1992).

49. Graham Allison, *Essence of Decision: Explaining the Cuban Missile Crisis*, 1st ed. (Boston: Little, Brown, 1971), 164. This perspective is similar to theories that "view the organization as a coalition." Richard M. Cyert and James G. March, *A Behavioral Theory of the Firm* (Englewood Cliffs, NJ: Prentice-Hall, 1963), 27.

50. Robert J. Art, "Bureaucratic Politics and American Foreign Policy: A Critique," *Policy Sciences* 4 (1973): 467–90, 486. For a similar critique, see Jonathan Bendor and Thomas H. Hammond, "Rethinking Allison's Models," *American Political Science Review* 86, no. 2 (1992): 301–22. Causal ambiguity is common because many references to "bureaucratic politics" describe a collage of different factors and outcomes rather than a coherent or causal theory.

51. This narrow definition is justified by David A. Welch, "The Organizational Process and Bureaucratic Politics Paradigms: Retrospect and Prospect," *International Security* 17, no. 2 (1992): 112–46, 121; Art, "A Critique," 473. For a broader definition, see Edward Rhodes, "Do Bureaucratic Politics Matter? Some Disconfirming Findings from the Case of the US Navy," *World Politics* 47, no. 1 (1994): 1–41.

52. Here "independence" corresponds to what Wilson calls "the external aspect of autonomy." In contrast, the internal aspect of autonomy refers to how bureaucracies use this independence, which Wilson argues is a function of their identity or culture: ideational variables that he cites to criticize the claim that bureaucrats only try to maximize their budget or size. These are related but distinct strands of argument. See James Q. Wilson, *Bureaucracy: What Government Agencies Do and Why They Do it* (New York: Basic Books, 1989), xviii, 180–82. For the sort of size- or budget-maximizing claims that he criticizes, see work by Anthony Downs and William A. Nishanen Jr., among others.

53. Conversely, Posen and Snyder make virtually no mention of identity or culture. Even prestige—an ideational variable—is, for Posen, merely a means for maintaining

independence. Posen, *Sources of Military Doctrine*, 45, 58; Jack Snyder, *The Ideology of the Offensive: Military Decision Making and the Disaster of 1914* (Ithaca: Cornell University Press, 1991), 24.

54. Harvey M. Sapolsky, *The Polaris System Development: Bureaucratic and Programmatic Success in Government* (Cambridge: Harvard University Press, 1972), 14.

55. Ibid., 15, 246; Allison, *Essence of Decision*, 144–45, 168.

56. Eugene Gholz, "The Curtiss-Wright Corporation and Cold War-Era Defense Procurement: A Challenge to Military-Industrial Complex Theory," *Journal of Cold War Studies* 2, no. 1 (2000): 37, 45, 74–75.

57. Michael H. Armacost, *The Politics of Weapons Innovation: The Thor-Jupiter Controversy* (New York: Columbia University Press, 1969), 14.

58. Sapolsky, *Polaris System Development*, 40. Also see Armacost, *Politics of Weapons Innovation*; and Owen R. Cote, Jr., "The Politics of Innovative Military Doctrine: The US Navy and Fleet Ballistic Missiles" (PhD diss., Massachusetts Institute of Technology, 1996). The benefits of "sequential" and thus competitive bomber development are also highlighted by Brown, *Flying Blind*.

59. Wilson, *Bureaucracy*, xix. Studies of military science and technology—particularly those sympathetic to a bureaucratic perspective—often warn against simple explanations. See Ted Greenwood, *Making the MIRV: A Study of Defense Decision Making* (Lanham, MD: University Press of America, 1975), 80–81; Theo Farrell, *Weapons without a Cause: The Politics of Weapons Acquisition in the United States* (New York: St. Martin's Press, 1997), 175; Donald MacKenzie, *Inventing Accuracy: A Historical Sociology of Nuclear Missile Guidance*, 4th ed. (Cambridge: MIT Press, 1990), 3, 399–401; and Graham Spinardi, *From Polaris to Trident: The Development of US Fleet Ballistic Missile Technology* (New York: Cambridge University Press, 1994), 13–14, 180.

60. Brown, *Flying Blind*, 311.

61. Morton H. Halperin, *Bureaucratic Politics and Foreign Policy* (Washington, DC: Brookings Institution, 1974); Carl H. Builder, *The Masks of War: American Military Styles in Strategy and Analysis* (Baltimore: Johns Hopkins University Press, 1989). For one application, see Farrell, *Weapons without a Cause*.

62. Even if we assume that interests in funding and autonomy are one kind of idea, there are other types to consider as well. It is therefore important to distinguish between them and ask what kind of ideational factor best explains key outcomes.

63. Halperin, *Bureaucratic Politics and Foreign Policy*, 30–34, 57.

64. Allison, *Essence of Decision*, 169.

65. A similar concept is organizational identity. "In spite of its widespread usage in organizational studies, however, organizational identity is not consistently defined, theorized, or modeled." Kevin G. Corley et al., "Guiding Organization Identity through Aged Adolescence," *Journal of Management Inquiry* 15, no. 2 (2006): 85–99, 86.

66. Sociological institutionalism is summarized in Paul J. DiMaggio and Walter W. Powell, eds., *The New Institutionalism in Organizational Analysis* (Chicago: University of Chicago Press, 1991). For applications of sociological institutionalism and social constructivism to national security, see, among others, Peter J. Katzenstein, ed. *The Culture of National Security: Norms and Identity in World Politics* (New York: Columbia University Press, 1996). On scientific paradigms and technological frames, see Thomas S. Kuhn, *The Structure of Scientific Revolutions*, 3rd ed. (Chicago: University

of Chicago Press, 1962); and Wiebe E. Bijker, "The Social Construction of Bakelite: Towards a Theory of Invention," in *The Social Construction of Technological Systems,* ed. Wiebe E. Bijker, Thomas P. Hughes, and Trevor J. Pinch (Cambridge: MIT Press, 1987).

67. Similar definitions are provided by Lynn Eden, *Whole World on Fire: Organizations, Knowledge, and Nuclear Weapons Devastation* (Ithaca: Cornell University Press, 2004); Robert M. Entman, "Framing: Toward Clarification of a Fractured Paradigm," *Journal of Communication* 43, no. 4 (1993): 51–58; and Paul Shirvastava and Susan Schneider, "Organizational Frames of Reference," *Human Relations* 37, no. 10 (1984): 795–809.

68. Eden, *Whole World on Fire,* 55. She also argues that knowledge-laden routines are interpretive, not merely procedural, and so they differ from "dumb" standard operating procedures.

69. "The concept of framing provides an operational definition of the notion of *dominant meaning,*" which "consists of the problems, causal, evaluative, and treatment interpretations with the highest probability of being noticed, processed, and accepted by the most people." Entman, "Framing," 56. Therefore, organizational frames are relatively uncontested (especially in a setting like the military) in contrast to the conflict that characterizes bureaucratic competition over turf.

70. Frames of reference are multidimensional, and they may lack clear boundaries, so this inside/outside distinction is a matter of degree. Bijker, "Social Construction of Bakelite," 174.

71. Eden, *Whole World on Fire,* 56. Similarly, see "competency traps" in Barbara Levitt and James G. March, "Organizational Learning," *Annual Review of Sociology* 14 (1988): 319–40.

72. While the notion of stereotypes as collective phenomena is not new, my application of this concept to decision making in otherwise sophisticated organizations is relatively novel. Among other literature reviews, see Charles Stangor and Mark Schaller, "Stereotypes as Individual and Collective Representations," in *Stereotypes and Stereotyping,* ed. C. Neil Macrae, Charles Strangor, and Miles Hewstone (New York: Guilford Press, 1996); and David J. Schneider, *The Psychology of Stereotyping* (New York: Guilford Press, 2004). For another approach to stereotypes as a semantic category, see Kathleen M. Carley and David S. Kaufer, "Semantic Connectivity: An Approach for Analyzing Symbols in Semantic Networks," *Communication Theory* 3, no. 3 (1993): 183–213.

73. For one attempt to impose consistency on inconsistent categories, see W. Seth Carus, *Defining "Weapons of Mass Destruction,"* Occasional paper 4 (Washington DC: National Defense University Press, 2006).

74. Diane Vaughan, *The Challenger Launch Decision: Risk, Technology, Culture, and Deviance at NASA* (Chicago: University of Chicago Press, 1996), 62. Similarly, on the absorption of uncertainty through these categories, see James G. March and Herbert A. Simon, *Organizations,* 2nd ed. (Cambridge: Blackwell, 1993), 186.

75. See Eden, *Whole World on Fire,* 50, 56, along with Karl E. Weick, *Sensemaking in Organizations* (Thousand Oaks, CA: Sage, 1995).

76. For example, Vogel explains how a "biotech revolution frame" contributed to the US intelligence failure that fueled the 2003 Iraq War, that is, the assessment that Iraq had BW when it did not. This particular frame may be better described as a stereotype, however, since the simple and inaccurate ideas that Vogel describes were influential in part because biology was peripheral at the CIA. Only a few intelligence

analysts worked on BW. Those who did were not specialists (the Agency preferred generalists). "There is no evidence that . . . [they] consulted or worked closely with former US and Soviet bioweapons scientists to draw on their specialized weapons know-how." And, when these analysts shared their conclusions with biological experts outside the organization, the experts were "surprised to see what they considered an erroneous depiction of an Iraqi mobile bioweapons capability in the CIA's briefing." Vogel, *Phantom Menace or Looming Danger?*, 178–79, 211. Reliance on other inaccurate stereotypes might help explain why the US intelligence community also failed to accurately estimate the size, scope, and sophistication of the Soviet BW program.

77. Of course, ideas cannot act by themselves—nor can interests, for that matter, or threat perceptions. But the ideas that I describe do work by enabling or constraining the actions of organizations and their members in important ways.

78. If individual cognition does not determine aggregate outcomes, then any given model of individual decision making (e.g., bounded rationality, cybernetics, even "dreaded risks") might support different theories of group behavior. To simplify my analysis, I treat schema as if they are primitive units, thereby bracketing the otherwise infinite regress of analysis into the constituent parts of individual cognition. See Lawrence W. Barsalou, "Frames, Concepts, and Conceptual Fields," in *Frames, Fields, and Contrasts: New Essays in Semantic and Lexical Organization*, ed. Adrienne Lehrer and Eva Feder Kittay (Hillsdale, NJ: Lawrence Erlbaum Associates, 1992), 41; and Paul Di-Maggio, "Culture and Cognition," *Annual Review of Sociology* 23 (1997): 263–87.

79. In order for the meaning of these symbols and practices to be intelligible, they must be shared (at least as a "thinly coherent" network of semiotic relations). As a subset of culture, however, organizational frame theory can posit that some shared assumptions and heuristics are coherent—even dominant—without assuming the same about their cultural context. I also acknowledge the potential for alternatives frames and resistance. For debate on these issues see, among others, William H. Sewell, "The Concept(s) of Culture," in *Beyond the Cultural Turn: New Directions in the Study of Society and Culture*, ed. Victoria E. Bonnell and Lynn Hunt (Berkeley: University of California Press, 1999); and Lisa Wedeen, "Conceptualizing Culture: Possibilities for Political Science," *American Political Science Review* 96, no. 4 (2002): 713–28.

80. Jeffrey W. Legro, "Military Culture and Inadvertent Escalation in World War II," *International Security* 18, no. 4 (1994): 108–42, 116.

81. Elizabeth Kier, *Imagining War: French and British Military Doctrine between the Wars* (Princeton: Princeton University Press, 1997).

82. For example, see Michael C. Desch, "Culture Clash: Assessing the Importance of Ideas in Security Studies," *International Security* 23, no. 1 (1998): 141–70.

83. Martin Van Creveld, *The Transformation of War* (New York: Free Press, 1991), 80–83.

84. Wayne E. Lee, "Mind and Matter—Cultural Analysis in American Military History: A Look at the State of the Field," *Journal of American History* 93, no. 4 (2007): 1116–42, 1123. Also see Russell F. Weigley, *The American Way of War: A History of United States Military Strategy and Policy* (New York: Macmillan, 1973).

85. Robert H. Scales, Jr., *Firepower in Limited War* (Washington, DC: National Defense University Press, 1990), 4.

86. Eden, *Whole World on Fire*, 2, 53.

87. US Army, *Counterinsurgency*, FM 3–24/MCWP 3-33.5 (Washington, DC: Department of the Army, 15 December 2006), ix, 1.27.

88. Andrew F. Krepinevich, *The Army and Vietnam* (Baltimore: Johns Hopkins University Press, 1986); John A. Nagl, *Counterinsurgency Lessons from Malaya and Vietnam: Learning to Eat Soup with a Knife* (Westport, CT: Praeger, 2002). For an alternative explanation that faults democracy rather than the military for this suboptimal strategy, see Jonathan D. Caverley, "The Myth of Military Myopia: Democracy, Small Wars, and Vietnam," *International Security* 34, no. 3 (2009): 119–57.

89. Ironically, by the 1980s, the Soviet Union was bogged down fighting and losing its own counterinsurgency campaign in Afghanistan, further diminishing the conventional threat that the USSR posed to Western Europe.

90. Among others, see Colin Jackson, "From Conservatism to Revolutionary Intoxication: The US Army and the Second Interwar Period," in *US Military Innovation since the Cold War: Creation without Destruction*, ed. Harvey M. Sapolsky, Benjamin H. Friedman, and Brendan Rittenhouse Green (New York: Routledge, 2009); and Fred Kaplan, *The Insurgents: David Petraeus and the Plot to Change the American Way of War* (New York: Simon & Schuster, 2013).

91. Air-Sea Battle Office, "Air-Sea Battle: Service Collaboration to Address Anti-Access & Area Denial Challenges (version 9.0)," May 2013, http://navylive.dodlive.mil/files/2013/06/ASB-26-June-2013.pdf, i; and similarly, Greg Jaffe, "US Model for a Future War Fans Tensions with China and Inside Pentagon," *Washington Post*, 1 August 2012.

92. Robert H. Scales, *Yellow Smoke: The Future of Land Warfare for America's Military* (Lanham, MD: Rowman & Littlefield, 2003), xii.

93. Jackson, "From Conservatism to Revolutionary Intoxication," 48.

94. Kaplan, *Insurgents*, 26, 45. Also see Deborah D. Avant and James H. Lebovic, "US Military Responses to Post-Cold War Missions," in *The Sources of Military Change: Culture, Politics, Technology*, ed. Theo Farrell and Terry Terriff (Boulder, CO: Lynne Rienner, 2002).

95. Stephen P. Rosen, *Winning the Next War: Innovation and the Modern Military* (Ithaca: Cornell University Press, 1991), 7, 21, 104.

96. Herman H. Goldstine, *The Computer: From Pascal to von Neumann* (Princeton: Princeton University Press, 1972).

97. Jack Ward, "An Interview with Walter MacWilliams: Developing the First 'Working' Transistor Application," Transistor Museum, http://www.semiconductormuseum.com/Transistors/BellLabs/OralHistories/MacWilliams/MacWilliams_Page5.htm.

98. Walter H. MacWilliams, "A Transistor Gating Matrix for a Simulated Warfare Computer," *Bell Laboratories Record* 35 (1957): 94.

99. M. M. Irvine, "Early Digital Computers at Bell Telephone Laboratories," *IEEE Annals of the History of Computing* 23, no. 3 (2001): 34, 40.

100. Theo Farrell, "World Culture and Military Power," *Security Studies* 14, no. 3 (2005): 448–88, 448.

101. Matthew R. Smallman-Raynor and Andrew D. Cliff, *War Epidemics: An Historical Geography of Infectious Diseases in Military Conflict and Civil Strife, 1850–2000* (Oxford: Oxford University Press, 2004), 217; K. David Patterson, "Typhus and Its Control in Russia, 1870–1940," *Medical History* 37 (1933): 361–81, 373; Alibek and Handelman, *Biohazard*, 32.

102. Leitenberg and Zilinskas, *Soviet Biological Weapons Program*, 26, 44.

103. However, unlike arguments about the cult of the offensive that privilege bureaucratic interests such as autonomy, an offensive frame hypothesis would highlight shared assumptions and heuristics that privilege attack. Jack Snyder, "Civil-Military Relations and the Cult of the Offensive, 1914 and 1984," *International Security* 9, no. 1 (1984): 108–46; Stephen Van Evera, "The Cult of the Offensive and the Origins of the First World War," *International Security* 9, no. 1 (1984): 58–107.

104. Eden, *Whole World on Fire*, 53.

2. Stereotypical Neglect of Military Research, Development, and Acquisition

1. Jeffery K. Smart, "History of Chemical and Biological Warfare: An American Perspective," in *Medical Aspects of Chemical and Biological Warfare*, ed. Frederick R. Sidell, Ernest T. Takafuji, and David R. Franz (Washington, DC: Office of the Surgeon General, 1997), 28, 32; Leon A. Fox, "Bacterial Warfare: The Use of Biologic Agents in Warfare," *Military Surgeon* 72, no. 3 (1933): 189–207.

2. Sheldon H. Harris, *Factories of Death: Japanese Biological Warfare 1932–45 and the American Cover-Up* (New York: Routledge, 1994), 150, 264.

3. See Olivier Lepick, "French Activities Relating to Biological Warfare, 1919–45," in *Biological and Toxin Weapons: Research, Development and Use from the Middle Ages to 1945*, ed. Erhard Geissler and John Ellis van Courtland Moon, SIPRI Chemical and Biological Warfare Studies (Oxford: Oxford University Press, 1999); and Brian Balmer, *Britain and Biological Warfare: Expert Advice and Science Policy, 1930–65* (New York: Palgrave, 2001). Plus, Germany had used BW against livestock during World War I.

4. Harris, *Factories of Death*, 150; George W. Merck, "Activities of the United States in the Field of Biological Warfare: A Report to the Secretary of War," n.d. draft, RG 165, box 182, Records of the War Department General and Special Staffs, National Archives and Records Administration (hereafter NARA), 4; Sanders Marble, "Brigadier General James Stevens Simmons (1890–1954), Medical Corps, United States Army: A Career in Preventive Medicine," *Journal of Medical Biography* 20 (2012): 3–10, 4.

5. James S. Simmons, Memorandum for Mr. H. H. Bundy. Subject: Comments on Biological Warfare, 18 August 1941, Committees on Biological Warfare, series 1, WBC Committee, National Academies Archive. Also see SGO Liaison Officer, "History of the Relation of the SGO to BW Activities," n.d. draft (ca. 1946), RG 112, box 12, Records of the Office of the Surgeon General (Army), Biological Warfare Specialized Files 1941–47, NARA, 7–11, 69–71. Skepticism about the Bern Report increased with time, and differences of opinion about BW in the surgeon general's office were reported after the fact.

6. Merck, "Report to the Secretary of War," 5–7.

7. Ibid., 8.

8. Ibid., 8–9.

9. SGO Liaison Officer, "History of the Relation of the SGO to BW Activities," 30.

10. Merck, "Report to the Secretary of War," 8. In contrast, according to one biologist, "the idea of using biological agents to kill people represented a complete shift in thinking. But it took me only about twenty-four hours to think my way through

[150]

it. After all, the immorality of war is war itself. . . . Would I rather have a dagger stuck in me, or be hit by a high explosive, or be hit with fire and badly burned, or would I rather have any disease that I could think of. To me it was very simple. I'd rather have any disease. . . . I, in imagination, went into a hospital. You go into an accident ward and everyone is moaning and suffering. They're in pain. You walk through a contagious disease ward. . . . They're weak, they're desperately ill, but they aren't really suffering. . . . So if it's a question of how much you suffer, it is then clear that biological warfare is a more humane weapon than any that we commonly use." Ira L. Baldwin, *My Half Century at the University of Wisconsin*, ed. Donna Taylor Harts-horne, privately published by Ira L. Baldwin, printed by Omnipress, Madison, Wisconsin. Copy located in 13-II BP, folder 8.2, Presidents—Housewright, BW Materials—Ft. Detrick, American Society for Microbiology (hereafter ASM) Archives, 1995, 124. Similarly, see Brian Balmer, "Killing 'Without the Distressing Preliminaries': Scientists' Defence of the British Biological Warfare Programme," *Minerva* 40, no. 1 (2002): 57–75.

11. Merck, "Report to the Secretary of War," 13. At the time, these activities were referred to as "anti-biological warfare." See A. S. Behrman Lt. Col., "Summary of ABW Work and Recommendations for the Manner of Its Continuance," 1944, RG 165, box 182, Records of the War Department General and Special Staffs, NARA; SGO Liaison Officer, "History of the Relation of the SGO to BW Activities," 28.

12. Ira L. Baldwin, "Meeting of the Committee on Biological Warfare in the Pentagon, Room 3E-1060," 13-II, folder 2, ASM Archives, 1951, 11. Merck's letter to this effect, dated 10 December 1942, was preceded by verbal instructions to the chief of the Chemical Warfare Service in late November. Merck, "Report to the Secretary of War," section 1, 1.

13. Merck, "Report to the Secretary of War," 16.

14. Ibid., 19; SGO Liaison Officer, "History of the Relation of the SGO to BW Activities," 54.

15. Secretary of War, Memorandum for the Chief of Staff. Subject: Biological Warfare, 13 January 1944, RG 165, box 182, Records of the War Department General and Special Staffs, NARA, 2 (emphasis added). Also see Maj. Thomas F. M. Scott, Subject: Chronological summary of the assumption of responsibility by the SGO for the medical and defense aspects of BW, 1945, RG 112, box 2, Records of the Office of the Surgeon General (Army), Biological Warfare Specialized Files 1941–47, NARA; N. Paul Hudson, "Report of Activities of Dr. N. Paul Judson, Special Consultant, 22 January 1944 to 30 June 1945 in Connection with the Responsibilities of the Office of the Surgeon General in Defense against Biological Warfare," 1945, RG 112, box 2, Records of the Office of the Surgeon General (Army), Biological Warfare Specialized Files 1941–47, NARA.

16. Merck, "Report to the Secretary of War," 20–21.

17. Frederic J. Brown, *Chemical Warfare: A Study in Restraints*, 2nd ed. (New Brunswick: Transaction, 2006), 19.

18. Leo P. Brophy, "Origins of the Chemical Corps," *Military Affairs* 20, no. 4 (1956): 217–26, 226, 222.

19. Brown, *Chemical Warfare*, 82.

20. Brophy, "Origins of the Chemical Corps," 225. Initially, the Army surgeon general and the Medical Department were responsible for gas masks for chemical defense, but these functions were transferred to the CWS in 1918. Stanhope

Bayne-Jones, *The Evolution of Preventive Medicine in the United States Army, 1607–1939* (Washington, DC: Office of the Surgeon General, Department of the Army, 1968), 157.

21. Leo P. Brophy and George L. B. Fisher, *The Chemical Warfare Service: Organizing for War* (Washington, DC: Center of Military History, United States Army, 1959), 25, 22. The British Chemical Defense Research Department seemed to suffer a similar plight.

22. Brown, *Chemical Warfare*, 151.

23. Lt. Col. Oram C. Woolpert, Subject: Immunization against 'X', to Office of the Surgeon General, Attention: Brig. General James S. Simmons, 1943, RG 112, box 1, Records of the Office of the Surgeon General (Army), Biological Warfare Specialized Files 1941–47, NARA; A. M. Pappenheimer, "The Story of a Toxic Protein, 1888–1992," *Protein Science* 2 (1993): 292–98, 295.

24. Accounts vary as to how much vaccine and what type (i.e., mono- or bivalent) was eventually produced, ranging from several hundred thousand doses to more than a million.

25. SGO Liaison Officer, "History of the Relation of the SGO to BW Activities," 104–9.

26. Lt. William B. Sarles, Memorandum. Re: Meeting in Dr. Fred's Office, 1944, RG 165, box 188, Records of the War Department General and Special Staffs, WRS Basic Documents to "X" Toxoid, NARA, 3; "Camp Detrick Meeting," 1945, RG 165, box 184, Records of the War Department General and Special Staffs, Correspondence File of Dr. G. W. Merck, Special Consultant to the Secretary of War, 1942–46, NARA, 4.

27. Major Arthur N. Gorelick, Lt. Walter L. Bloom, and Lt. S. S. Chapman, Subject: Report on Conference with Merck & Company, to Chief, D Division, Camp Detrick, 1944, RG 112, box 1, Records of the Office of the Surgeon General (Army), Biological Warfare Specialized Files 1941–47, NARA; D. F. Robertson, "Letter from Merck & Co Inc Medical Department, to N. Paul Hudson, Special Consultant, Army Service Forces," 1944, RG 112, box 1, Records of the Office of the Surgeon General (Army), Biological Warfare Specialized Files 1941–47, NARA. Likewise, on penicillin and anthrax, see "Camp Detrick Meeting," 4.

28. For summaries of this work, see "Agent: UL," RG 112, box 1, Records of the Office of the Surgeon General (Army), Biological Warfare Specialized Files 1941–47, NARA; "Report on 'N' Immunization," 1944, RG 112, box 1, Records of the Office of the Surgeon General (Army), Biological Warfare Specialized Files 1941–47, NARA.

29. Merck, "Report to the Secretary of War," section 1, 6, 15–16; SGO Liaison Officer, "History of the Relation of the SGO to BW Activities," 119, 26.

30. Merck, "Report to the Secretary of War," section 1, 6; "Research and Development Program of the Chemical Warfare Service in Biological Warfare," 1944, RG 165, box 185, Record of the War Department General and Special Staffs, Correspondence File of Dr. G. W. Merck, Special Consultant to the Secretary of War, 1942–46, NARA.

31. Merck, "Report to the Secretary of War," section 1, 6.

32. Baldwin, *My Half Century at the University of Wisconsin*, 128.

33. See Sarles, Memorandum. Re: Meeting in Dr. Fred's Office, 3; Maj. Murray Sanders, Subject: Rapid Detection of X, 1944, RG 112, box 1, Records of the Office of the Surgeon General (Army), Biological Warfare Specialized Files 1941–47, NARA; Col. Oram C. Woolpert, Subject: Detection of Human Pathogens in BW, to Technical Director, Camp Detrick, 1945, RG 112, box 2, Records of the Office of the Surgeon General (Army), Biological Warfare Specialized Files 1941–47, NARA.

34. Col. James B. Mason, Memorandum. For Brig. General Bliss, Operations Service, SGO, 1944, RG 112, box 1, Records of the Office of the Surgeon General (Army), Biological Warfare Specialized Files 1941–47, NARA, 3; "Report of a meeting held at Camp Detrick on February 11, 1944, 2:15 p.m. to discuss policy with regard to 'N' production, manufacture of British 4 lb. Type F Mark 1 bomb and manufacture of 'X' toxoid," 1944, RG 165, box 182, Records of the War Department General and Special Staffs, NARA.

35. Ed Regis, *The Biology of Doom: The History of America's Secret Germ Warfare Project* (New York: Henry Holt, 1999), 32.

36. Rexmond C. Cochrane and Leo P. Brophy, *Biological Warfare Research in the United States*, rough draft (Army Chemical Center, MD: Historical Section, 24 November 1947), 482; Regis, *Biology of Doom*, 68.

37. Cochrane and Brophy, *Biological Warfare Research in the United States*, 482.

38. Ibid., 438. Similarly, see US Army, *US Army Activities in the US Biological Warfare Programs*, vol. 1 (Washington, DC: Department of the Army, 24 February 1977), 77.

39. According to William Patrick, "such an agent powder can be disseminated from any number of devices that require only small amounts of energy. The ABC fire extinguisher is a good example and can achieve a plus 40% aerosol recovery of a standard *Bacillus subtilis* var *niger* powder using +/- 20 psi." William C. Patrick III, "Biological Terrorism and Aerosol Dissemination," *Politics and the Life Sciences* 15, no. 2 (1996): 208–10, 209.

40. Cochrane and Brophy, *Biological Warfare Research in the United States*, 482.

41. Ibid., 440–42; Regis, *Biology of Doom*: 70; Jeanne Guillemin, *Biological Weapons: From the Invention of State-Sponsored Programs to Contemporary Bioterrorism* (New York: Columbia University Press, 2005), 64.

42. Baldwin, *My Half Century at the University of Wisconsin*, 130.

43. Maj. Thomas F. M. Scott, Subject: The modification of the work at Camp Detrick contingent on the Japanese surrender and plans for the future, 1945, RG 112, box 2, Records of the Office of the Surgeon General (Army), Biological Warfare Specialized Files 1941–47, NARA; Maj. Thomas F. M. Scott, Subject: Joint meeting with CWS on a postwar plan for BW research, 1945, RG 112, box 2, Records of the Office of the Surgeon General (Army), Biological Warfare Specialized Files 1941–47, NARA; SGO Liaison Officer, "History of the Relation of the SGO to BW Activities," 133.

44. "Telephone conversation between Mr. George W. Merck and Gen. Simmons on 14 August 1945," RG 112, box 2, Records of the Office of the Surgeon General (Army), Biological Warfare Specialized Files 1941–47, NARA.

45. Henry L. Stimson, Memorandum for the Chief of Staff. Subject: Research and Development in Biological Warfare, 1945, RG 112, box 2, Records of the Office of the Surgeon General (Army), Biological Warfare Specialized Files 1941–47, NARA; Cochrane and Brophy, *Biological Warfare Research in the United States*, 503; US Army, *US Army Activities in the US Biological Warfare Programs*, 32–33.

46. George W. Merck, Memorandum to Mr. H. H. Bundy, Special Assistant to the Secretary of War. Subject: Chemical Warfare Service BW Activities, 1945, RG 165, box 186, Records of the War Department General and Special Staffs, Correspondence file of Dr. G. W. Merck, Special Consultant to the Secretary of War, 1942–46, NARA.

47. During the war, the CWS clashed with the Army surgeon general's office over their respective responsibilities, overall control, and the establishment of a Medical Division in CWS. See James S. Simmons, Memorandum for General Kirk, RG 112,

box 2, Biological Warfare Specialized Files, NARA; Karl R. Lundeberg, Memorandum for file. Subject: SGO Committee on BW, RG 112, box 2, Biological Warfare Specialized Files, NARA; SGO Liaison Officer, "History of the Relation of the SGO to BW Activities," 76, 83, 88–91.

48. Maj. Gen. William N. Porter, Subject: Recommended Peacetime Program of Research and Development in Biological Warfare, 1945, RG 165, box 186, NARA; Scott, Subject: Joint meeting with CWS on a postwar plan for BW research.

49. Ross T. McIntire, Memorandum for Commander William B. Sarles, 1945, RG 165, box 186, NARA (emphasis added). Similar conclusions are noted in the response by Comdr. William B. Sarles, Memorandum for Vice Admiral Ross T. McIntire (MC) USN, Surgeon General, 1945, RG 165, box 186, NARA.

50. Norman T. Kirk, Letter to Commanding General, Army Service Forces, 1945, RG 165, box 186, NARA, 1–2. On the Army surgeon general's alternative plan, see SGO Liaison Officer, "History of the Relation of the SGO to BW Activities," 138.

51. US Army, *US Army Activities in the US Biological Warfare Programs*, 30–31. On the evolution of the CWS Advisory Committee on BW Research and Development in 1949 into the Research and Development Board under the newly established DoD, see Simon M. Whitby, *Biological Warfare against Crops* (New York: Palgrave, 2002), 97.

52. The Soviet Union initially placed biological weapons under its Military Chemical Agency as well. However, "in the highly compartmentalized Soviet system, different departments were responsible for these two weapons systems and . . . there was very little interchange between them." Milton Leitenberg and Raymond A. Zilinskas, *The Soviet Biological Weapons Program: A History* (Cambridge: Harvard University Press, 2012), 741.

53. Col. Karl R. Lundeberg, Memorandum for Col. Stone, Director, Army Medical Research & Development Bd. SGO. Subject: Withdrawal of Medical Dept. Non-Concurrence in Project Q, 1946, RG 112, box 3, Records of the Office of the Surgeon General (Army), Biological Warfare Specialized Files 1941–47, NARA.

54. Dorothy L. Miller, *History of Air Force Participation in the Biological Warfare Program: 1951–1954* (Wright-Patterson Air Force Base: Historical Division, Air Materiel Command, January 1957), 73.

55. Baldwin, "Meeting of the Committee on Biological Warfare," 19–20; Dorothy L. Miller, *History of Air Force Participation in Biological Warfare Program: 1944–1951* (Wright-Patterson Air Force Base: Historical Office, Air Materiel Command, September 1952), 21–22.

56. Earl P. Stevenson et al., "Report of The Secretary of Defense's Ad Hoc Committee on Chemical, Biological, and Radiological Warfare," 30 June 1950, US Department of Energy, Office of Scientific and Technological Information, https://www.osti.gov/opennet/servlets/purl/16008529-aMEBjr/16008529.pdf, 7.

57. Milton Leitenberg, "False Allegations of US Biological Weapons Use during the Korean War," in *Terrorism, War, or Disease? Unraveling the Use of Biological Weapons*, ed. Anne L. Clunan, Peter R. Lavoy, and Susan B. Martin (Stanford: Stanford University Press, 2008), 132–33.

58. Miller, *History of Air Force Participation: 1951–1954*, 69–70.

59. Ibid., 13–15.

60. Conrad C. Crane, " 'No Practical Capabilities': American Biological and Chemical Warfare Programs during the Korean War," *Perspective in Biology and Medicine* 45, no. 2 (2002): 241–49, 22–25.

61. Miller, *History of Air Force Participation: 1951–1954*, 62. To a limited extent, the military's first BW capability had been achieved in 1951 with the standardization of an anticrop agent that caused wheat rust. US Army, *US Army Activities in the US Biological Warfare Programs*, 36.

62. Miller, *History of Air Force Participation: 1951–1954*, 40.

63. Ibid., 53–56, 75, 67.

64. Ibid., 181–82, 52, 69. Also see US Army, *US Army Activities in the US Biological Warfare Programs*, 38, 46.

65. Balmer, *Britain and Biological Warfare*, 142.

66. US Army, *US Army Activities in the US Biological Warfare Programs*, 40.

67. This name change may have been prompted by a new communications center that the Army built at Detrick, however, rather than any recognition of the BW program. Richard M. Clendenin, *Science and Technology at Fort Detrick, 1943–1968* (Frederick, MD: Technical Information Division, April 1968), 38, 42.

68. NSC 5602/1, "Basic National Security Policy," *Foreign Relations of the United States, 1955–1957*, vol. 19, doc. 120, US Department of State, Office of the Historian, http://history.state.gov/historicaldocuments/frus1955-57v19/d120. Also see John Ellis Van Courtland Moon, "The US Biological Weapons Program," in *Deadly Cultures: Biological Weapons Since 1945*, ed. Mark Wheelis, Lajos Rozsa, and Malcolm Dando (Cambridge: Harvard University Press, 2006), 12; Miller, *History of Air Force Participation: 1951–1954*, 58; US Army, *US Army Activities in the US Biological Warfare Programs*, 41.

69. Guillemin, *Biological Weapons*, 103.

70. Miller, *History of Air Force Participation: 1951–1954*, 91.

71. 435th meeting of the National Security Council, 18 February 1960, *Foreign Relations of the United States, 1958–1960*, vol. 3, doc. 92, US Department of State, Office of the Historian, http://history.state.gov/historicaldocuments/frus1958-60v03/d92.

72. On BW and flexible response, see Moon, "US Biological Weapons Program," 32; David I. Goldman, "The Generals and the Germs: The Army Leadership's Response to Nixon's Review of Chemical and Biological Warfare Policies in 1969," *Journal of Military History* 73, no. 2 (2009): 531–69, 535.

73. US Army Chemical Corps, *Summary of Major Events and Problems: Fiscal Years 1961–1962* (Army Chemical Center, MD: Historical Office, 1962), 9.

74. Among others, see William F. Page, Heather A. Young, and Harriet M. Crawford, *Long-Term Health Effects of Participation in Project SHAD (Shipboard Hazard and Defense)* (Washington, DC: National Academies Press, 2007), 11–12.

75. William C. Patrick III, private papers, provided courtesy of Joel McCleary.

76. David R. Franz, Cheryl D. Parrott, and Ernest T. Takafuji, "The US Biological Warfare and Biological Defense Programs," in *Medical Aspects of Chemical and Biological Warfare*, ed. Frederick R. Sidell, Ernest T. Takafuji, and David R. Franz (Washington, DC: Office of the Surgeon General at TMM Publications, 1997), 428; US Army, *US Army Activities in the US Biological Warfare Programs*, 177.

77. Dan Crozier, "Commission on Epidemiological Survey," in *The Armed Forces Epidemiological Board*, ed. Theodore E. Woodward (Washington, DC: Office of the Surgeon General, 1994), 220.

78. Hundreds of Seventh-Day Adventists also worked as medical technicians in Project Whitecoat. US Army, *US Army Activities in the US Biological Warfare Programs*,

182. Although the majority of the human subjects involved were military draftees, Detrick also participated in studies using volunteers from at least one civilian prison. Crozier, "Commission on Epidemiological Survey," 242.

79. Crozier, "Commission on Epidemiological Survey," 221.

80. Ibid., 223, 29, 34; US Army, *US Army Activities in the US Biological Warfare Programs*, 179, 81.

81. See Milton Puziss and George G. Wright, "Anaerobic process for production of a gel-adsorbed anthrax immunizing antigen," United States Patent Office, 3,208,909, filed 19 May 1961, patented 28 September 1965. The anthrax vaccine absorbed (AVA) is a filtrate that contains a mixture of cellular products (but no bacteria) that is absorbed using aluminum hydroxide as an adjuvant.

82. Crozier, "Commission on Epidemiological Survey," 253–54, 240. VEE vaccine could be readily produced and stored because a tiny amount of live attenuated virus is diluted down to produce large quantities of the vaccine. The size of this stockpile might therefore represent a case of "technology push" as much or more so than "demand pull" due to the BW threat.

83. Miller, *History of Air Force Participation: 1951–1954*, 136.

84. Several detection methods were tried during this period; they failed due to technical problems such as high false alarm rates (i.e., lack of specificity) and reagent requirements. See Robert E. Boyle and Leo L. Laughlin, *History and Technical Evaluation of the US Bio/Toxin Detection Program* (Arlington, VA: Battelle Memorial Institute, 1995).

85. Jeffery K. Smart, "History of Chemical and Biological Detectors, Alarms, and Warning Systems," Aberdeen Proving Ground MD, US Army Soldier and Biological Chemical Command, https://www.hsdl.org/?view=docs/dod/detectors.pdf& code=4aa6be7a426cf2f2730b2ef1547f397d, 21; Miller, *History of Air Force Participation: 1951–1954*, 140, 27.

86. Sonia Ben Ouagrham-Gormley, "Barriers to Bioweapons: Intangible Obstacles to Proliferation," *International Security* 36, no. 4 (2012): 80–114, 90–92.

87. "Confidential memorandum for Dr. Colin MacLeod to be used at his discretion," 13-IIBP, folder 8.8, Presidents—Housewright, BW materials, ASM Archives, 1962. At the time, MacLeod was a prominent member of the Commission on Epidemiological Survey.

88. Melvin Laird, "Memorandum for Assistant to the President for National Security Affairs," 30 April 1969, National Security Archive, George Washington University, http://www.gwu.edu/~nsarchiv/NSAEBB/NSAEBB58/RNCBW1.pdf; Tom Mangold and Jeff Goldberg, *Plague Wars: The Terrifying Reality of Biological Warfare* (New York: St. Martin's Press, 1999), 54.

89. Henry A. Kissinger, "National Security Study Memorandum [NSSM] 59: US Policy on Chemical and Biological Warfare and Agents," National Security Council, 28 May 1969, National Security Archive, George Washington University, http:// www.gwu.edu/~nsarchiv/NSAEBB/NSAEBB58/RNCBW4.pdf.

90. Interviews with former Detrick officials, Vienna, Virginia, and Frederick, Maryland, June 2007. Also see Goldman, "Generals and the Germs"; Jonathan B. Tucker, "A Farewell to Germs: The US Renunciation of Biological and Toxin Warfare, 1969–70," *International Security* 27, no. 1 (2002): 107–48; and Forrest Russel Frank, "US Arms Control Policymaking: The 1972 Biological Weapons Convention Case" (PhD diss., Stanford University, 1974).

91. Goldman, "Generals and the Germs," 544.

92. Frank, "US Arms Control Policymaking," 119.

93. Goldman, "Generals and the Germs," 557, 55.

94. Ibid., 561n110. Detrick had already received guidance on demilitarization from the Army Munitions Command on 12 November. US Army, *US Army Activities in the US Biological Warfare Programs*, 225.

95. Goldman, "Generals and the Germs," 562–65.

96. Henry A. Kissinger, "National Security Decision Memorandum 35: United States Policy on Chemical Warfare Program and Bacteriological/Biological Research Program," 25 November 1969, National Security Archive, George Washington University, http://www.gwu.edu/~nsarchiv/NSAEBB/NSAEBB58/RNCBW8.pdf.

97. Melvin R. Laird, "Chemical Warfare and Biological Research—Terminology." 9 December 1969, National Security Archive, George Washington University, http://www.gwu.edu/~nsarchiv/NSAEBB/NSAEBB58/RNCBW12.pdf (emphasis added).

98. Interdepartmental Political-Military Group, "US Policy on Chemical and Biological Warfare and Agents," Report to the National Security Council in response to NSSM 59, 10 November 1969, National Security Archive, George Washington University, http://www2.gwu.edu/~nsarchiv/NSAEBB/NSAEBB58/RNCBW6a.pdf, 23.

99. Robert A. Lovett, "Memorandum, Biological Warfare Intelligence," 16 August 1952, RG 218, box 152, Records of the US Joint Chiefs of Staff, Central Decimal File 1951–53, NARA; Walter B. Smith, "Memorandum, Biological Warfare Intelligence," 25 October 1952, RG 218, box 153, Records of the US Joint Chiefs of Staff, Central Decimal File 1951–53, NARA.

100. Ronald M. Atlas and Malcolm Dando, "The Dual-Use Dilemma for the Life Sciences: Perspectives, Conundrums, and Global Solutions," *Biosecurity and Bioterrorism: Biodefense Strategy, Practice, and Science* 4, no. 3 (2006): 276–86, 282.

101. Granted, in 1975, the CIA discovered that it retained a small supply of pathogens and toxins after Nixon ordered them destroyed. For one account, see Regis, *Biology of Doom*, 232.

102. US Army, *US Army Activities in the US Biological Warfare Programs*, 51, 58; Congressional Research Service: "Chemical and Biological Warfare: Issues and Developments during 1974" (Library of Congress, 1974), 22–24, 87; "Chemical and Biological Warfare: Issues and Developments during 1975" (Library of Congress, 1976), 64, 75, 94, 97; "Chemical and Biological Warfare: Issues and Developments during 1976 and January 1–June 30, 1977" (Library of Congress, 1977), 4.

103. Interview with a former official who worked at Detrick and Edgewood, Vienna, Virginia, June 2007.

104. Norman M. Covert, "Scientist's Work Lives On after His Death," *Fort Detrick Standard*, 29 May 1987.

105. Quoted in Albert J. Mauroni, *Chemical-Biological Defense: US Military Policies and Decisions in the Gulf War* (Westport, CT: Praeger, 1998), i, also see 1.

106. Smart, "History of Chemical and Biological Warfare," 65.

107. *Biological Defense Research Program: Final Programmatic Environmental Impact Statement* (Fort Detrick, MD: US Army Medical Research and Development Command, April 1989), 5.19, 5.21.

108. GAO, *US Forces Are Not Adequately Equipped to Detect All Threats* (Washington, DC: GAO, 1993), 4.

109. Albert J. Mauroni, *America's Struggle with Chemical-Biological Warfare* (Westport, CT: Praeger, 2000). 157; DoD, *Annual Report on Chemical Warfare—Biological Defense Research Program Obligations* (Washington, DC: DoD, 1987), annex B, 3; annex C, 3. The Navy failed to even specify formal requirements for chemical or biological defense, relying instead on ad hoc assessments of need. Past programs guided future funding decisions, but research records were incomplete, their guidance was inconsistent, and these nonkinetic capabilities suffered as a result. EAI Corporation, *Final Report on Review of CBW Defense Research Information System Needs of the Navy Program Element Manager* (Bethesda, MD: Naval Medical Research and Development Command, 1983), 26–27, 35.

110. US Army, *US Army Activities in the US Biological Warfare Programs*, 58; Interdepartmental Political-Military Group, "Annual Review of United States Chemical Warfare and Biological Research Programs as of 1 November 1970," 5 December 1970, 23.

111. Smart, "History of Chemical and Biological Detectors, Alarms, and Warning Systems," 26; Mauroni, *Chemical-Biological Defense*, 213.

112. Michael E. Brown, *Flying Blind: The Politics of the US Strategic Bomber Program* (Ithaca: Cornell University Press, 1992), 26.

113. Donald MacKenzie, *Inventing Accuracy: A Historical Sociology of Nuclear Missile Guidance*, 4 ed. (Cambridge: MIT Press, 1990), 384; Harvey M. Sapolsky, *The Polaris System Development: Bureaucratic and Programmatic Success in Government* (Cambridge: Harvard University Press, 1972), 44.

114. On the "irrational" imbalance of spending on missile defense versus biodefense, see Richard A. Falkenrath, Robert D. Newman, and Bradley A. Thayer, *America's Achilles' Heel: Nuclear, Biological, and Chemical Terrorism and Covert Attack*, ed. Sean M. Lynn-Jones Michael E. Brown, and Steven E. Miller (Cambridge: MIT Press, 1998), 218; National Research Council, *Giving Full Measure to Countermeasures: Addressing Problems in the DoD Program to Develop Medical Countermeasures against Biological Warfare Agents* (Washington, DC: National Academies Press, 2004), 34.

115. According to the GAO, "the fact that current detection technology was lacking should not have precluded the Chemical School from establishing a mission area requirement. Further, the lack of technology should have indicated . . . that it needed to initiate research to develop the technology." GAO, *US Forces Are Not Adequately Equipped to Detect All Threats*, 7.

116. Wayne H. Griest and Stephen A. Lammert, "The Development of the Block II Chemical Biological Mass Spectrometer," in *Identification of Microorganisms by Mass Spectrometry*, ed. Charles L. Wilkins and Jackson O. Lay (Hoboken, NJ: John Wiley & Sons, 2006), 66; M. G. Louis J. Del Rosso, "Biological Threat," 16 October 1990, Gulf-LINK, http://www.gulflink.osd.mil/declassimages/otsg/19961108/110596_sep96_decls12_0001.html.

117. EAI Corporation, "Final Report," 1.

118. Norman M. Covert, *Cutting Edge: The History of Fort Detrick*, 4th ed. (Fort Detrick, MD: US Army, 2000).

119. Civil Service Standards Committee of the American Academy of Microbiology, "Fort Detrick Report,"13-II, folder 8.2, Presidents—Housewright, BW Materials—Ft. Detrick, ASM Archives, 1976.

120. Among other sources, see budget data from Richard O. Spertzel, "RDTE Program Data Sheet: Medical Defense Against Biological Agents," January 1977, RG

112, box 3, Records of the Office of the Surgeon General (Army), Program Development Files FY 1967–1975, NARA.

121. GAO, *Biological Warfare: Role of Salk Institute in Army's Research Program* (Washington DC: GAO, 1991), 8; Stacy M. Okutani, "Structuring Biodefense: Legacies and Current Policy Choices" (PhD diss., University of Maryland, 2007), 122. Interview with former USAMRIID official, Frederick, Maryland, June 2007.

122. On these incidents, see Rebecca Katz and Burton Singer, "Can an Attribution Assessment Be Made for Yellow Rain? Systematic Reanalysis in a Chemical-and-Biological-Weapons Use Investigation," *Politics and the Life Sciences* 26, no. 1 (2007): 24–42.

123. At the time, opposition included a lawsuit filed by Jeremy Rifkin, as well as attempts by Representative Wayne Owens to have Congress strip biodefense from DoD, give the funding to the NIH, and require greater transparency (HR 806 and HR 5241). Senator John Glenn also requested a review of the DoD Biological Defense Research Program that criticized the scope of infectious agents under investigation. See GAO, *Biological Warfare: Better Controls in DOD's Research Could Prevent Unneeded Expenditures* (Washington, DC: GAO, 1990), 3.

124. Interviews with former USAMRIID officials, Washington, DC, and Frederick, Maryland, June 2007. Also, Judith Miller, Stephen Engelberg, and William Broad, *Germs: Biological Weapons and America's Secret War* (New York: Simon & Schuster, 2001), 84–85.

125. Experimental vaccines had been stored and, in rare instances like VEE, produced in bulk at the Swiftwater facility. But these supplies were typically small and only intended for use by laboratory staff—not the armed forces at large.

126. Interview with Anna Johnson-Winegar, Frederick, Maryland, July 2007. Credit for this decision also appears due to Major Robert Eng. See Miller, Engelberg, and Broad, *Germs*, 85–86.

127. Robert Eng, "Medical Biological Warfare (BW) Defense Readiness for US Forces in Operation Desert Shield/Storm," 5 April 1991, GulfLINK, http://www.gulflink.osd.mil/declassimages/otsg/19961211/120396_sep96_decls47_0001.html.

128. On Soviet spending, see Ken Alibek and Stephen Handelman, *Biohazard* (New York: Dell, 1999), 118; David E. Hoffman, *The Dead Hand: The Untold Story of the Cold War Arms Race and Its Dangerous Legacy* (New York: Doubleday, 2009), 333.

129. Gregory D. Koblentz, *Living Weapons: Biological Warfare and International Security* (Ithaca: Cornell University Press, 2009), 22.

130. CENTCOM, "After Action Report: Medical Defense against Biological Warfare," 12 March 1991, GulfLINK, http://www.gulflink.osd.mil/bw_ii/bw_refs/n23en070/960315_doc04_05_0000004.htm; CIA, "Prewar Status of Iraq's Weapons of Mass Destruction," 20 March 1991, National Security Archive, George Washington University, http://www.gwu.edu/~nsarchiv/NSAEBB/NSAEBB80/wmd04.pdf, iii–iv.

131. Mauroni, *Chemical-Biological Defense*, 34–35, 51, 71, 83; Rosso, "Biological Threat"; Miller, Engelberg, and Broad, *Germs*, 107.

132. Interview with Jack E. Berndt, Bel Air, Maryland, July 2007. Also see Bernard Rostker, "The Use of Modeling and Simulation in the Planning of Attacks on Iraqi Chemical and Biological Warfare Targets," 23 February 2000, GulfLINK, http://www.gulflink.osd.mil/aircampaign/index.htm.

133. Mauroni, *Chemical-Biological Defense*, 51, 64–65, 86.

134. "Lead Report: Defense Special Weapons Agency Modeling Support for Gulf War," 9 February 1998, GulfLINK, http://www.gulflink.osd.mil/aircampaign/aircampaign_refs/n24en033/8040_035_0000002.htm, 2; Mauroni, *Chemical-Biological Defense*, 86; Ken Silvernail, "Memorandum for Colonel Phillip: ANBACIS II Computer Downwind Prediction Feedback," 5 February 1991, GulfLINK, http://www.gulflink.osd.mil/declassdocs/af/19960214/aaapm_01.html.

135. Joint Staff, "Chronology of Key Events," 1992, GulfLINK, http://www.gulflink.osd.mil/declassimages/otsg/19961211/120396_sep96_decls1_0001.html, 2–3; J. Pitt Tomlinson, "Memorandum for Lieutenant General Frank F. Ledford: Recommendations of the AD HOC Working Group for the Medical Defense against Biological Warfare," 24 August 1990, GulfLINK, http://www.gulflink.osd.mil/declassimages/otsg/19961211/120396_sep96_decls31_0001.html.

136. Miller, Engelberg, and Broad, *Germs*, 103.

137. Susan A. Iliff, "An Additional 'R': Remembering the Animals," *ILAR Journal* 43, no. 1 (2002): 38–47, 44.

138. Quoted in Miller, Engelberg, and Broad, *Germs*, 106.

139. Office of the Surgeon General, "Medical Biological Warfare Defense Action Plan for Operation Desert Shield," 1990, GulfLINK, http://www.gulflink.osd.mil/declassimages/otsg/19961108/110596_sep96_decls24_0011.html; Robert R. Eng, "Memorandum for Record," 15 December 1990, GulfLINK, http://www.gulflink.osd.mil/declassimages/otsg/19961230/123096_sep96_decls52_0001.html.

140. Miller, Engelberg, and Broad, *Germs*, 108.

141. Robert Eng, "Status of the Procurement of Horses for Production of Botulinum Antitoxin," 12 December 1990, GulfLINK, http://www.gulflink.osd.mil/declassimages/otsg/19970101/970101_sep96_decls30_0001.html.

142. Interview with former USAMRIID official, Washington, DC, May 2008.

143. Colonel Harry Dangerfield, quoted in Miller, Engelberg, and Broad, *Germs*, 108.

144. Ibid. For similar decisions and critiques, see Kendall Hoyt, *Long Shot: Vaccines for National Defense* (Cambridge: Harvard University Press, 2012), 128–29.

145. Interview with Anna Johnson-Winegar, Frederick, Maryland, July 2007.

146. See Public Law 103–160, "National Defense Authorization Act for Fiscal Year 1994," 30 November 1993, GulfLINK, http://www.gulflink.osd.mil/declassimages/otsg/19961230/123096_sep96_decls57_0002.html.

147. National Research Council, *Giving Full Measure to Countermeasures*, 29. Also see Al Mauroni, *Where Are the WMDs? The Reality of Chem-Bio Threats on the Home Front and the Battlefront* (Annapolis, MD: Naval Institute Press, 2006), chaps. 2 and 3.

148. Interviews with former DoD officials, Frederick, Maryland, July 2007, and Washington, DC, May 2008.

149. Mauroni, *Where Are the WMDs?*, 74.

150. See GAO, *Chemical and Biological Defense: Emphasis Remains Insufficient to Resolve Continuing Problems* (Washington, DC: GAO, 1996), 7; Martin Enserink, "On Biowarfare's Frontline," *Science* 296 (June 2002): 1954–56. In contrast, overall military RDT&E only declined about 20%, R-1 tables, 1993, 1995, 1997, Defense Technical Information Center, http://www.dtic.mil/cgi-bin/GetTRDoc?AD=ADA247271&

Location=U2&doc=GetTRDoc.pdf; http://www.dtic.mil/cgi-bin/GetTRDoc?AD=
ADA277105&Location=U2&doc=GetTRDoc.pdf; and http://dodreports.com/pdf/
ada320886.pdf.

151. Interview with former USAMRIID official, Frederick, Maryland, June 2007.

152. Mauroni, *Chemical-Biological Defense*, 181–82.

153. Lynn Eden, *Whole World on Fire: Organizations, Knowledge, and Nuclear Weapons Devastation* (Ithaca: Cornell University Press, 2004), 269–77.

154. Likewise, during the Great Depression, "the cut applied to the CWS was much greater . . . than the cut contemplated for any other regular army activity." Brown, *Chemical Warfare*, 141–42.

155. Miller, Engelberg, and Broad, *Germs*, 196, 158, 201.

156. Interview with Richard J. Danzig, Washington, DC, June 2007.

157. Miller, Engelberg, and Broad, *Germs*, 155, 158, 188.

158. Interview with Danzig, June 2007. Lederberg had already lobbied the DoD for several years to invest in biodefense.

159. Barry R. Posen, *The Sources of Military Doctrine* (Ithaca: Cornell University Press, 1984), 174.

160. Stephen P. Rosen, *Winning the Next War: Innovation and the Modern Military* (Ithaca: Cornell University Press, 1991), 251, 20.

161. Interview with former USAMRIID official, Washington, DC, May 2008. Also note Michael H. Vodkin and Stephen H. Leppla, "Cloning of the Protective Antigen Gene of Bacillus anthracis," *Cell* 34 (September 1983): 693–97.

162. For example, see Harry G. Dangerfield, "Memorandum Thru HQDA: Seventh Tri-Service Task Force (Project Badger) Meeting," 29 November 1990, GulfLINK, http://www.gulflink.osd.mil/declassimages/otsg/19961030/102596_sep96_ decls12_0001.html, 2.

163. Hoyt, *Long Shot*, 126.

164. Joint Staff, "Chronology of Key Events," 31; "Memorandum for Colonel Warden," 11 December 1990, GulfLINK, http://www.gulflink.osd.mil/declassimages/ af/19970729/970729_aadev_05.html.

165. JPO-BioDefense, "Vaccine Production Facility Cost Estimate," ca. 1993, Gulf-LINK, http://www.gulflink.osd.mil/declassimages/otsg/19961230/123096_sep96_ decls47_0023.html; Klenke, "Biological Defense Vaccine Production Facility," 7 January 1993, GulfLINK, http://www.gulflink.osd.mil/declassimages/otsg/19961211/ 120396_sep96_decls73_0001.html.

166. Interview with former DoD official, Frederick, Maryland, July 2007. Also Miller, Engelberg, and Broad, *Germs*, 142.

167. Interview with former DoD official, Frederick, Maryland, July 2007.

168. Robert J. Lieberman, "Defense Anthrax Vaccine Contracting," Senate Committee on Armed Services, 12 July 2000, US Senate Committee on Armed Services, http://www.armed-services.senate.gov/statemnt/2000/000712rl.pdf, 4.

169. National Research Council, *Giving Full Measure to Countermeasures*, 29.

170. Quoted in John Cohen and Eliot Marshall, "Vaccines for Biodefense: A System in Distress," *Science* 294 (October 2001): 498–501, 498.

171. Franklin H. Top et al., "DoD Acquisition of Vaccine Production: Report to the Deputy Secretary of Defense by the Independent Panel of Experts," in DoD, *Report on Biological Warfare Defense Vaccine Research and Development Programs*, (July 2000), ii, 16, 21. Like the Project Badger proposal, however, "the DoD ultimately shelved the Top Report." Hoyt, *Long Shot*, 131.

172. Interview with former HHS official, Washington, DC, May 2008. Also, Cohen and Marshall, "Vaccines for Biodefense."

173. John D. Grabenstein and William Winkenwerder, "US Military Smallpox Vaccination Program Experience," *JAMA* 289, no. 24 (2003): 3278–82; GAO, *Smallpox Vaccination: Review of the Implementation of the Military Program* (Washington, DC: GAO, 2003); and Colonel Erik A. Henchal in Eric Schmitt, "Threats and Responses: Biowarfare—Military Says It Can't Make Enough Vaccines for Troops," *New York Times*, 9 January 2003. BioPort was renamed Emergent BioSolutions in 2004.

174. Elaine M. Grossman, "Pentagon Pulls $1B from WMD-Defense Efforts to Fund Vaccine Initiative," *Global Security Newswire*, 27 August 2010; Donald S. Burke et al., *Protecting the Frontline in Biodefense Research: The Special Immunizations Program* (Washington, DC: National Academies Press, 2011), 105–6.

175. Erika Check Hayden, "Pentagon Rethinks Bioterror Effort," *Nature* 477 (September 2011): 380–81.

176. Interview with Johnson-Winegar, 2007.

177. On critical shortages of protective equipment, for example, see GAO, *Chemical and Biological Defense: Emphasis Remains Insufficient*; GAO, *Chemical and Biological Defense: Improved Risk Assessment and Inventory Management Are Needed* (Washington, DC: GAO, 2001); Mauroni, *Where Are the WMDs?*, 48–49.

178. Mark L. Grotke and Bruce W. Jezek, "The Biological Integrated Detection System," in *Director's Series on Proliferation*, ed. Kathleen C. Bailey (Livermore, CA: Lawrence Livermore National Laboratory, 1994); Richard D. Howell, "BIDS—What Is It? How Does It Work?," *CML Army Chemical Review* (January 1995); Mark L. Malatesta, Daniel F. Mack, and Lavon Harbor, "BIDS—Identifying BW Agents on the Battlefield," *CML Army Chemical Review* (July 1995).

179. DoD, *Chemical and Biological Defense Program, Annual Report to Congress*, March 2000, http://www.defense.gov/pubs/chembio02012000.pdf, A2; David R. Walt and David R. Franz, "Biological Warfare: A Host of Detection Strategies Have Been Developed, but Each Has Significant Limitations," *Analytical Chemistry* (1 December 2000): 738–47.

180. For example, see Miller, Engelberg, and Broad, *Germs*, 283.

181. The acquisition phase for this system has regressed. Compare the dates and descriptions of the Joint Biological Standoff Detection System in 2010 with the 2012 Army Weapon Systems Handbook: Federation of American Scientists, https://www.fas.org/man/dod-101/sys/land/wsh2010/156.pdf; http://www.fas.org/man/dod-101/sys/land/wsh2012/170.pdf.

182. Interview with Johnson-Winegar, 2007. Also, Mauroni, *Where Are the WMDs?*, 83.

183. Quoted in Hoyt, *Long Shot*, 133.

184. Rosen, *Winning the Next War*, 11.

185. Interview with former USAMRIID official, Frederick, Maryland, June 2007.

3. Fatal Assumptions: Military Doctrine

1. Barry R. Posen, *The Sources of Military Doctrine* (Ithaca: Cornell University Press, 1984), 13. This definition is also consistent with how the US military defines doctrine, namely, as "fundamental principles by which the military forces or elements thereof guide their actions in support of national objectives." DoD, *Department of Defense Dictionary of Military and Associated Terms*, Joint Publication 1-02 (amended through 15 December 2013), 78.

2. Posen, *Sources of Military Doctrine*, 67; Eugene Gholz, "The Curtiss-Wright Corporation and Cold War-Era Defense Procurement: A Challenge to Military-Industrial Complex Theory," *Journal of Cold War Studies* 2, no. 1 (2000): 35–75, 45–46.

3. Lynn Eden, *Whole World on Fire: Organizations, Knowledge, and Nuclear Weapons Devastation* (Ithaca: Cornell University Press, 2004), 53. This difference is mitigated by the observation that organizational frame theory ultimately describes a circular process, whereby frames shape action (e.g., decisions about doctrine), which shapes capabilities, which shape frames. See Eden, *Whole World on Fire,* 56; Wiebe E. Bijker, "The Social Construction of Bakelite: Towards a Theory of Invention," in *The Social Construction of Technological Systems*, ed. Wiebe E. Bijker, Thomas P. Hughes, and Trevor J. Pinch (Cambridge: MIT Press, 1987), 173.

4. Posen, *Sources of Military Doctrine*, 14.

5. The US military produced little doctrine for using biological weapons when it had an offensive BW program. However, selection bias may qualify this observation because offensive doctrine is more likely to remain classified.

6. F. M. Day for R. C. Lindsay, "Memorandum for General Schuyler, Admiral Ingersoll, General Smith, Concept for Employment of Chemical Warfare," 1950, RG 218, box 206, Records of the US Joint Chiefs of Staff, Central Decimal File 1948–50, NARA(emphasis added).

7. For example, see Douglas R. Lewis, "The Shaping of United States Biodefense Posture" (PhD diss., George Mason University, 2012).

8. US Army, *NBC Defense*, FM 21-40 (Washington, DC: Department of the Army, 14 October 1977), C1–3.

9. Ibid., 6–7. Similarly, see US Army et al., *Multiservice Tactics, Techniques, and Procedures for Nuclear, Biological, and Chemical (NBC) Protection*, FM 3-11.4 / MCWP 3-37.2 / NTTP 3-11.27 / AFTTP (I) 3-2.46 (2 June 2003), II-3.

10. See War Department, *Basic Field Manual: Defense against Chemical Attack*, FM 21-40 (Washington, DC: Government Printing Office, 1940), 84; US Army and US Air Force, *Defense against CBR Attack*, FM 21-40 / AFM 355-9 (Washington DC: Departments of the Army and the Air Force, 17 August 1954), 181–84.

11. These hazard markers are cited repeatedly in doctrine over the years.

12. US Army and US Air Force, *Technical Aspects of Biological Defense* TM 3-216 / AFM 355-6 (Washington, DC: Departments of the Army and the Air Force, 12 January 1971), 60.

13. US Army and US Air Force, *Defense against CBR Attack*, 100.

14. US Army, *NBC Decontamination*, FM 3-5 (Washington, DC: Department of the Army, 24 June 1985), 1–5.

15. John Vitko et al., *Sensor Systems for Biological Agent Attacks: Protecting Buildings and Military Bases* (Washington, DC: National Academies Press, 2005). 1.

16. US Army et al., *Armed Forces Doctrine for Chemical Warfare and Biological Defense*, FM 101-40 / NWP 36 (D) / AFR 355-5 / FMFM 11-6 (Washington, DC: Departments of the Army, the Navy, and the Air Force, 30 June 1976), 4–1. Although the military did not start stockpiling vaccine for biodefense until the late 1980s, doctrine dating back to the 1950s suggested that vaccines were readily available. See US Army and US Air Force, *Defense against CBR Attack*, 87.

17. US Army, *Soldier's Handbook for Nuclear, Biological, and Chemical Warfare*, FM 21-41 (Washington, DC: Department of the Army, 19 December 1958), 161.

18. US Army, *Chemical, Biological, Radiological and Nuclear Defense*, FM 21-40 (Washington, DC: Department of the Army, 20 December 1968), 5–2.

19. US Army and US Air Force, *Technical Aspects of Biological Defense*, 57.

20. "The NBCWRS is used to report biological attacks. However, the number of potential agents, the various dissemination methods and techniques, and the lack of automated detection and identification devices have thwarted an all-encompassing simplified biological hazard prediction. So, the use of the NBCWRS will be extremely limited." US Army, *Chemical and Biological Contamination Avoidance*, FM3-3 / FMFM 11-17 (Washington, DC: Department of the Army, 16 November 1992), 4–9. For an older version of this system, see "DA form 890" in US Army and Air Force, *Defense against CBR Attack*, 186.

21. US Navy, *ABC Warfare Defense*, NAVPERS 10099 (Bureau of Naval Personnel, 1960), 36.

22. Ibid., 42–43. Shortly after the Vietnam War, the military argued that "smoke, flame, incendiary, riot control agents, and chemical herbicides are not to be considered chemical warfare agents." US Army et al., *Armed Forces Doctrine for Chemical Warfare and Biological Defense*, 1. By the 1980s, however, these nonkinetic agents all reappeared together in doctrine. See US Army, *NBC Operations*, FM 3-100 (Washington, DC: Department of the Army, 17 September 1985).

23. Al Mauroni, *Where Are the WMDs? The Reality of Chem-Bio Threats on the Home Front and the Battlefront* (Annapolis, MD: Naval Institute Press, 2006), 53; War Department, *Defense against Chemical Attack*, 23.

24. DoD, *Joint Doctrine for Operations in Nuclear, Biological, and Chemical (NBC) Environments*, Joint Publication 3-11 (11 July 2000), III-13.

25. On the impersonal language of nuclear strategy, for example, see Carol Cohn, "Sex and Death in the Rational World of Defense Intellectuals," *Signs* 12, no. 4 (1987).

26. DoD, *Joint Doctrine for Nuclear, Biological, and Chemical (NBC) Defense*, Joint Publication 3-11 (10 July 1995), II-1, V-1. Similarly, see DoD, *Joint Doctrine for Operations in Nuclear, Biological, and Chemical (NBC) Environments*, II-4, IV-1; US Air Force, *Counter Nuclear, Biological, and Chemical Operations*, AFDD 2-1.8 (Washington, DC: Secretary of the Air Force, 16 August 2000), 1, 25.

27. Consider the military's official definition of "biological agent," namely, "a microorganism (or a toxin derived from it) that causes disease in personnel, plants, or animals or causes the deterioration of materiel. See also 'chemical agent.'" DoD, *Department of Defense Dictionary of Military and Associated Terms*, 27. The reverse is not true: the definition of "chemical agent" does not refer back to BW (i.e., the reference is directional and not reciprocal).

28. Interview with former official from USAMRIID, Frederick, Maryland, July 2007.

29. According to Mauroni, after 1980, "the new doctrine . . . emphasized that combat forces should continue the mission even if contaminated," which he argues "was a major change from the past, when combat units had expected to be completely de-contaminated before continuing operations." Albert J. Mauroni, *Chemical-Biological Defense: US Military Policies and Decisions in the Gulf War* (Westport, CT: Praeger, 1998), 2. However, this was no major change: doctrine had always emphasized that defensive measures only be taken "without undue interference with the mission." US Army and US Air Force, *Defense against CBR Attack*, 12. The priority placed on the mission is also evident in the military's name for individual protective equipment, that is, *mission-oriented* protective posture.

30. Lee Ben Clarke, *Mission Improbable: Using Fantasy Documents to Tame Disaster* (Chicago: University of Chicago Press, 1999).

31. Ibid., 414. Whereas Clarke treats uncertainty as an independent variable, I argue that uncertainty depends in part on the knowledge that an organization chooses to create. And these choices are, in turn, functions of organizational frames and stereo-types. (Clarke also emphasizes power and conflict more than I do here.)

32. Albert J. Mauroni, *America's Struggle with Chemical-Biological Warfare* (Westport, CT: Praeger, 2000), 222.

33. See Judith Miller, Stephen Engelberg, and William Broad, *Germs: Biological Weapons and America's Secret War* (New York: Simon & Schuster, 2001), 106, 116, 118.

34. For example, "The BW Warning and Detection System *will* provide advance no-tification," Office of the Surgeon General, "Interim Medical Doctrine, Biological Warfare (BW) Defense against Anthrax and Botulinum Toxin for Operation Desert Shield," 23 December 1990, GulfLINK, http://www.gulflink.osd.mil/declassim ages/otsg/19961230/123096_sep96_decls12_0001.html, 3–1 (emphasis added). In contrast, "will" is replaced with "may" in a later version. DoD, "Interim Medical Doctrine, Tactics, Techniques, and Procedures: Biological Warfare Defense for Opera-tion Desert Storm," 26 January 1991, GulfLINK, http://www.gulflink.osd.mil/decl-assimages/otsg/19970101/970101_sep96_decls2_0001.html, 2–1. On CENTCOM's insistence that emphasis remain on masking procedures as the "prime defensive measure," see Joint Staff, "Chronology of Key Events," 1992, http://www.gulf link.osd.mil/declassimages/otsg/19961211/120396_sep96_decls1_0001.html, 24.

35. See DoD, "Interim Medical Doctrine, Tactics, Techniques, and Procedures." On the ad hoc effort to develop doctrine for BW detection that began in December 1990, see Joint Staff, "Chronology of Key Events," 16; and Mauroni, *Chemical-Biological Defense*, 72.

36. For a similar critique, see National Research Council, *Naval Forces' Defense Capa-bilities against Chemical and Biological Warfare Threats* (Washington, DC: National Academies Press, 2004), 20.

37. DoD, *Smallpox Response Plan* (Washington, DC: Department of Defense, 29 Sep-tember 2002), 1.

38. US Army, *Chemical, Biological, Radiological and Nuclear Defense*, 5–4. Variations of this quote appear repeatedly over the years.

39. US Army et al., *Treatment of Biological Warfare Agent Casualties*, FM 8-284 / NAVMED P-5042 / AFMAN (I) 44-156 / MCRP 4-11.1C (Washington, DC: Departments of the Army, the Navy, the Air Force, and the Commandant, Marine Corps, 17 July 2000), 1–12; DoD, *Joint Doctrine for Nuclear, Biological, and Chemical (NBC) Defense*, V-2.

40. GAO, *Chemical and Biological Defense: DOD Should Clarify Expectations for Medical Readiness* (Washington, DC: GAO, 2001), 2.

41. See US Army et al., *Multiservice Tactics, Techniques, and Procedures for Chemical, Biological, Radiological, and Nuclear Contamination Avoidance*, FM 3-11.3 / MCRP 3-37. 2A / NTTP 3-11.25 / AFTTP (I) 3-2.56 (Washington, DC: Department of the Army, US Marine Corps, US Navy, US Air Force, February 2006); *Multiservice Tactics, Techniques, and Procedures for Nuclear, Biological, and Chemical (NBC) Protection,*; and *Multiservice Tactics, Techniques, and Procedures for Chemical, Biological, Radiological, and Nuclear Decontamination*, FM 3-11.5 / MCWP 3-37.3 / NTTP 3-11.26 / AFTTP (I) 3-2.60 (4 April 2006).

42. For example, US Army et al., *Multiservice Tactics, Techniques, and Procedures for Biological Surveillance*, FM 3-11.86 / MCWP 3.37.1C / NTTP 3-11.31 / AFTTP (I) 3-2.52 (4 October 2004).

43. Correspondence with former OSD official, December 2013.

44. For critiques of this approach, see Al Mauroni, "The Changing Face of Biological Warfare Defense," *CML Army Chemical Review* (April 2004), 2; *Where Are the WMDs?*, 85–87.

45. On the pros and cons of half-masks, see Karl Lowe, Graham S. Pearson, and Victor Utgoff, "Potential Values of a Simple Biological Warfare Protective Mask," in *Biological Weapons: Limiting the Threat*, ed. Joshua Lederberg (Cambridge, MA: Belfer Center for Science and International Affairs, 2000); Jim A. Davis and Bruce W. Bennett, "Needed Now: The '85% Quick Fix' in Bio-Defense," in *The War Next Time: Countering Rogue States and Terrorists Armed with Chemical and Biological Weapons*, ed. Barry R. Schneider and Jim A. Davis (Maxwell Air Force Base, AL: USAF Counterproliferation Center, 2004).

46. Mauroni, "Changing Face of Biological Warfare Defense," 2. In addition, bureaucratic interests probably played a role in the demise of this biodefense concept. It was proposed by the Office of the Secretary of Defense, but "the military had combat development centers, at least in theory, to examine new concepts and develop doctrine, and were unused to having OSD challenging their concepts and recommending drastic changes." Mauroni, *Where Are the WMDs?*, 86. But here, as elsewhere, organizational frames and stereotypes help explain why this proposal (1) would have been such a drastic change to begin with, and (2) failed while the Chemical School prevailed.

47. In particular, DoD, *Joint Doctrine for Operations in Nuclear, Biological, and Chemical (NBC) Environments*.

48. The Joint Requirements Oversight Council approved the 4S concept during the summer of 2003. On this concept, see Chemical Corps, "Chemical Vision 2010" (1999); Mauroni, *Where Are the WMDs?*, 255–57; DoD *Operations in Chemical, Biological, Radiological, and Nuclear (CBRN) Environments*, Joint Publication 3-11 (26 August 2008).

49. Correspondence with former OSD official, December 2013.

50. US Army, *NBC Defense*, 6–2.

51. Mauroni, *Chemical-Biological Defense*, 18; "Changing Face of Biological Warfare Defense"; and *Where Are the WMDs?*, 86.

52. Network text analysis describes a family of related methods that are also referred to as cognitive maps, mental models, frame analysis, and semantic networks, among others. Kathleen Carley, "Coding Choices for Textual Analysis: A Comparison of Content Analysis and Map Analysis," *Sociological Methodology* 23 (1993): 75–126.

53. Stanley Wasserman and Katherine Faust, *Social Network Analysis: Methods and Applications*, ed. Mark Granovetter (New York: Cambridge University Press, 1994).

54. On the pros and cons of using different units of text to define a relationship, see Steven R. Corman et al., "Studying Complex Discursive Systems: Centering Resonance Analysis of Communication," *Human Communication Research* 28, no. 2 (2002): 157–206. Sentences have several advantages for this analysis, since they are meaningful units of text that do not require tagging or chunking phrases into different parts of speech (an imperfect process that would be complicated by the technical content of military doctrine).

55. Kathleen M. Carley, "Network Text Analysis: The Network Position of Concepts," in *Text Analysis for the Social Sciences: Methods for Drawing Statistical Inferences from Texts and Transcripts*, ed. Carl W. Roberts (Mahwah, NJ: Lawrence Erlbaum Associates, 1997).

56. Data for network text analysis was prepared using custom algorithms coded in Python, with the files then exported to Pajek for calculation. Coding rules for network text analysis were similar to those used for term counts, coupled with functions to identify the relationships between words (i.e., appearance in the same sentence) and filter the output (e.g., deleting stop words and applying a Porter Stemmer). Depending on the length and content of each document, the resulting networks ranged in size, with some containing more than 3,300 nodes. See Wouter de Nooy, Andrej Mrvar, and Vladimir Batagelj, *Exploratory Social Network Analysis with Pajek* (New York: Cambridge University Press, 2005); Steven Bird, Ewan Klein, and Edward Loper, *Natural Language Processing in Python*, O'Reilly Media, 2009, http://www.nltk.org/book/.

57. Words with the highest degree centrality are those with the most ties to other terms. Whereas this is a local measure, closeness centrality takes the global structure of the network into account, defining the most central words as those that are proximate to all of the other terms in the document. Another aspect of global structure is reflected in betweenness centrality, for which the most central words are those that serve as bridges between otherwise disconnected terms in the document.

58. These measures for statistical significance assume that the preconditions of independent sampling from a normal distribution apply here. Either way, this is a conservative test. These centrality measures do not address the frequency of each tie (i.e., edge width). Since "chem-" is more frequent than "bio-," the differences between them stand to be even greater if centrality were calculated for the subset of ties above a given frequency threshold, such as the network in figure 3.2. I thank James Evans for his invaluable insight into these metrics.

59. One of the best examples of improved doctrine is US Air Force, *Disease Containment Planning Guidance*, AFI 10-2604 (6 April 2007). It draws explicitly on planning guidance from the civilian CDC and makes very few references to stereotypes. Nevertheless, this document was published more than four years after the invasion of Iraq, and it remains to be seen whether it—or the Air Force Counter-Biological Warfare Concepts of Operations that this guidance claims to support—will counterbalance all of the multiservice doctrine that still relies on nonkinetic stereotypes.

60. Carl H. Builder, *The Masks of War: American Military Styles in Strategy and Analysis* (Baltimore: Johns Hopkins University Press, 1989), 31. Also see NRC, *Naval Forces' Defense Capabilities*, 37.

61. Training programs dedicated to biological warfare were established during World War II and the Korean War, but these were short lived. For example, see the

first "bacteriological warfare school," described in George W. Merck, "Activities of the United States in the Field of Biological Warfare: A Report to the Secretary of War," n.d., RG 165, box 182, Records of the War Department General and Special Staffs, NARA, section 1, 11; Maj. General William N. Porter, "Subject: Bacteriological Warfare School," in *To: Chief of Staff, United States Army*, 1944, RG 112, box 1, Records of the Office of the Surgeon General (Army), Biological Warfare Specialized Files, 1941–47, NARA; and the Air Force "100-man Program," described in Dorothy L. Miller, *History of Air Force Participation in the Biological Warfare Program: 1951–1954* (Wright-Patterson Air Force Base: Historical Division, Air Materiel Command, 1957), 53–56, 224. BW training was also incorporated into established courses at the Army Chemical School in 1947. Rexmond C. Cochrane and Leo P. Brophy, *Biological Warfare Research in the United States*, rough draft (Army Chemical Center, MD: Historical Section, 24 November 1947), 514.

62. US Army, *Planning and Conducting Chemical, Biological, and Radiological (CBR) and Nuclear Defense Training*, FM 21–48 (Washington, DC: Department of the Army, 1973), 2–2, 2–3, B-4. This manual also suggests that, in order to practice collecting and reporting "intelligence" on BW, "empty soda or beer cans can be painted with a grey background and a code name in Esperanto or a foreign language. . . . These cans should be placed in designated places in the exercise area where participating personnel can find them. This will permit units to implement biological defense procedures" (E-4). In another exercise, "biological attack is probable: send one platoon every 30 minutes to the aid station for immunization," even though vaccines were not readily available at the time and multiple doses were required over several months for full immunity (2–12).

63. Granted, if training is consistent with doctrine, then despite the problems inherent to that doctrine, it is still possible to conclude that "the Services generally have met the requirements placed on them by Joint, multi-Service and Service specific doctrine." Deena S. Disraelly et al., *Nuclear, Chemical, and Biological Education and Training: A Review across the Services and Joint Community* (Alexandria, VA: Institute for Defense Analysis, 2007), ES-2.

64. Interview with Jack E. Berndt, Bel Air, Maryland, July 2007.

65. See GAO, *Army Training: Evaluations of Units' Proficiency Are Not Always Reliable* (Washington, DC: GAO, 1991), 3; DoD, Office of the Inspector General, *Unit Chemical and Biological Defense Readiness Training*, Report No. 98-174 (1998), 6; GAO, *Chemical and Biological Defense: Army and Marine Corps Need to Establish Minimum Training Tasks and Improve Reporting for Combat Training Centers* (Washington, DC: GAO, 2005), 17; Disraelly et al., *Nuclear, Chemical, and Biological Education and Training*, ES-3.

66. "Cross Service Identification of Chemical, Biological, Radiological, Nuclear, and (High Yield) Explosives (CBRN) Training Commonalities and GAP Analysis Report," quoted in Disraelly et al., *Nuclear, Chemical, and Biological Education and Training*, 9. For similar conclusions, see GAO, *Chemical and Biological Defense: Emphasis Remains Insufficient to Resolve Continuing Problems* (Washington, DC: GAO, 1996), 5; and GAO, *DOD Should Clarify Expectations for Medical Readiness*, 3.

67. Disraelly et al., *Nuclear, Chemical, and Biological Education and Training*, 132.

68. US Public Health Service, "Seminar Proceedings, 'Responding to the Consequences of Chemical and Biological Terrorism'" (1995), 1–13.

69. Interview with Berndt, 2007

70. Theresa Hitchens, "Exercise Finds US Falls Short in BioWar—Officials Address Realm of Germ Attack against US by Lesser Powers," *Army Times*, 9 November 1995.

71. Quoted in Tom Mangold and Jeff Goldberg, *Plague Wars: The Terrifying Reality of Biological Warfare* (New York: St. Martin's Press, 1999), 325.

72. Mauroni, *Chemical-Biological Defense*, 171. Exercises like Global 95 illustrate how, "in workshop games, red players saw NBC capabilities as important weapons to assail US vulnerabilities and to reduce the significance of US conventional technological superiority. The same players, when cast in the role of blue planners, consistently minimized the difficulties of operations in NBC environments." Robert G. Joseph, "The Impact of NBC Proliferation on Doctrine and Operations," *Joint Force Quarterly* (Autumn 1996): 78. Thus, for biological warfare in particular, "the trend to date has been to downplay the potential magnitude of the BW challenge or overestimate the efficacy of US countermeasures in exercises and training." National Defense University, *The Counterproliferation Imperative—Meeting Tomorrow's Challenges* (Washington, DC: Center for Counterproliferation Research, 2001), 39.

73. GAO, *DOD Should Clarify Expectations for Medical Readiness*, 3. Army and Marine Corps training for the nonmedical aspects of NBC defense is variable if not deficient at their combat training centers, and wars in Iraq and Afghanistan may have compounded these problems. GAO, *Army and Marine Corps Need to Establish Minimum Training Tasks and Improve Reporting for Combat Training Centers*. Furthermore, as the DoD admits, "currently the Professional Military Education (PME) provides only limited CBRN defense considerations and does not adequately address the CBRN threat or US response capability in their curricula, associated wargames, or workshops." DoD, *Chemical and Biological Defense Program: Annual Report to Congress* (April 2007), 97.

74. Disraelly et al., *Nuclear, Chemical, and Biological Education and Training*, 127.

75. Amy Smithson and Leslie-Anne Levy, *Ataxia: The Chemical and Biological Terrorism Threat and the US Response*, Stimson Report 35 (Washington, DC: Henry L. Stimson Center, 2000), 176. For additional critiques, see GAO, *Combating Terrorism: Opportunities to Improve Domestic Preparedness Program Focus and Efficiency* (Washington, DC: GAO, 1998). For a defense of this training program by one of its organizers, see Al Mauroni, "A Rebuttal to 'Ataxia': The Smithson Report on US Response to Chem/Bio Terrorism," *Journal of Homeland Security* (December 2000).

76. Smithson and Levy, *Ataxia*, 176.

77. Interview with D. A. Henderson, Baltimore, Maryland, November 2009. Also see D. A. Henderson, *Smallpox—The Death of a Disease: The Inside Story of Eradicating a Worldwide Killer* (Amherst: Prometheus Books, 2009), 277; Smithson and Levy, *Ataxia*, 178, 80.

78. National Guard WMD Civil Support Teams (previously named Rapid Assessment and Initial Detection, or RAID, teams) represent another military foray into civil defense that was in trouble at the time. DoD Inspector General, *Management of National Guard Weapons of Mass Destruction-Civil Support Teams*, Report No. D-2001-043 (31 January 2001); Smithson and Levy, *Ataxia*, 141. One possible exception to this pattern of poor performance was the Marine Corps' Chemical/Biological Incident Response Force (CBIRF). Jonathan B. Tucker, "National Health and Medical Services Response to Incidents of Chemical and Biological Terrorism," *JAMA* 278, no. 5 (6 August 1997): 362–68.

79. Mauroni, *Where Are the WMDs?*, 245.

80. US Army, *Chemical, Biological, Radiological, Nuclear, and High Yield Explosives Operational Headquarters*, FM 3-90.10 (Washington, DC: Department of the Army, 24 January 2008), vii. Also Mauroni, *Where Are the WMDs?*, 150. Likewise, before

the 1991, "no one had considered what exactly combat units should do with munitions filled with biological agents," and no guidance was provided until the last days of Operation Desert Storm. Mauroni, *Chemical-Biological Defense*, 112, 222.

81. Interview with Berndt, 2007.

82. Bernard Rostker, "Information Paper: The Fox NBC Reconnaissance Vehicle," 1997, GulfLINK, http://www.gulflink.osd.mil/foxnbc/.

83. Mauroni, *Chemical-Biological Defense*, 83.

84. "513th Military Intelligence Brigade after Action Report, Chronology of Key Events," n.d., GulfLINK, http://www.gulflink.osd.mil/declassimages/army/1996 1203/120396_aug96_decls4_0001.html, III-87. For more on the training and operations of the 9th Chemical Company, see Development and Engineering Center Chemical Research, "XM2/PM10 (BGI) Biological Aerosol Samper in Desert Storm," 1991, GulfLINK, http://www.gulflink.osd.mil/bw_ii/bw_refs/n23en044/7316_010_0000001.htm; Cpt. Jon Drushal, "Biological Operations During Desert Storm," *CML Army Chemical Review* (January 1997); Dale A. Vesser, "Close-Out Report: Biological Warfare Investigation," 2001, GulfLINK, http://www.gulflink.osd.mil/bw_ii/index.html. The Air Force fielded its own team at the end of January, which may have used a prototype anthrax detector called Morning Song. CENTCOM, "After Action Report: Medical Defense against Biological Warfare," 1991, GulfLINK, http://www.gulflink.osd.mil/bw_ii/bw_refs/n23en070/960315_doc04_05_0000004.htm, 2; Robert E. Boyle and Leo L. Laughlin, *History and Technical Evaluation of the US Bio/Toxin Detection Program* (Arlington, VA: Battelle Memorial Institute, 1995), 51; Mauroni, *Chemical-Biological Defense*, 52.

85. Rodney D. Hudson, "513th Military Intelligence Brigade Chemical Officer, Memorandum for Record, Subject: 'Biological Monitoring,'" 1991, GulfLINK, http://www.gulf link.osd.mil/bw_ii/bw_refs/n23en065/091896_jul96_decls2_0000001.htm; Vesser, "Close-Out Report: Biological Warfare Investigation." Initially, every "hot" sample associated with a positive SMART card was transported to the Naval Theater Laboratory for additional testing and evacuated to Fort Detrick by the Technical Escort Unit. Drushal, "Biological Operations during Desert Storm," 37. On 8 December 1991, TEU also delivered to USAMRIID blood samples from Iraqi deserters—provided by Saudi officials, later prompting "grave concern" about the treatment of prisoners of war—to test if they were immunized against potential BW agents (including smallpox); they were not. CENTCOM, "After Action Report: Medical Defense against Biological Warfare," 3; Joint Staff, "Chronology of Key Events," 17, 21, 26.

86. Smithson and Levy, *Ataxia*, 185.

87. Interview with former UNSCOM inspector, Frederick, Maryland, June 2007.

88. After processing a positive sample, the additional time required for a report to reach CENTCOM HQ was not to exceed one hour. See Development and Engineering Center Chemical Research, "XM2/PM10 (BGI) Biological Aerosol Samper in Desert Storm."

89. Most chemical companies are either in the Army Reserve or Army National Guard.

90. Mauroni, *Where Are the WMDs?*, 59.

91. Ibid., 202.

92. Ibid., 202, 306.

93. Interview with DoD official, Washington, DC, May 2008. Also see Miller, Engelberg, and Broad, *Germs*, 283. In general, according to another source, "field detectors are still not reliable, even in 2007." Interview with former UNSCOM inspector, 2007.

94. Like BIDS, Portal Shield was initially deployed in limited numbers and "not available to all required sites." US Air Force, *USAF Operations in a Chemical and Biological (CB) Warfare Environment: Defense Equipment* Handbook 32-4014, vol. 3 (1 February 1998), 78. Automated detection systems rely on laboratory confirmation for the samples they collect, and so, as an increasing number of biological detection systems are deployed, "the Army, Air Force, and Navy, together with their forward medical laboratories, have trouble dealing with the current load of samples." Mauroni, "Changing Face of Biological Warfare Defense," 4.

95. Quoted in Elizabeth A. Fenn, *Pox Americana: The Great Smallpox Epidemic of 1775–82* (New York: Hill and Wang, 2001), 91.

96. George Washington, letter to William Shippen Jr., 6 January 1777. Quoted in Stanhope Bayne-Jones, *The Evolution of Preventive Medicine in the United States Army, 1607–1939* (Washington, DC: Office of the Surgeon General, Department of the Army, 1968). 52.

97. The sickness and contagion caused by inoculation is why this practice was banned within the Continental Army until January 1777. The logistic challenges it imposed also caused Washington to change his mind later that month, but he ordered inoculations to resume a few days later. Fenn, *Pox Americana*, 47, 70, 93.

98. Ibid., 134. For similar conclusions, see Bayne-Jones, *Evolution of Preventive Medicine in the United States Army, 1607–1939*, 54; and Ann M. Becker, "Smallpox in Washington's Army: Strategic Implications of the Disease during the American Revolutionary War," *Journal of Military History* 68 (April 2004): 381–430.

99. Organizational continuity is a critical scope condition for organizational frame theory. It also helps reconcile this theory's path dependency with other cultural accounts of military behavior. According to Farrell, for example, world culture compelled the Irish military to adopt a conventional force posture that violated its "heritage of unconventional warfare." Yet if the Irish army was born into a civil war, as Farrell notes, and the units steeped in unconventional warfare split from the government and rebelled, then there may have been little practical continuity—particularly in terms of personnel—between this guerrilla heritage and the national military that adopted a conventional posture. See Theo Farrell, "World Culture and Military Power," *Security Studies* 14, no. 3 (2005): 448–88.

100. "[Most] physicians and surgeons of the Revolutionary Army . . . neglected to record and transmit their experiences and observations." Bayne-Jones, *Evolution of Preventive Medicine in the United States Army*, 77, 62.

101. Ibid., 75, 79. On the professionalization of the Army and Navy during the late nineteenth century, see Wayne E. Lee, "Mind and Matter—Cultural Analysis in American Military History: A Look at the State of the Field," *Journal of American History* 93, no. 4 (2007): 1116–42, 1123.

102. SGO Liaison Officer, "History of the Relation of the SGO to BW Activities," n.d. (ca. 1946), RG 112, box 12, Records of the Office of the Surgeon General (Army), Biological Warfare Specialized Files 1941–47, NARA, 6, also 16–17, 24–25.

103. James E. Norman et al., "Mortality Follow-up of the 1942 Epidemic of Hepatitis B in the US Army," *Hepatology* 18, no. 4 (1993): 790–97, 791.

104. William J. Klenke, "Memorandum for Record," in *Drug and Vaccine Usage during Operation Desert Shield/Storm*, 1991, GulfLINK, http://www.gulflink.osd.mil/declassimages/otsg/19961230/123096_sep96_decls33_0001.html.

105. Mauroni, *Where Are the WMDs?*, 55.

106. Joint Staff, "Chronology of Key Events," 2–3; Col. Pitt Tomlinson and Maj. Robert Eng, "Medical Defense against Biological Warfare Threat—EXSUMS," 1990, GulfLINK, http://www.gulflink.osd.mil/declassimages/otsg/19961230/123096_sep96_decls9_0001.html, 4; J. Pitt Tomlinson, "Memorandum for Lieutenant General Frank F. Ledford: Recommendations of the AD HOC Working Group for the Medical Defense against Biological Warfare," 1990, GulfLINK, http://www.gulflink.osd.mil/declassimages/otsg/19961211/120396_sep96_decls31_0001.html.

107. "Memorandum for Colonel Warden," 1990, GulfLINK, http://www.gulflink.osd.mil/declassimages/af/19970729/970729_aadev_05.html, 5. Also see Joint Staff, "Chronology of Key Events," 17–19.

108. Miller, Engelberg, and Broad, *Germs*, 112, 16. Meanwhile, the military launched a concerted public affairs campaign that misrepresented its biodefense capabilities—regarding both vaccines and detection—to help allay fears and deter Iraq from using BW. See "Public Affairs Guidance—Chemical and Biological Defense Program," 1990, GulfLINK, http://www.gulflink.osd.mil/declassimages/army/19961108/110596_mar96_decls3_0002.html.

109. CENTCOM, "After Action Report: Medical Defense against Biological Warfare."

110. Robert Eng, "Letter to COL Dievendorf," 1991, GulfLINK, http://www.gulflink.osd.mil/declassimages/otsg/19961108/110596_sep96_decls7_0002.html; Thomas V. Inglesby et al., "Anthrax as a Biological Weapon: Medical and Public Health Management," *JAMA* 281, no. 18 (1999):1735–45, 1741; also Miller, Engelberg, and Broad, *Germs*, 119.

111. Joint Staff, "Chronology of Key Events," 30; Miller, Engelberg, and Broad, *Germs*, 133.

112. William J. Perry, "Subject: DoD Immunization Program for Biological Warfare Defense," Directive Number 6205.3, 1993.

113. William S. Cohen, "Memorandum for Secretaries of the Military Departments, Subject: Implementation of the Anthrax Vaccination Program for the Total Force, 18 May 1998; Hearing before the Military Personnel Subcommittee, Committee on Armed Services, House of Representatives, *Department of Defense Anthrax Vaccine Immunization Program*, 30 September 1999, Federation of American Scientists, http://www.fas.org/spp/starwars/congress/1999_h/has273020_0.htm, 25, 80.

114. For example, the assistant commandant of the Marine Corps argued for making vaccinations mandatory, and later, General Randall West insisted on keeping them that way. Interview with Richard J. Danzig, Washington, DC: June 2007, and interview with Anna Johnson-Winegar, Frederick, Maryland, July 2007. The issue of mandatory versus voluntary vaccination first arose during the 1991 Gulf War, at which time vaccinations were believed to be mandatory. Joint Staff, "Chronology of Key Events," 27.

115. James H. Binns et al., *Gulf War Illness and the Health of Gulf War Veterans: Scientific Findings and Recommendations*, (Washington, DC: US Government Printing Office, 2008).

116. David S.C. Chu, "Memorandum for Secretaries of the Military Departments, Subject: Anthrax Vaccine Immunization Program," 23 December 2003, http://www.

vaccines.mil/documents/327stoppage.pdf; Paul Wolfowitz, "Memorandum for Secretaries of the Military Departments, Subject: Resumption of the Anthrax Vaccine Immunization Program (AVIP) under Emergency Use Authorization (EUA)," 25 April 2005, http://www.vaccines.mil/documents/737Wolfowitz07425-05.pdf; William Winkenwerder, "Memorandum for Surgeon[s] General of the Army, Navy, Air Force, Subject: Continuation of the Anthrax Vaccine Immunization Program (AVIP)," 22 December 2005, http://www.vaccines.mil/documents/853continuation.pdf; David S.C. Chu, "Memorandum for Secretaries of the Military Departments, Subject: Implementation of the Anthrax Vaccine Immunization Program (AVIP)," 6 December 2006, http://www.vaccines.mil/documents/979AVIP%20Implementation%20Guidance%206%20Dec%2006.pdf; DoD, "Individual's Briefing: Anthrax Vaccine," 2009, http://www.anthrax.mil/documents/1281Anthrax%20Individuals%20Brief-%2014%20Sep%2009_printable.pdf.

117. Interview with Johnson-Winegar, 2007. Elaine Sciolino, "Anthrax Vaccination Program Is Failing, Pentagon Admits," *New York Times,* 13 July 2000; James Dao, "Anthrax Vaccination Program Is Further Cut by the Pentagon," *New York Times,* 1 December 2000; Jim Garamone, "DoD Slows Anthrax Vaccination Program Again," American Forces Press Service, 11 June 2001.

118. Eric Schmitt, "Threats and Responses: Biowarfare—Military Says It Can't Make Enough Vaccines for Troops," *New York Times,* 9 January 2003.

119. DoD, *Smallpox Response Plan,* 9.

120. John D. Grabenstein and William Winkenwerder, "US Military Smallpox Vaccination Program Experience," *JAMA* 289, no. 24 (2003): 3278–82; GAO, *Smallpox Vaccination: Review of the Implementation of the Military Program* (Washington, DC: GAO, 2003).

121. The military's vaccination program was also facilitated by only one dose of smallpox vaccine being required (unlike the multiple doses needed for immunity against other BW agents) and DoD plans drawing explicitly on guidelines provided by the CDC.

122. Interview with Johnson-Winegar, 2007.

123. DoD, "Q&A: DoD Resumes Anthrax Vaccinations," 2004, http://www.anthrax.mil/media/pdf/ResumptionQA.pdf.

124. For example, the M12 Heavy Decontamination System "is inadequate to support all of the Army's heavy decontamination requirements." Even though "DOD has long recognized the need to replace its aging decontamination systems," its decade-long effort to do so was unsuccessful and terminated in 2003. GAO, *Chemical and Biological Defense: Management Actions are Needed to Close the Gap between Army Chemical Unit Preparedness and Stated National Priorities* (Washington, DC: GAO, 2007), 24, 27. Likewise, "at the end of the 20th century, the Army did not have a standardized biological specific decontaminant in case of a biological attack. Instead, the Army relied on the standardized chemical decontaminants DS2 and STB for biological decontamination." Jeffery K. Smart, "History of Decontamination," Aberdeen Proving Ground: US Army, Soldier and Biological Chemical Command, n.d., 28.

4. An Unlikely Sponsor?

1. Tara Kirk Sell and Matthew Watson, "Federal Agency Biodefense Funding, FY 2013–FY 2014," *Biosecurity and Bioterrorism: Biodefense Strategy, Practice, and Science* 11, no. 3 (2013): 1–21.

2. For its part, realist literature may focus on the military, but the underlying theory assumes that states are unitary and rational actors. Therefore, the distribution of functions across domestic organizations is largely irrelevant, so long as it is rational. This means that realist hypotheses about fear and self-help are as applicable to civilian organizations involved with national security as they are to the armed services.

3. Among others, see George L. Engel, "The Need for a New Medical Model: A Challenge for Biomedicine," *Science* 196, no. 4286 (1977): 129–36; Cheryl Mattingly, "What Is Clinical Reasoning?," *American Journal of Occupational Therapy* 45, no. 11 (1991): 979–86; and Neil Pearce, "Traditional Epidemiology, Modern Epidemiology, and Public Health," *American Journal of Public Health* 86, no. 5 (1996): 678–83.

4. Allan M. Brandt and Martha Gardner, "Antagonism and Accommodation: Interpreting the Relationship between Public Health and Medicine in the United States during the 20th Century," *American Journal of Public Health* 90, no. 5 (2000): 707–15, 711.

5. Priscilla Wald, *Contagious: Cultures, Carriers, and the Outbreak Narrative* (Durham: Duke University Press, 2008).

6. Elizabeth W. Etheridge, *Sentinel for Health: A History of the Centers for Disease Control* (Berkeley: University of California Press, 1992), xv.

7. Ibid., 15–17, 28–30; also, Alexander D. Langmuir, "The Epidemic Intelligence Service of the Center for Disease Control," *Public Health Reports* 95, no. 5 (1980): 470–77, 471.

8. "Whether pursued independently or in cooperation with NIH, projects in medicine and science [at CDC] dominated the institution." Etheridge, *Sentinel for Health*, 49. Similarly, see Pearce, "Traditional Epidemiology, Modern Epidemiology, and Public Health"; and Brandt and Gardner, "Interpreting the Relationship between Public Health and Medicine."

9. R. E. Dyer, Letter to the PHS Surgeon General, 16 December 1940, Committees on Biological Warfare, series 1, WBC Committee, National Academies Archive.

10. Ed Regis, *The Biology of Doom: The History of America's Secret Germ Warfare Project* (New York: Henry Holt and Company, 1999), 37; Rexmond C. Cochrane and Leo P. Brophy, *Biological Warfare Research in the United States*, rough draft (Army Chemical Center, MD: Historical Section, 24 November 1947), 315, 30, 83.

11. Robert E. Boyle and Leo L. Laughlin, *History and Technical Evaluation of the US Bio/Toxin Detection Program* (Arlington, VA: Battelle Memorial Institute, 1995), 3; US Army, *US Army Activities in the US Biological Warfare Programs*, vol. 1 (Washington, DC: Department of the Army, 24 February 1977), 155–65.

12. Etheridge, *Sentinel for Health*, 41; Elizabeth Fee and Theodore M. Brown, "Preemptive Biopreparedness: Can We Learn Anything from History?," *American Journal of Public Health* 91, no. 5 (2001): 721–26, 723.

13. Langmuir, quoted in Etheridge, *Sentinel for Health*, 42, 61.

14. Alexander D. Langmuir and Justin M. Andrews, "Biological Warfare Defense: The Epidemic Intelligence Service of the Communicable Disease Center," *American Journal of Public Health* 42 (1952): 235–38, 238; Stephen B. Thacker, Andrew L. Dannenberg, and Douglas H. Hamilton, "Epidemic Intelligence Service of the Centers for Disease Control and Prevention: 50 Years of Training and Service in Applied Epidemiology," *American Journal of Epidemiology* 154, no. 11 (2001): 985–92.

15. Etheridge, *Sentinel for Health*, 62, 98–99. Also Max Moody, Morris Goldman, and B. M. Thomason, "Staining Bacterial Smears with Fluorescent Antibody," *Journal of Bacteriology* 72, no. 3 (1956): 525–32.

16. Etheridge, *Sentinel for Health*, 42, 67.

17. Donald A. Henderson, "Biopreparedness and Public Health," *American Journal of Public Health* 91, no. 12 (2001): 1917–18, 1917.

18. Ruth L. Berkelman and Phyllis Freeman, "Emerging Infections and the CDC Response," in *Emerging Illnesses and Society: Negotiating the Public Health Agenda*, ed. Randall M. Packard, et al. (Baltimore: Johns Hopkins University Press, 2004), 350.

19. Among others, see Judith Miller, Stephen Engelberg, and William Broad, *Germs: Biological Weapons and America's Secret War* (New York: Simon & Schuster, 2001), chap. 1; and W. Seth Carus, *Bioterrorism and Biocrimes: The Illicit Use of Biological Agents since 1900*, working paper (Washington, DC: Center for Counterproliferation Research, National Defense University, 2001), 50–58.

20. Thomas J. Torok et al., "A Large Community Outbreak of Salmonellosis Caused by Intentional Contamination of Restaurant Salad Bars," *JAMA* 278, no. 5 (1997): 389–95.

21. Leonard A. Scheele, Letter to Dr. Karl T. Compton, 18 August 1949, RG 218, box 206, Records of the US Joint Chiefs of Staff, Central Decimal File 1948–50, NARA. In this letter, Scheele also suggests that emphasizing the similarities of "CEBAR" weapons "seems logical," but, even so, he chooses to focus on BW and recommends that future studies include "professional health personnel, especially epidemiologists."

22. Interview with former USAMRIID official, Frederick, Maryland, June 2007. Also, interview with D. A. Henderson, Baltimore, Maryland, November 2009.

23. Neither the president nor Congress appeared to demand civilian biodefense at the time. Although civil defense plans delegated this responsibility to the Department of Health, Education, and Welfare, they did not confer authority, and details for the National Biological and Chemical Warfare Defense Plan were never finalized. See Office of Civil and Defense Mobilization, *1961 Annual Report*, http://www.hsdl.org/?view&did=34676, 40, 93.

24. Stephen S. Morse and Ann Schluederberg, "Emerging Viruses: The Evolution of Viruses and Viral Diseases," *Journal of Infectious Diseases* 162, no. 1 (1990): 1–7.

25. Barbara J. Culliton, "Emerging Viruses, Emerging Threat," *Science* 247, no. 4940 (1990): 279–80, 279.

26. Quoted in ibid., 279.

27. Robert B. Tesh, "In Memoriam: Robert E. Shope, MD," *Vector-Borne and Zoonotic Diseases* 4, no. 2 (2004): 91–94. Also, correspondence with ProMED cofounder and associate editor, October 2011.

28. Miller, Engelberg, and Broad, *Germs*, 111. Apparently, Lederberg had some access to intelligence on the Soviet BW program during the 1980s (he helped debrief Vladimir Pasechnik), but he was also skeptical of hawkish assessments by the Reagan administration. For one critical view of Lederberg as an "alarmist," see Susan Wright, "Terrorists and Biological Weapons: Forging the Linkage in the Clinton Administration," *Politics and the Life Sciences* 25, no. I-2 (2007): 57–114.

29. Joshua Lederberg, Robert E. Shope, and Stanley C. Oaks, Jr., eds., *Emerging Infections: Microbial Threats to Health in the United States* (Washington, DC: National Academy Press, 1992).

30. Berkelman and Freeman, "Emerging Illnesses and Society," 365. Similarly, see James M. Hughes and D. Peter Dortman, "In Memoriam: Joshua Lederberg (1925–2008)," *Emerging Infectious Diseases* 14, no. 6 (June 2008): 981–83, 982. The relationship

that American scientists constructed between emerging infectious diseases and national security also had international ramifications. After the US government started characterizing infectious disease as a security threat, international institutions such as the United Nations and World Health Organization started to do the same. For example, see National Intelligence Estimate, *The Global Infectious Disease Threat and Its Implications for the United States*, NIE 99-17D (January 2000); also UN Security Council Resolution 1308 (designated HIV/AIDS a security threat), analyzed in Stefan Elbe, "Should HIV/AIDS Be Securitized? The Ethical Dilemmas of Linking HIV/AIDS and Security," *International Studies Quarterly* 50, no. 1 (2006): 119–44.

31. Miller, Engelberg, and Broad, *Germs*, 112.

32. Testimony of Dr. Frank Young—A Review of Federal Bioterrorism Preparedness Programs from a Public Health Perspective, Subcommittee on Oversight and Investigations, 10 October 2001.

33. US Public Health Service, *Proceedings of the Seminar on Responding to the Consequences of Chemical and Biological Terrorism*, (11–14 July 1995), 2–177. For an analysis of this argument, see Mark Wheelis, "Biological Warfare at the 1346 Siege of Caffa," *Emerging Infectious Diseases* 8, no. 9 (September 2002).

34. These medical strike teams initially focused on chemical weapons, but they increasingly prepared for bioterrorism as the program expanded. See IOM, *Preparing for Terrorism: Tools for Evaluating the Metropolitan Medical Response System Program* (Washington, DC: National Academy Press, 2002).

35. "Meeting Between Hussein Kamal and UNSCOM and IAEA," Note for the File, 22 August 1995, http://www.un.org/depts/unmovic/new/documents/hk.pdf.

36. Tim Weiner, "Soviet Defector Warns of Biological Weapons," *New York Times*, 25 February 1998.

37. Leonard A. Cole, *The Anthrax Letters: A Medical Detective Story* (Washington, DC: Joseph Henry Press, 2003), 126.

38. Interview with Henderson, 2009.

39. Margaret A. Hamburg, "Challenges Confronting Public Health Agencies," *Public Health Reports* 116, supplement 2 (2001): 59–63, 62. Also see Miller, Engelberg, and Broad, *Germs*, 279.

40. Again, although US intelligence on Iraq's BW facilities was weak, assessment of the agents that were deployed was reasonably accurate. Gregory D. Koblentz, *Living Weapons: Biological Warfare and International Security* (Ithaca: Cornell University Press, 2009), 169–76.

41. Jonathan B. Tucker, "National Health and Medical Services Response to Incidents of Chemical and Biological Terrorism," *JAMA* 278, no. 5 (6 August 1997): 352–68; Amy Smithson and Leslie-Anne Levy, *Ataxia: The Chemical and Biological Terrorism Threat and the US Response*, Stimson Report 35 (Washington, DC: Henry L. Stimson Center, 2000), 118–20.

42. Presidential Decision Directive NSTC-7, Emerging Infectious Diseases, 12 June 1996. The novelty here—later highlighted in Clinton's announcement of PDD 62—is the growing association between disease and terrorism. This association was absent from earlier inputs into the policy process, including the National Science and Technology Council's *Report on International Science: Global Microbial Threats in the 1990s*, http://clinton4.nara.gov/WH/EOP/OSTP/CISET/html/toc.html.

43. White House, Presidential Decision Directive 62, Combating Terrorism, 22 May 1998.

44. See Miller, Engelberg, and Broad, *Germs*, 225, 35–44.

45. William Jefferson Clinton, "Commencement Address at the United States Naval Academy in Annapolis, Maryland," 22 May 1998, http://www.gpo.gov/fdsys/pkg/WCPD-1998-05-25/pdf/WCPD-1998-05-25.pdf.

46. William Jefferson Clinton and Joshua Lederberg, "Keeping America Secure for the 21st Century," *Proceedings of the National Academy of Sciences* 96 (March 1999): 3486–88.

47. Henderson, quoted in Cole, *Anthrax Letters*, 126. President Clinton's counterterrorism adviser was also dissatisfied with the federal response to threats such as bioterrorism. Richard A. Clarke, *Against All Enemies: Inside America's War on Terror* (New York: Free Press, 2004), 163.

48. Bill Frist, "Public Health and National Security: The Critical Role of Increased Federal Support," *Health Affairs* 21, no. 6 (2002): 117–30, 120.

49. GAO, *Bioterrorism: Federal Research and Preparedness Activities* (Washington, DC: GAO, 2001), 60.

50. Tommy G. Thompson, "Civilian Preparedness for Biological Warfare and Terrorism: HHS Readiness and Role in Vaccine Research and Development," Testimony before the United States House of Representatives, Committee on Government Reform Subcommittee on National Security, Veterans Affairs and International Relations, 23 October 2001, http://www.hhs.gov/asl/testify/t011023.html.

51. CDC, "Preventing Emerging Infectious Diseases: A Strategy for the 21st Century," *Morbidity and Mortality Weekly Report* 47, no. RR-15 (1998): 1–14.

52. Stephen A. Morse, quoted in Cole, *Anthrax Letters*, 130–31.

53. Jeffrey Koplan, "CDC's Strategic Plan for Bioterrorism Preparedness and Response," *Public Health Reports* 116, supplement 2 (2001): 9–16; Stephen A. Morse et al., "Detecting Biothreat Agents: The Laboratory Response Network," *ASM News* 69, no. 9 (2003): 433–37.

54. Steven D. Bice, "The US National Pharmaceutical Stockpile Program: Buying Is the Easy Part," ADP013451, in Chemical and Biological Medical Treatment Symposium: Industry II World Congress on Chemical and Biological Terrorism, 2001, http://handle.dtic.mil/100.2/ADP013451; David Rosner and Gerald Karkowitz, *Are We Ready? Public Health since 9/11* (Berkeley: University of California Press, 2006), 134.

55. Richard A. Clarke, Janet Reno, and Donna E. Shalala, "Briefing on the Emerging Threats of Biological, Chemical, and Cyber Terrorism," 22 January 1999, Federation of American Scientists, http://www.fas.org/spp/starwars/program/news99/99012207_tlt.htm.

56. Thomas V. Inglesby, Rita Grossman, and Tara O'Toole, "A Plague on Your City: Observations from TOPOFF," *Clinical Infectious Diseases* 32, no. 3 (2001): 436–45; Testimony of Margaret A. Hamburg regarding the biological weapons threat, House Government Reform Committee, Subcommittee on National Security, Veterans Affairs and International Relations, 23 July 2001, http://www.nti.org/analysis/testimonies/prepared-testimony-dr-peggy-hamburg-regarding-biological-weapons-threat/; Tara O'Toole, Michael Mair, and Thomas V. Inglesby, "Shining Light on 'Dark Winter,'" *Clinical Infectious Diseases* 34, no. 7 (2002): 972–83.

57. Interview with Henderson, 2009. Also see comments by Scott Lillibridge, quoted in Rosner and Karkowitz, *Are We Ready?*, 132.

58. For example, see Kenneth W. Bernard, "Health and National Security: A Contemporary Collision of Cultures," *Biosecurity and Bioterrorism: Biodefense Strategy, Practice, and Science* 11, no. 2 (2013): 157–62.

59. FDA, "Talk Paper, Next Year's Budget Request for FDA," T00-9, 7 February 2000; Rosner and Karkowitz, *Are We Ready?*, 137–38.

60. Interview with former HHS official, Washington, D.C., May 2008. However, there was a gap between administrations because the new National Security Council staff retained no health expertise. Interview with Kenneth Bernard, Monterey, California, October 2008.

61. HHS, "Fact Sheet, HHS Initiative Prepares for Possible Bioterrorism Threat," 16 August 2001.

62. Interview with former HHS official, May 2008; also, interview with Henderson, 2009.

63. Judith F. English, Mae Y. Cundiff, John D. Malone, and Jeanne A. Pfeiffer, *Bioterrorism Readiness Plan: A Template for Healthcare Facilities*, 13 April 1999, http://emergency.cdc.gov/bioterrorism/pdf/13apr99APIC-CDCBioterrorism.pdf; Ali S. Khan, Alexandra M. Levitt, and Michael J. Sage, "Biological and Chemical Terrorism: Strategic Plan for Preparedness and Response, Recommendations of the CDC Strategic Planning Workgroup," *Morbidity and Mortality Weekly Report* 49, no. RR-4 (April 2000): 1–14; HHS and CDC, *The Public Health Response to Biological and Chemical Terrorism: Interim Planning Guidance for State and Public Health Officials*, July 2001, http://emergency.cdc.gov/Documents/Planning/PlanningGuidance.PDF.

64. The CDC plans to detect a biological attack through epidemiology and disease surveillance, that is, through knowledge-laden routines that date back to the founding of the organization. One goal is early detection, but here "early" is relative: in this context, it is still assumed to occur after the victims are exposed.

65. According to PDD 39 and the Federal Response Plan, HHS must provide medical services if an attack overwhelms state and local capacity. HHS response plans discuss several possible responses, including mobilizing medical strike teams, delivering supplies from the Strategic National Stockpile, managing mass-casualty care, providing public information, and enforcing quarantine, among other actions. The quality of these plans is open to question, but at least they acknowledge the jurisdiction of various federal, state, and local agencies, whereas the military has traditionally paid little attention to this issue despite its dependence on civilian infrastructure both at home and abroad.

66. Here the sample used for quantitative analysis consists of HHS, *Health and Medical Services Support Plan for the Federal Response to Acts of Chemical/Biological (C/B) Terrorism*, 21 June 1996; English et al., *Bioterrorism Readiness Plan*; Khan, Levitt, and Sage, "Biological and Chemical Terrorism: Strategic Plan"; and HHS and CDC, *The Public Health Response to Biological and Chemical Terrorism: Interim Planning Guidance*.

67. Furthermore, when terms are conjoined in HHS documents, "bio-" often comes first in the phrase, so the order of words is "biological and/or chemical," unlike ubiquitous references to "chemical and biological" in military doctrine. More important, because biology is inside the organizational frame at HHS, links between "bio-" and "chem-" stand to be less damaging to the secondary concept than at the DoD, where both categories fall outside of the military's kinetic frame. At worst, "chem-" is at the periphery of the conceptual core at HHS, whereas "bio-" is at the periphery of the periphery at the DoD.

68. NIAID, *NIAID Strategic Plan for Biodefense Research*, NIH Publication No. 03-5306, February 2002, 1.

69. Interview with Henderson, 2009.

70. HHS and CDC, *The Public Health Response to Biological and Chemical Terrorism: Interim Planning Guidance*, 45. On the Global Emerging Infectious Surveillance and Response System, see National Research Council, *Review of the DoD-GEIS Influenza Programs: Strengthening Global Surveillance and Response* (Washington, DC: National Academies Press, 2007). For evidence of the military's relatively late acknowledgement of the relationship between emerging infectious diseases and BW, see references to Andrew Weber, Assistant to the Secretary of Defense for Nuclear and Chemical and Biological Defense Programs, "Memorandum Subject: Including Emerging Infectious Disease into the Biodefense Mission Set," 26 October 2009; and, for one critique of the separation between the military's approach to countermeasures for BW and naturally occurring diseases, see Col. Kenneth E. Hall, "The Dangerous Decline in the Department of Defense's Vaccine Program for Infectious Diseases," *Air & Space Power Journal* (Spring 2011).

71. Thompson, "Civilian Preparedness for Biological Warfare and Terrorism."

72. Stephen A. Morse, quoted in Cole, *Anthrax Letters*, 129.

73. D. A. Henderson, *Smallpox: The Death of a Disease: The Inside Story of Eradicating a Worldwide Killer* (Amherst, NY: Prometheus Books, 2009), 286; Cole, *Anthrax Letters*, 117.

74. The first victims of inhalation anthrax were Ernesto Blanco and Bob Stevens, but it was later learned that the earliest cases were cutaneous infections suffered by Johanna Huden and Erin O'Connor. See Leonard A. Cole, "The US Anthrax Letters: A Confirmed Case of BW Agent Use," in *Terrorism, War, or Disease? Unraveling the Use of Biological Weapons*, ed. Anne L. Clunan, Peter R. Lavoy, and Susan B. Martin (Stanford: Stanford University Press, 2008), 29.

75. See Cole, *Anthrax Letters*, 17–18, 21; IOM, *Preparing for Terrorism*, 59.

76. Wil S. Hylton, "How Ready Are We for Bioterrorism?," *New York Times*, 30 October 2011.

77. H. Clifford Lane, John La Montagne, and Anthony S. Fauci, "Bioterrorism: A Clear and Present Danger," *Nature Medicine* 7, no. 12 (2001): 1271–73, 1273.

78. NIAID, "Appropriations history," in NIAID FY 2010 Budget, http://www.niaid.nih.gov/about/whoWeAre/budget/Documents/fy2010cj.pdf; NIH, "Actual Obligations by Budget Mechanism, FY 2000–FY 2012," http://officeofbudget.od.nih.gov/pdfs/spending_history/Mechanism%20Detail%20for%20Total%20NIH%20FY%202000%20-%20FY%202012%20%283%29.pdf.

79. Ceci Connolly, "Smallpox Vaccine Plan Called Lacking; CDC Head Says $600 Million More Is Needed," *Washington Post*, 30 November 2001.

80. This phrase is often—though perhaps inaccurately—attributed to Everett Dirksen. See http://www.dirksencenter.org/print_emd_billionhere.htm.

81. Interview with Anna Johnson-Winegar, Frederick, Maryland, July 2007.

82. CDC Office of Public Health Preparedness and Response, *Public Health Preparedness: Strengthening the Nation's Emergency Response State by State*, September 2010, http://emergency.cdc.gov/publications/2010phprep/, 16; Crystal Franco and Tara Kirk Sell, "Federal Agency Biodefense Funding, FY 2012–FY 2013," Biosecurity and Bioterrorism: Biodefense Strategy, Practice, and Science 10, no. 2 (2012): 162–81, 169.

83. Interview with Bernard, 2008; interview with Michael Ascher, Walnut Creek, California, October 2008. For mixed reviews of BioWatch, see Dana A. Shea and Sarah A. Lister, *The BioWatch Program: Detection of Bioterrorism*, CRS Report for Congress, 19 November 2003; Department of Homeland Security, Office of the Inspector General, *DHS' Management of BioWatch Program*, OIG-07-22, January 2007; National Research Council, *BioWatch and Public Health Surveillance: Evaluating Systems for the Early Detection of Biological Threats* (Washington, DC: National Academies Press, 2011). The Laboratory Response Network is now managed by the CDC's National Center for Emerging and Zoonotic Infectious Diseases, which was established in 2010 when the National Center for Infectious Diseases was reorganized and retired.

84. Franco and Sell, "Federal Agency Biodefense Funding, FY 2012–FY 2013," 169.

85. NIAID, *Congressional Justification: FY 2012,* http://www.niaid.nih.gov/about/who weare/budget/Pages/default.aspx, 18.

86. NIAID, *Congressional Justification: FY 2008,*" http://www.niaid.nih.gov/about/ whoweare/budget/Pages/default.aspx, 3.

87. NIAID, *Congressional Justification: FY 2013,* http://www.niaid.nih.gov/about/ whoweare/budget/Pages/default.aspx, 14.

88. National Research Council, *The Smallpox Vaccination Program: Public Health in an Age of Terrorism* (Washington, DC: National Academies Press, 2005), 16, 24, 27.

89. William J. Broad, "US To Vaccinate 500,000 Workers against Smallpox," *New York Times*, 7 July 2002.

90. Anita Manning and Steve Sternberg, "Officials Ponder Timing, Sequence of Immunizations," *USA Today*, 7 October 2002.

91. Henderson, *Smallpox: The Death of a Disease*, 295–96. Similarly, interview with Henderson, 2009, as well as Lawrence K. Altman, "Action Delayed on Vaccination Advice," *New York Times*, 25 August 2002; Laura Meckler, "US Divided on Smallpox Policy," Associated Press, 5 October 2002; and National Research Council, *Smallpox Vaccination Program*, 29.

92. GAO, *Smallpox Vaccination: Implementation of National Program Faces Challenges* (Washington, DC: GAO, 2003), 5, 11.

93. National Research Council, *Smallpox Vaccination Program*, 57.

94. Interview with former HHS official, 2008. Also instrumental to this process was retired PHS Admiral Kenneth Bernard, then serving on the president's Homeland Security Council.

95. Interview with former HHS official, 2008. Also see Statement by Tommy G. Thompson on Project Bioshield, House Committee on Energy and Commerce and House Select Committee on Homeland Security, 27 March 2003, http://www.hhs. gov/asl/testify/t030327a.html.

96. In addition, BioShield provided for the emergency use of unlicensed products and expedited procedures for research and development, including the peer review process for NIH grants and contracts. White House, "President Details Project BioShield," 3 February 2003, http://georgewbush-whitehouse.archives.gov/news/ releases/2003/02/20030203.html.

97. Quoted in Jon Cohen, "Reinventing Project BioShield," *Science* 333, no. 6047 (2011): 1216–18, 1217. Fauci reached a similar conclusion about BioShield: "The Mercks and the GlaxoSmithKlines and others looked at it and said, 'Forget it.'" Quoted

in Hylton, "How Ready Are We for Bioterrorism?" For debate over how much money is enough, see Jason Matheny, Michael Mair, and Bradley Smith, "Cost/ Success Projections for US Biodefense Countermeasure Development," *Nature Biotechnology* 26, no. 9 (2008): 981–83; and Lynn C. Klotz and Alan Pearson, "BARDA's budget," *Nature Biotechnology* 27, no. 8 (2009): 698–99.

98. Among others, see Cohen, "Reinventing Project BioShield," 1217; Kendall Hoyt, *Long Shot: Vaccines for National Defense* (Cambridge: Harvard University Press, 2012), 151–53.

99. Quoted in David Willman, "New Anthrax Vaccine Doomed by Lobbying," *Los Angeles Times*, 2 December 2007. Also see Eric Lipton, "Bid to Stockpile Bioterror Drugs Stymied by Setbacks," *New York Times*, 18 September 2006; and Elizabeth MacDonald and Robert Langreth, "Spore Wars," *Forbes*, 6 June 2005.

100. Michael S. Rosenwald, "Rockville Biotech Buys Rival's Anthrax Vaccine" *Washington Post*, 5 May 2008.

101. Quoted in Hylton, "How Ready Are We for Bioterrorism?"

102. HHS Office of the Assistant Secretary for Preparedness and Response, *Project BioShield Annual Report to Congress: January 2011–December 2011*, https://www.med icalcountermeasures.gov/media/10061/pbs_report_2011_final_9-6-2012.pdf, 4–5. Also, on the anthrax and smallpox vaccine stockpiles, see Hylton, "How Ready Are We for Bioterrorism?"

103. Frank Gottron, *The Project BioShield Act: Issues for the 112th Congress*, Congressional Research Service, Report for Congress, 13 March 2012, 10.

104. Bob Graham and Jim Talent, *Prevention of WMD Proliferation and Terrorism Report Card*, Commission on the Prevention of Weapons of Mass Destruction Proliferation and Terrorism, January 2010, 6.

105. Randall Larsen, quoted in Hylton, "How Ready Are We for Bioterrorism?"

106. Hoyt, *Long Shot*, 135, 150–51.

107. Though it is consistent with the biomedical frame, I do not argue that NIH/ NIAID's stance on basic research—criticized by Hoyt—is the only compatible approach. It is possible to imagine more integrated if not centralized programs; it is also possible to envision an approach that pays greater heed to tacit knowledge and the bottlenecks between basic research and practical applications. Kathleen M. Vogel, "Framing Biosecurity: An Alternative to the Biotech Revolution Model?," *Science and Public Policy* 35, no. 1 (2008): 45–54.

108. For example, see comments by Fauci, Danzig, and others quoted in Hylton, "How Ready Are We for Bioterrorism?" Also see Erika Check Hayden, "Biodefence since 9/11: The Price of Protection," *Nature* 477 (September 2011): 150–51; Hoyt, *Long Shot*, 27–29; Philip K. Russell and Gigi Kwik Gronvall, "US Medical Countermeasure Development since 2001: A Long Way Yet to Go," *Biosecurity and Bioterrorism: Biodefense Strategy, Practice, and Science* 10, no. 1 (2012): 66–76, 74.

109. Michael E. Brown, *Flying Blind: The Politics of the US Strategic Bomber Program* (Ithaca: Cornell University Press, 1992); Thomas L. McNaugher, *The M16 Controversies: Military Organizations and Weapons Acquisition* (New York: Praeger, 1984).

110. On the failure to achieve aspirations as a key trigger, see Richard M. Cyert and James G. March, *A Behavioral Theory of the Firm* (Englewood Cliffs, NJ: Prentice-Hall, 1963); and Barbara Levitt and James G. March, "Organizational Learning," *Annual Review of Sociology* 14 (1988).

111. Quoted in Hayden, "Biodefence since 9/11." An internal review also acknowledged that "filling the discovery and developmental pipeline with needed product candidates eligible for Project BioShield . . . has been slower and more costly than anticipated." HHS, *The Public Health Emergency Medical Countermeasures Enterprise Review*, August 2010, https://www.medicalcountermeasures.gov/media/1138/mcmreviewfinalcover-508.pdf, 5.

112. Catherine Shaffer, "US Biodefense Contracts Continue to Lure Biotechs," *Nature Biotechnology* 28, no. 3 (2010): 187–88. Though easily overlooked, the rate of change is a key distinction between the DoD and HHS.

113. HHS, *Fiscal Year 2012: Public Health and Social Services Emergency Fund: Justification of Estimates for Appropriations Committees*, http://www.hhs.gov/about/budget/fy2012/phssef_cj_fy2012.pdf, 20.

114. See FDA and NIH, "NIH and FDA Announce Collaborative Initiative to Fast-Track Innovations to the Public," 24 February 2010, http://www.fda.gov/NewsEvents/Newsroom/PressAnnouncements/2010/ucm201706.htm; Bipartisan WMD Terrorism Research Center, *Bio-Response Report Card* (Washington, DC: WMD Center, 2011), 43. Similarly, NIAID has started highlighting the drug candidates that it successfully transitions to BARDA. NIAID, *Congressional Justification: FY 2013*, 18.

115. Interview with Henderson, 2009.

116. HHS, *Justification of Estimates for Appropriations Committees*, 55; HHS, press release, "HHS Creates New Centers to Develop, Manufacture Medical Countermeasures," 18 June 2012, http://www.hhs.gov/news/press/2012pres/06/20120618a.html.

Biodefense and Beyond

1. Donald MacKenzie, *Inventing Accuracy: A Historical Sociology of Nuclear Missile Guidance*, 4th ed. (Cambridge: MIT Press, 1990), 169.

2. Alexander Wendt, *Social Theory of International Politics* (Cambridge: Cambridge University Press, 1999), 111.

3. Abraham H. Maslow, *Psychology of Science: A Reconnaissance* (New York: Harper and Row, 1966), 15.

4. Lee Ben Clarke, *Mission Improbable: Using Fantasy Documents to Tame Disaster* (Chicago: University of Chicago Press, 1999), 167.

5. See Susan Wright and Stuart Ketcham, "The Problem of Interpreting the US Biological Defense Research Program," in *Preventing a Biological Arms Race*, ed. Susan Wright (Cambridge: MIT Press, 1990); and Charles Piller and Keith R. Yamamoto, *Gene Wars* (New York: Beech Tree Books, 1988).

6. Frederic J. Brown, *Chemical Warfare: A Study in Restraints*, 2nd ed. (New Brunswick, NJ: Transaction, 2006), 293.

7. Given the power and global footprint of the US military, its ideas can also affect international norms. This is illustrated by Allied Technical Protocol 45 (ATP-45), for example, which defines the NATO standard for warning and reporting nuclear, biological, and chemical hazards based on US military doctrine.

8. "The mechanisms of education, socialization, and participation that develop, maintain, and undermine shared identities are obviously more weakly developed at the international level than within individual nation-states." James G. March and

Johan P. Olsen, "The Institutional Dynamics of International Political Orders," *International Organization* 52, no. 4 (1998): 943–69, 961. Also see Jeffrey T. Checkel, "Social Constructivisms in Global and European Politics: A Review Essay," *Review of International Studies* 30, no. 2 (2004): 229–44, 237; and "second wave" social constructivism, including Amitav Acharya, "How Ideas Spread: Whose Norms Matter? Norm Localization and Institutional Change in Asian Regionalism," *International Organization* 58, no. 2 (2004): 239–75; and Jeffrey W. Legro, "Which Norms Matter? Revisiting the 'Failure' of Internationalism," *International Organization* 51, no. 1 (1997): 31–63.

9. Among others, see Lynn C. Klotz and Edward J. Sylvester, *Breeding Bio Insecurity: How U.S. Biodefense Is Exporting Fear, Globalizing Risk, and Making Us All Less Secure* (Chicago: University of Chicago Press, 2009), 83. Biodefense involves important trade-offs and thus risks that demand careful consideration. But Klotz and Sylvester go so far as to claim that "from Soviet Russia to apartheid South Africa to twenty-first-century America, almost nothing has changed," which disregards substantial evidence to the contrary.

10. Gregory D. Koblentz, *Living Weapons: Biological Warfare and International Security* (Ithaca: Cornell University Press, 2009), 3.

11. James Q. Wilson, *Bureaucracy: What Government Agencies Do and Why They Do It* (New York: Basic Books, 1989), 106.

12. Carl H. Builder, *The Masks of War: American Military Styles in Strategy and Analysis* (Baltimore: Johns Hopkins University Press, 1989), back cover.

13. Ibid., 202, 131.

14. Among others, see Michael Moss, "Many Missteps Tied to Delay in Armor for Troops in Iraq," *New York Times*, 7 March 2005; and "Safer Vehicles for Soldiers: A Tale of Delay and Glitches," *New York Times*, 26 June 2005.

15. Matthew Evangelista, "Case Studies and Theories of the Arms Race," *Security Dialogue* 17, no. 2 (1986): 197–206, 199.

16. Robert J. Art and Robert Jervis, eds., *Innovation and the Arms Race* (Ithaca: Cornell University Press, 1988), 245.

17. The nonkinetic effects of neutron bombs were not the only reason to oppose these weapons; for one critique of their strategic logic, see Fred M. Kaplan, "Enhanced-Radiation Weapons," *Scientific American* 238, no. 5 (1978): 44–51. However, questionable strategic logic does not prevent many kinetic systems from being deployed (consider national missile defense) or advanced by the armed services (a recent example of which might include prompt global strike using ICBMs). Amy F. Woolf, *Conventional Prompt Global Strike and Long-Range Ballistic Missiles: Background and Issues*, Congressional Research Service, 26 April 2013.

18. Evangelista, *Innovation and the Arms Race* (Ithaca: Cornell University Press, 1988), 248.

19. Sam Cohen, *F*** You! Mr. President: Confession of the Father of the Neutron Bomb*, 3rd. ed., 2006, http://www.AthenaLab.com/Confessions_Sam_Cohen_2006_Third_Edition.pdf, 125, 54. As the title suggests, this autobiography is more of a personal rant than a scholarly source. But it is instructive. Similarly, see Sam Cohen, *The Truth about the Neutron Bomb* (New York: William Morrow & Co., 1983). It is also interesting to note that the USSR "amassed much more information on the relative biological effectiveness (RBE) of neutrons at different energies . . . and at higher dose levels than the United States," which, like the Soviet BW program, might be indicative of subtle but significant differences in the dominant frames and stereotypes at work

inside opposing organizations during the Cold War. Glen I. Reeves, "Medical Implications of Enhanced Radiation Weapons," *Military Medicine* 175, no. 12 (2010): 964–70, 964.

20. Among many others, see John Arquilla and David Ronfeldt, "Cyberwar Is Coming!," *Comparative Strategy* 12, no. 2 (1993): 141–65; Richard A. Clarke and Robert K. Knake, *Cyber War: The Next Threat to National Security and What to Do about It* (New York: HarperCollins, 2010); and Elisabeth Bumiller and Thom Shanker, "Panetta Warns of Dire Threat of Cyberattack on US," *New York Times*, 11 October 2012.

21. James Bret Michael et al., "From Chaos to Collective Defense," *Computer* 43, no. 8 (2010): 91–94.

22. Martin C. Libicki, "Cyberspace Is Not a Warfighting Domain," *I/S: Journal of Law and Policy for the Information Society* 8, no. 2 (2012): 321–36, 332.

23. Ibid., 326, 336. Libicki argues that this terminology has become more discriminate over time. In contrast to this book, he also suggests that "the influence of concepts and doctrine on what people actually do on a day-to-day basis is limited," and the primacy of kinetic effects is self-evident.

24. For a classic account, see Cliff Stoll, *The Cuckoo's Egg: Tracking a Spy through the Maze of Computer Espionage* (New York: Pocket Books, 1990).

25. GAO, *Information Security: Computer Attacks at Department of Defense Pose Increasing Risks* (Washington, DC: GAO, 1996), 22–24.

26. See Clarke and Knake, *Cyber War*, 110–11. For more recent examples, see Thom Shanker and Elisabeth Bumiller, "Hackers Gained Access to Sensitive Military Files," *New York Times*, 14 July 2011; Ellen Nakashima, "Cyber-Intruder Sparks Massive Federal Response—And Debate over Dealing with Threats," *Washington Post*, 9 December 2011; and "Pentagon Aircraft, Missile Defense Programs Said Target of China Cyber Threat," *Associated Press*, 29 May 2013.

27. Lynn Eden, *Whole World on Fire: Organizations, Knowledge, and Nuclear Weapons Devastation* (Ithaca: Cornell University Press, 2004), 303.

28. Plus, differentiation can enable the fruitful cross-fertilization of ideas. Cross-fertilization requires heterogeneity, but this conceptual diversity is lacking when different problems and solutions are simply assumed to be the same.

29. This may also facilitate communication between different organizations, as discussed by M. Gunnar Andersson et al, "Separated by a Common Language: Awareness of Term Usage Differences between Languages and Disciplines in Biopreparedness," *Biosecurity and Bioterrorism: Biodefense Strategy, Practice, and Science* 11, sup. 1 (2013): S276–S285.

30. For example, Army et al., *Multiservice Tactics, Techniques, and Procedures for Biological Surveillance*, FM 3-11.86 / MCWP 3.37.1C / NTTP 3-11.31 / AFTTP (I) 3-2.52 (4 October 2004).

31. See US Air Force, *Disease Containment Planning Guidance*, AFI 10-2604 (6 April 2007).

32. For one critical view on the history of all-hazard planning, see Clarke, *Mission Improbable*.

Index

Acambis Corporation, 121
Advisory Committee on Immunization Practices, 121, 122
Afghanistan, 21, 32, 57, 99, 133, 149n89
AIDS, 103, 108, 119, 125
Air Force Information Warfare Center, 136
Al Qaeda, 21. *See also* September 11 attacks
Alibekov, Kanatjan (a.k.a. Ken Alibek), 20, 34, 108, 110–111
Allied Technical Protocol 45 (ATP-45), 59, 182n7
Allison, Graham, 24
Animal Efficacy Rule, 126
anthrax (*Bacillus anthracis*), 5–7; accident at Sverdlovsk, 20, 54, 107, 144n32; Aum Shinrikyo terrorism with, 21; detection of, 7, 94, 105; during Gulf War, 1–2, 110; testing of, 48; treatment of, 41, 122, 124; vaccines for, 50, 56, 57, 60, 63–66, 97–99, 112, 123; during World War II, 42–43
anthrax letters (2001), 2, 21, 82–83, 118, 127, 142n15, 145n43. *See also* Bruce Ivins
Anthrax Vaccine Immunization Program (AVIP), 98–100
antibiotic. *See* medical countermeasures
Appel, John, 55
Armed Forces Epidemiology Board, 60, 66

arms races, 15, 132
Army Chemical School, 83
Army Medical Research and Development Command, 57
Army Medical Service, 49
atropine, 76, 90, 114
Aum Shinrikyo, 21, 108, 110, 117
Automated Nuclear, Biological, and Chemical Information System (ANBACIS), 59

Bacillus anthracis. See anthrax
Bacillus globigii, 7, 48
Bacillus subtilis var. *niger*, 48, 153n39
BACUS exercise, 22, 145n45, 145n47
Baldwin, Ira L., 41, 43, 151n10
Base Closure and Realignment Commission, 62
Berkelman, Ruth, 109
Bern Report, 37, 39
Bernard, Kenneth, 180n94
biodefense: definition of, 5, 17; during war, 38, 40–41, 51, 58–61, 67, 92–100; feasibility of, 56, 67–68; funding for, 22, 45, 54, 55, 57–58, 60–69, 102, 112–115, 118–120, 122–124, 127; military versus civilian, 2, 4, 11, 13, 38–39, 50, 102, 115–116, 124–127; other kinds of defense versus, 5–9, 45, 53, 72, 74–79, 116, 129; predictions about, 15, 25, 35. *See also* physical

against, 7–9, 39, 75, 80, 83, 89–90;
international law and, 18–19
Cheney, Dick, 121, 122
Chikungunya virus, 57
China, 32
ciprofloxacin, 60, 98
civilian intervention, 15, 63–65, 69, 70,
81, 141n7
Civil War (US), 31
CIVIX 93 (anthrax training exercise), 109
Clark, William, 109
Clarke, Lee, 80
Clarke, Lee Ben, 129, 165n31
Clinton, Bill, 65, 109; counterterrorism
policies of, 111, 114, 115
Clostridium botulinum, 5–6. *See also*
botulinum toxin
Cochrane, Rexmond, 42
Cohen, Samuel, 133
Cohen, William, 65
Commission on Epidemiological Sur-
vey, 49, 50
computer systems, 26, 30, 33–34, 58–60.
See also cybersecurity
confirmation bias, 28
Convention on the Prohibition of the
Development, Production and Stock-
piling of Bacteriological and Toxin
Weapons and on Their Destruction.
See Biological Weapons Convention
Counter-Biological Warfare Concept of
Operations, 137
counterinsurgency, 32, 132, 137, 149n89
Coxiella burnetii (Q fever), 19, 48, 49
cybersecurity, 32, 34, 135–136

Danzig, Richard, 63, 65, 91, 98, 111
Dark Winter exercise (2001), 144
decontamination, 5, 7, 41, 54, 75–76,
173n124. *See also* physical protection
Defense Advanced Research Projects
Agency (DARPA), 67
Defense Against Weapons of Mass De-
struction Act (1996), 91–92, 112
Defense Information Systems Agency,
136
Defense Medical Readiness and Train-
ing Institute, 90
Defense Nuclear Agency, 59, 62
Defense Science Board, 108
Defense Threat Reduction Agency
(DTRA), 62, 67, 69

Department of Agriculture, 13, 102
Department of Defense (DoD), 2, 4, 10,
61; Domestic Preparedness Program of, 92, 112; HHS and, 2–4, 26,
35, 102–103, 110–111, 114, 117, 119,
124–127, 130; kinetic frame of, 3,
30–35
Department of Health and Human
Services. *See* Health and Human
Services
Department of Homeland Security
(DHS), 11, 102, 123, 131–132, 138;
CDC and, 120; funding of, 119, 123
Deseret Test Center, Fort Douglas,
Utah, 48
detection systems: for biological weapons, 7, 17, 41, 50, 55–56, 59, 68–69,
76–81, 93–95, 105–107; light detection
and ranging as, 50, 56, 68, 95
deterrence, 18
Detrick. *See* Fort Detrick
"dirty bombs," 9. *See also* radiological
weapons
doctrine. *See* military doctrine
Domestic Preparedness Program, 92,
112
Dryvax smallpox vaccine, 121
dual-use, 9, 54, 131–132
Dugway Proving Ground, Utah, 40, 48,
55, 62, 104
DynPort Corporation, 67

Ebola (*Zaire ebolavirus*), 5–6, 57,
122
Eden, Lynn, 26, 27, 31, 62; on military doctrine, 72; on organizational
frames, 26, 31, 72, 137
Edgewood Arsenal, Aberdeen, Md., 40,
54, 62
Eisenhower, Dwight D., 47, 48
El Salvador, 50
Emergent Bio-Solutions, 123, 124, 126,
127
emerging infectious diseases, 11,
107–109, 115, 117, 120, 130, 176n30.
Eng, Robert, 159n126
enhanced-radiation weapons (ERW), 9,
133–134, 183n17. *See also* radiological
weapons
ENIAC computer, 33
Environmental Protection Agency
(EPA), 102, 120

justification for, 2; medical counter-measures during 2, 62, 67, 99–100, 121–122.
isopropyl methylphosphonofluridate. *See* sarin
Israel, 95
Ivins, Bruce, 21, 131

Japan, 41, 52, 97; Aum Shinrikyo sarin attack in, 21, 108, 110, 117; Unit 731 of, 19, 37
Jefferson, Thomas, 95
Johns Hopkins Center for Civilian Biodefense Strategies, 118
Johnson-Winegar, Anna, 57, 67, 99, 119
Joint Biological Point Detection System (JBPDS), 68, 95
Joint Biological Standoff Detection System, 68
Joint Program Office for Biological Defense (JPO-BD), 61, 68
Joint Vaccine Acquisition Program (JVAP), 67
Jordan, 95
Joseph, Stephen, 63

Kadlec, Robert, 123
Kamel, Hussein, 108, 110–111
Kennedy, John F., 48
Kier, Elizabeth, 29
kinetic frame of reference, 3–4, 10, 30–36, 132–135; biomedical frame versus, 4, 11, 30, 102, 103, 112; learning and, 4, 27, 31–32, 35, 56, 70, 74, 84, 89, 100, 126, 129
Kissinger, Henry, 51, 52
Kliewe, Heinrich, 20
Klotz, Lynn C., 183n9
Koblentz, Gregory, 18, 132
Koplan, Jeffrey, 114, 115, 118, 119
Korea, North, 21
Korea, South, 99
Korean War, 11, 45–47, 53, 126; civilian biodefense and, 104–105, 107, 108, 127
Krulak, Charles, 63, 65

Laboratory Response Network, 113, 118, 120
Laird, Melvin, 51–52, 69
Langmuir, Alexander, 105, 107, 108, 127

Lederberg, Joshua, 61, 63, 65, 98, 108–111, 116–117, 175n28
Legro, Jeffrey, 29
Leitenberg, Milton, 22, 46
LeMay, Curtis, 46
Levy, Leslie-Anne, 92
Libby, I. Lewis "Scooter," 122
Libicki, Martin C., 135–136, 184n23
light detection and ranging (LIDAR), 50, 56, 68, 95
Lillibridge, Scott, 112, 115, 118
"linear model" of innovation, 125
Lysenko, Trofim, 19

MacKenzie, Donald, 129
malaria, 104, 119
Manhattan Project, 18
Marburg virus, 19
March, James G., 182n8
Martin, Susan, 18
Mathieson Chemical Company, 47
Mauroni, Albert, 55; on detection equipment, 80, 93; on military doctrine, 84, 87, 165n29; on vaccination, 97; on war games, 91
McNamara, Robert, 48–49, 51
medical countermeasures, 5, 7, 17, 56–58, 76–77, 80, 83, 120–122, 125–127; during Gulf War, 58, 60–61, 65, 81–84, 97–98; during Iraq War, 62, 67, 100; Project BioShield and, 121, 123–124
Merck, George, 38–39, 41, 43, 151n12
Merrell National Laboratories, 50
Meselson, Matthew, 107
Metropolitan Medical Strike Teams, 109, 111
Michigan Biologic Products Institute, 57, 66
Miles' law, 23
military doctrine, 11, 41, 71–72, 163n1; "chem centric," 84–89, 100, 117; compared to civilian plans, 115–117
Military Operations Other than War (MOOTW), 33
Miller, Dorothy, 46–47
mining of seaways, 132–134
mission-oriented protective posture (MOPP), 7–9, 75, 83, 100; during Gulf War, 97; training with, 90, 92. *See also* physical protection

Moltke, Helmuth von, 90
Monath, Thomas, 69
"monitor, mitigate, and respond" proposal, 83
Morse, Stephen S., 108
M31 Biological Integrated Detection System (BIDS), 68, 94–95
M12 Heavy Decontamination System, 173n124

National Academy of Sciences, 37
National Biodefense Analysis and Countermeasure Center (NBACC), 131–132
National Cancer Institute, 56
National Center for Infectious Diseases, 112, 118
National Guard WMD Civil Support Teams, 169n78
National Institute of Allergy and Infectious Disease (NIAID), 103, 108, 112, 130; research by, 116, 119, 120, 124, 125, 181n107
National Institutes of Health (NIH), 11, 103–105, 108, 109, 112; budget for, 112, 119; mission of, 104
National Security Decision Memorandum (NSDM) 35, 52
National Security Study Memorandum (NSSM) 59, 51–52
National Smallpox Vaccination Program, 99–100, 121
NATO, 182n7
NBC Warning and Reporting System (NBCWRS), 78, 164n20, 167n56
network text analysis, 85–89, 166n52
neutron bomb, 9, 133–134, 183n17
Nixon, Richard, 11, 51–55, 69
nonkinetic stereotypes, 4, 28, 34–36, 40, 53, 78, 100–102, 112, 117, 129. See also kinetic frame of reference
Novartis Corporation, 127
nuclear, biological, and chemical (NBC), 28–29, 55, 73, 78–80, 83–87, 90–93, 137. See also stereotypes
nuclear weapons: biological weapons versus, 8–9, 22, 43; damage evaluation of, 31; development of, 18, 43; neutron bomb and, 9, 133–134, 183n17

Nunn-Lugar-Domenici Act. See Defense Against Weapons of Mass Destruction Act

Obama, Barack, 124, 126
Oklahoma City bombing (1995), 110
Olsen, Johan P., 183n8
operational level of warfare, 10, 17–20, 49, 81, 91, 102, 115
Operation Desert Shield (1990), 21, 58–60, 80, 93, 97–98. See also Gulf War
Operation Desert Storm (1991). See Gulf War
Operation Desert Thunder (1998), 2, 94, 98
Operation Sledgehammer (1942), 38
organizational frames of reference, 3–4, 10, 26–35, 70, 84, 126, 131; change and, 63, 65, 70 101, 137; Eden on, 26, 31, 72, 137; stereotypes and, 3, 10–12, 27–30, 74, 84, 129, 130
organizational learning, 4, 27–29, 31, 70, 74, 84, 126
Osterholm, Michael, 110, 111
Ouagrham-Gormley, Sonia Ben, 21–22, 51
Owens, Wayne, 159n123
Owens, William, 63

Panama Canal Zone, 38
Pandemic and All Hazards Preparedness Act (2006), 124
Pappenheimer, A.M., 40
Pasechnik, Vladimir, 20, 175n28
"passive defense," 78, 136
path dependency, 27, 30, 34, 80, 96, 119, 171n99
Patrick, William, 49, 153n39
Patterson, K. David, 34
peacekeeping missions, 32–33, 137
penicillin, 41
phosgene, 7
physical protection, 5, 7–9, 17, 41, 50, 54, 68, 75–76, 81; masks as, 50, 79, 83, 90. See also mission-oriented protective posture (MOPP) gear
Pine Bluff, Ark., 47, 48, 52, 54
plague (*Yersinia pestis*), 5–6, 31, 110, 114; antibiotic-resistant strains of, 19; during Middle Ages, 109; treatment of, 122